PLANNING FOR DISASTER:

HOW NATURAL AND MAN-MADE DISASTERS SHAPE THE BUILT ENVIRONMENT

by William G. Ramroth Jr.

KAPLAN

PUBLISHING

New York

This publication is designed to provide accurate and authoritative information in regard to the subject matter covered. It is sold with the understanding that the publisher is not engaged in rendering legal, accounting, or other professional service. If legal advice or other expert assistance is required, the services of a competent professional should be sought.

Editorial Director: Jennifer Farthing
Development Editor: Joshua Martino
Production Editor: Julio Espin
Production Artist: International Composition and Typesetting
Cover Designer: Rod Hernandez

Published by Kaplan Publishing,
a division of Kaplan, Inc.

Printed in the United States of America

May 2007
07 08 09   10 9 8 7 6 5 4 3 2 1

ISBN 13: 978-1-4195-9373-4
ISBN 10: 1-4195-9373-0

For a safer built environment for Amanda and Molly

The ancient Roman architect and engineer Marcus Vitruvius Pollio claimed that there are three principal factors that affect the art and science of building. He called them "firmness, commodity, and delight."[1]

By *firmness*, he meant that buildings must be strong enough to stand up. The strength and integrity of a building's construction materials and foundation affect its utility and durability—its firmness. A wooden shack is not as permanent as a building constructed of stone, and both are more durable than a tent hastily pitched for the night.

By *commodity*, Vitruvius meant *use* or *function*. Buildings are built for a purpose, to house and support a particular function. The intended function of a building determines its shape. For example, coliseums, houses, and temples—three building types with which Vitruvius was very familiar—are built to support different functions, and consequently, their shapes are different.

By *delight*, Vitruvius was referring to artistic beauty. Proportion, ornament, and expression of building materials contribute greatly to a building's aesthetic appearance. When architecture is aesthetically well executed, it lifts the human spirit like a great painting or sculpture.

Good architecture, Vitruvius argued, must respond nobly to these three primary drivers—firmness, commodity, and delight—however, Vitruvius appears to have omitted one. There is a fourth force that shapes architecture: disaster. Throughout history, disaster has affected the design of buildings and the planning of cities.

The way disaster shapes architecture is very different from Vitruvius's firmness, commodity, and delight. Disaster works as a wrecking ball, destroying everything in its path that fails to anticipate and respect its power and destructive nature. In its wake, the survival of buildings and cities depends on how well their designers anticipated and prepared to resist disaster's wrecking ball.

After a disaster destroys buildings and cities, we are left with few choices. We can give up or pick up the pieces and rebuild again. Throughout history, some cities did not pick up the pieces. The city of

Pompeii is a notable example. Located near Naples, Italy, Pompeii was completely destroyed in 79 AD when Mount Vesuvius erupted, showering the city with rock and completely burying it in volcanic ash. Yet, cities generally rebuild, and when they do, they usually employ improved planning and design principles, which result from a better understanding and respect for a disaster's force. For its victims, a disaster's wrecking ball is both terrorizing and life threatening. Yet, ironically, good often comes out of disaster. Disaster provides opportunities. Often the rebuilding that takes place afterward improves living conditions for both the survivors and future generations.

Three of this book's chapters are titled "Fire," "Earthquake," and "Wind and Water" in deference to the ancient Greek's four natural elements: fire, earth, air, and water. The Greeks experienced these elements in everything they saw and touched, heard, tasted, and smelled. They experienced them at work in the formation of natural disasters—in earthquakes, gale-force winds, raging fires, and floods. Understandably, they believed that everything in the cosmos was built from the various combinations of these four elemental building blocks.

Today, fire, earth, air, and water have been replaced by 109 known elements or atoms. The combinations of these atoms account for the universe we perceive. Nevertheless, when it comes to planning for disaster, the ancient Greeks were on to something. Their four elements are the basic forces of natural disasters. Understanding how to plan and design to control and resist their devastating effects yields a built environment that is a safer place in which to live.

Not all disasters are the result of natural forces. Some are strictly man made. Chapter 4, "Overcrowding," looks at the role that squalid and unsanitary living conditions in inner cities have played in shaping building codes, cities, and suburbs. Chapter 7, "Disasters of Another Kind," examines recent economic disasters, structural disasters, and the social disaster of Pruitt-Igoe, a low-cost, highrise housing complex in St. Louis, Missouri, that was dynamited out of existence in the early 1970s.

There also is another form of disaster caused by man: terrorism. Americans have vivid memories of the nightmare of September 11, 2001. We refer to many historical events as pre–9/11 and post–9/11. Chapter 8 examines the collapse of the World Trade Center and shows how we are just beginning to see 9/11's impact on how we plan and build tall buildings.

The 2004 Tsunami in Southern Asia and Hurricane Katrina in 2005 are two colossal disasters from which we have not yet recovered. Chapter 6 looks at hurricanes and tsunamis, and how they affect the way we build. Chapter 9 tells the story of Hurricane Katrina and how its destructive force was magnified by poor planning and the failure to heed the warnings of experts.

Nothing captures our collective attention more than a disaster. It shakes us awake, forces us to rethink how we plan and build, and propels us into action. Throughout this book, the word "great" appears over and over in association with this disaster or that. It is these really big disasters that have had the most significant impact on how we plan and design. With each great disaster, there is a special urgency to make changes to prevent another like it from ever occurring again. Sadly, it takes a disaster to spur us into action.

1

IT TAKES A DISASTER

Legend has it that the ancient Greek fabler Aesop was born into slavery around 620 BC. As a young man, he so impressed his master that he was eventually freed, allowing him to travel throughout the ancient world telling fabulous stories.

Aesop would have made a great disaster planner. In his tale about the grasshopper and the ant, Aesop explained the basic course of action any good disaster planner should take, summarizing it in a concise and easy-to-remember moral. In addition, the story points out a not-so-commendable aspect of human nature.

In Aesop's fable, the grasshopper never thought about the future. He played and sang all summer long in the warm sun, camping out under the stars at night. The ant, on the other hand, had different priorities. He planned and prepared for the inevitable winter. He gathered kernels of corn and excavated large caverns in the earth in which to live and store his food. When the bitter, cold days of winter set in, the ant had a warm and cozy subterranean home and plenty of food to eat. The grasshopper, on the other hand, had no shelter and nothing to eat. The grasshopper learned the importance of planning for disaster the hard way. Aesop's moral: It is best to prepare for the days of necessity.

Aesop never said what the grasshopper did the following summer. Perhaps he returned to his old ways, fiddling away his time. If the grasshopper did not plan for the next winter, he was doomed to relive the season's harsh reality.

This last bit of wisdom does not come from Aesop. It comes from an equally wise man, George Santayana (1863–1952), who grasped another essential tenet of disaster planning. Santayana, a Spanish philosopher and poet, said, "Those who cannot remember the past are condemned to repeat it."[1]

Unfortunately, human nature is much like grasshopper nature. We tend to learn the importance of planning the hard way: being unprepared and living with the consequences. We procrastinate instead of plan.

On a small scale, we postpone replacing that old, worn-out roof. "Certainly it can last one more winter," we rationalize. "It made it through last year, after all!" But, when the old roof leaks—as all old roofs eventually do—we are literally left out in the rain. With little recourse, we frantically run around the house with pots and pans trying to catch all the drops. After the storm, instead of replacing just the roof, we must now replace much more: the dry-rotted rafters, the mildewed ceilings and walls, the buckled floorboards, and the ruined furniture.

How We Are Like the Grasshopper

In 2006, the San Francisco Bay Area commemorated the 100th anniversary of the April 18, 1906, Great Earthquake and Fire that destroyed over half of the city. Although experts had warned Bay Area residents for years to assemble an earthquake survival kit for the inevitable next earthquake, estimates made in 2006 revealed that fewer than 10 percent had actually done so. Most are like the grasshopper: When the next "Big One" hits—and again experts say it is inevitable—Bay Area residents will scurry about frantically and wish they had stored away that portable radio and flashlight, those extra batteries, and enough food and water to last a few days.

We fail to take action on the large scale too. For at least ten years prior to the devastation caused by Hurricane Katrina, scientists, environmentalists, and concerned citizens warned of impending disaster if nothing was done to stop the erosion and make repairs to the Gulf Coast wetlands. Wetlands are nature's shock absorbers, and when they are healthy, they soften the blow of hurricanes. For the region around

New Orleans, the cost of wetland restoration was estimated at $14 billion. Funding was requested repeatedly, but never came.[2] Those holding the purse strings had other priorities, even if the cost was miniscule compared to the cost in lives and property if nothing was done.

After Hurricane Katrina, the online newsletter *Flows*, supported by organizations such as the International Institute for Environment and Development, the World Bank, and the Bank-Netherlands Watershed Partnership Program, wrote about the wetland debate:

> Long before the hurricane [Katrina], local public officials and newspaper headlines warned that it would be necessary to "pay now or later" and to either "repair the marshland or rebuild New Orleans."[3]

Like the grasshopper, we chose to pay later. Instead of spending $14 billion to lessen Katrina's impact, we will now spend many times more to clean up afterwards. Exactly how much is uncertain, but estimates are upwards of $200 billion. Reporting on September 10, 2005, 12 days after Katrina, the Associated Press compared the cost of rebuilding to 4 years of war in Afghanistan and Iraq,[4] giving new magnitude to the saying, "Penny wise but pound foolish."

We invite trouble because we are slow learners. Throughout the United States, many rivers overflow their banks almost yearly, yet we continue to build in their floodplains. In California, city planners and building officials still let developers build over fault lines. In the Great Plains, another tornado is certain to touch down, and hurricanes are guaranteed to slam into the Gulf Coast again. Once again, mobile homes set on cinder blocks will be tossed high into the air. Rather than take the necessary planning steps to prevent disaster or lessen its impact, we continue in our ways.

Unfortunately, it takes a disaster to grab our attention and shake us into action. The bigger it is, the more likely we will do something. The shrill ant alone cannot do it; the example of the Gulf Coast wetlands is just one of many examples illustrating this point. It was not until 70 downtown blocks of Baltimore burned to the ground in 1904 that fire departments saw the need to standardize firefighting equipment so that fire departments from one city could better assist neighboring cities. The Great Baltimore Fire destroyed over 1,500 buildings and 2,500 businesses, and left 35,000 without jobs during the dead of winter. Only then did city officials realize the need for national standards regarding the design and construction of buildings. It took the tragic deaths of 141 young women in the 1907 Triangle Shirtwaist Factory Fire for New York City to investigate and improve the safety of hundreds of unregulated garment factories scattered throughout lower Manhattan, located in overcrowded, converted tenement and loft buildings. The chapters that follow include many other examples of our failure to act until after a disaster.

THE PRAGMATIC PROCESS OF DISASTER PLANNING

Humans are a pragmatic lot. We learn from results. The philosophy of pragmatism states that the value of an idea is measured by its outcome. Good ideas create desirable outcomes. Undesirable outcomes render the ideas that created them as bad ideas.

Planners, architects, engineers, and government officials do not make decisions based solely on deduction and induction, the two basic tools of logic. There is a third tool, called abduction, and planners and designers rely on it most. There are few well-defined axioms about the built environment. The real world is a muddy place. Real-world problems are not like story problems found in high school math books. Most decisions are more like hypotheses, based on incomplete and sometimes conflicting information or facts. Abduction is educated guessing based on past experiences, and it is the basic tool of pragmatism. Charles Sanders Peirce, considered the father of pragmatism, explained it this way:

> A hypothesis . . . has to be adopted, which is likely in itself, and renders the facts likely. This step of adopting a hypothesis as being suggested by the facts, is what I call abduction. I reckon it as a form of inference.[5]
>
> If you carefully consider the question of pragmatism you will see that it is nothing else than the question of the logic of abduction.[6]

Decisions are made based on what the planners believe will bring about the outcome that is desired. Once a decision is made and implemented, it is tested in real-world situations. The value of the decision is determined by the outcome: Did it match expectations? If so, the decision was a good idea. If the outcome was unfavorable or outright objectionable, the decision was a bad one. Thus, improvements of the built environment lurch forward based on educated guesses.

Convolution and Compromise

The process is sometimes obscured or convoluted because some decisions regarding disaster planning are unspoken. There is the stated reason and the real reason, and sometimes the real reason has less-than-honorable intentions.

For example, in 1880, San Francisco enacted an ordinance requiring noncombustible buildings for laundries. The ordinance stated:

> It shall be unlawful, from and after the passage of this order, for any person or persons to establish, maintain, or carry on a laundry, within the corporate limits of the city and county of San Francisco, without having first obtained the consent of the board of supervisors, except the same be located in a building constructed either of brick or stone.[7]

The ordinance sounds reasonable at face value. Wooden buildings are much more vulnerable to fire than those of brick or stone. Like many other 19th-century cities, San Francisco was regularly beset with fires. Requiring buildings be built of noncombustible materials made sense. Note, however, that the ordinance was carefully worded in order to make it retroactive. It not only applied to new laundries in new buildings, it also applied to existing laundries in existing buildings.

At the time, Chinese immigrants were routinely discriminated against. The ordinance was just another cleverly disguised way to victimize them. In 1880, over 95 percent of the laundries in San Francisco were located in wood buildings, and the majority of these were owned by Chinese. Requiring consent from the board of supervisors for an exemption meant that board members would have the opportunity to see the faces or read the names of those requesting permission to continue operating their laundries in wooden buildings. All non-Chinese laundry owners except one were granted exemptions; however, not a single Chinese laundry owner was given permission to continue operations in a wooden building.

In 1886, the ordinance made its way to the U.S. Supreme Court in the case of *Yick Wo v. Hopkins*. While the ordinance was found constitutional, the way in which it was enforced was found to be in violation of the 14th Amendment, which guaranteed privileges and immunities of citizenship, due process, and equal protection for all persons born or naturalized in the United States. Yick Wo was able to keep his laundry.[8]

The process of disaster planning is also complicated by compromises. Decision makers often know what should be done but realize that it will cause hardships, so decisions are tempered by conciliation. For example, by the end of the 19th century, fire and health safety problems in tenement buildings in New York City neared catastrophic proportions. New York City's 1892 building code did not require walls between apartments to be solid or constructed of fireproof materials, even in fireproof buildings. Spaced, wood-stud wall framing was permitted, provided the walls extended from the fireproof floor below to the fireproof floor above. In 1900, Lawrence Veiller, a pioneer in housing reform, wrote:

> The [New York] Commission would have liked to have required that all partitions in new tenement houses should be solid and also fireproof. The advantages of such a form of construction are very great; it takes away one of the places where vermin may lodge, and also greatly reduces the danger from spread of fire. The Commission, however, in view of the additional expense that this would entail, have not seen their way clear to making such recommendation at the present time.[9]

Lawmakers made a compromise in the interest of economy—an all-too-familiar scenario.

ARCHITECTURE MATTERS

The built environment defines the way in which we live. Believe it or not, planners, architects, and engineers manipulate us every day. We live the way we do because they have created the living conditions.

Architecture matters; it affects us physically and influences our attitude about our lives and the world around us.

For example, when we attend a meeting, seminar, or training session at work, we sit in a larger-than-normal room, the conference room. Our comfort depends on the room's design. We are too hot or too cold based on the building's heating, ventilating, and air conditioning (HVAC) system, over which we have little or no control. We often cannot open a window for fresh air. We may be able to see the projection screen well or there might be a glare. We may be able to control the room's lighting system and window shades. We can or cannot hear the speaker over the whir of the HVAC system, which cycles on and off. The room's finish materials reflect or absorb sound, making the room's acoustics "dead," "alive," or just right. The room feels spacious or claustrophobic depending on the room's proportions and ceiling height. If too much of the ceiling is in view as we watch the speaker, the room feels cramped. When the ceiling is high enough to be out of view, we feel better. The ceiling's height affects the room's acoustics, as well. All of this affects our physical and mental comfort, and consequently, our attentiveness during the meeting.

Newspaper stories, magazine articles, and books that discuss disasters often ignore or downplay the importance of planning and design in the formulation and prevention of disasters. For example, the low-income housing project called Pruitt-Igoe in St. Louis, Missouri, was a social disaster of unprecedented proportions. (Chapter 7 discusses Pruitt-Igoe in more detail.) Built between 1951 and 1954, Pruitt-Igoe first opened to widespread praise, but it was deliberately destroyed only 18 years later. Some critics said racism caused the disaster, others pointed to politics, and some indicated crime and drugs were the culprits. Still others claimed that the St. Louis police department exacerbated the project's problems by arriving whenever they were called to the site with guns drawn. While all of these factors may have contributed, architecture was the primary cause. It was responsible for the tall institutional-looking buildings in which Pruitt-Igoe's tenants lived on a daily basis. Architecture created the environment that influenced what the tenants thought about themselves and how they could use or could not use the interior and exterior spaces that were created for them. The project's size, building heights, and physical layout drew sharp distinctions between its tenants' living conditions and those of its better-off neighbors.

DISASTER, CODES AND REGULATIONS

The planning and design of the built environment is governed by building codes and zoning regulations. They contribute to our physical comfort, health, and safety. Good planning and design create opportunities for living long, enjoyable, and productive lives. Bad planning and design do the opposite. As will become abundantly clear through the course of this book, they can also exacerbate and even create disasters.

Over the course of generations, disastrous events and the planning and design responses to them have worked their way into the very bricks and mortar of the built environment—and into the concrete, steel, and glass. Disaster planning has become such an integral part of building codes and zoning regulations that much of it is invisible, like the unseen threads that hold our clothes together.

To illustrate how pervasive disaster planning is and how much we take it for granted, let us imagine that each of us lives in a suburban house. For many of us, this is no stretch at all. Approximately one-half of all Americans live in the suburbs, but not many are aware of disaster's role in creating our suburban homes.

Prior to the early 20th century, few if any Americans lived in the suburbs. In 19th-century America, as in Europe at the time, the agricultural countryside was sparsely populated and the industrialized city overcrowded; there was nothing in between.

By the end of the 19th century, the water, air, and living conditions in overcrowded cities had become abysmal. Still, people flocked to cities in search of the jobs created by the quickly expanding industrial age. Cities became congested, dirty, and unsanitary. Smoke belched from unregulated factories. The urban working class lived in deplorable tenement buildings that were unsafe and unhealthy.

During this period, London was among the worst cities—over 140,000 Londoners died from cholera during the 19th century. Thousands more died from other communicable diseases, such as typhus, malaria, and tuberculosis (TB), that resulted from overcrowded and unsanitary living conditions.

In 1840, Dr. Southwood Smith spoke of London's deplorable living conditions to the House of Commons:

At present no more regard is paid in the construction of houses to the health of the inhabitants than is paid to the health of pigs in making sites for them. In point of fact there is not so much attention paid to it.[10]

Conditions in large cities in the United States were no better. In addition to rural citizens moving to cities, immigrants arrived in the United States literally by the boatload. In large cities, communicable diseases such as TB ran rampant. By the latter half of the 19th century, over 8,000 New Yorkers died every year from TB. For the working-class city dweller, cramped, filthy, and unsanitary living conditions were the norm, not the exception.

In 1898, a Londoner and amateur city planner named Ebenezer Howard proposed a radical alternative to living in overcrowded and unhealthy cities. His alternative called for the construction of town-country communities, which he called "Garden Cities." A movement spearheaded by concerned, socially minded individuals quickly evolved based on Howard's ideas. Over the ensuing decades, the movement followed a circuitous route, but eventually many of its principles, conceived to alleviate the chronic problem of overcrowded cities, led to land-use reforms in the United States and the suburbs of today. (For more about Garden Cities, see Chapter 4.)

Prior to World War II, only a few suburbs existed in the United States. After the war, when hundreds of thousands of servicemen returned home, the Servicemen's Readjustment Act of 1944, more commonly known as the GI Bill, not only guaranteed these returning veterans educations, but it also promised them loans of up to $7,500 for purchasing homes. With the GI Bill, the suburban housing boom was on. Suburban developments spread like wildfire around every major city in the United States.

We wake up in the morning to daylight pouring in through our bedroom windows. We have bedroom windows because modern building codes require all bedrooms to have them. Until the beginning of the 20th century, this was not the case. Countless thousands of 19th-century tenement residents, living in cities such as London, New York, and Boston, were denied windows.

It is hard to believe, but London actually imposed a tax on windows! Called the Window Tax Act of 1798, it imposed a tax on houses based on the number of windows. The rationale was that the more windows a house had, the higher the income of the owner, and consequently, the more tax the owner could afford to pay. The tax was a wonderful source of revenue. In 1815, it brought about £2 million to London's coffers.[11]

However, the tax had the unintended consequence of discouraging tenement building owners from installing windows in apartments. By the time the tax was repealed in 1851, there were thousands of window-less tenement apartments in London. Without healthful sunlight and ventilation, many tenement dwellers suffered and died from respiratory ailments and other diseases.

In the United States, tenement building owners also constructed windowless apartments. In the late 18th century, the Lower East Side of New York City was originally developed as modest, single-family row houses on narrow lots, generally 25 feet wide. By the 1820s, the houses on these lots were quickly being replaced with tenement buildings with one goal in mind: to squeeze in as many apartments as possible. Consequently, many rooms had no outside walls and few means of getting natural light and ventilation to them. In 1853, the New York City Association for Improving the Condition of the Poor reported:

> [T]he dwellings of the industrious classes in New York were not adapted to the wants of human beings, nor compatible with the health, or the social or moral improvement, of the occupants. . . . [T]he sleeping rooms . . . are frequently without means of ventilation, being dark or having windows 18 inches square with fixed lattices [sashes].[12]

A survey conducted around 1900 by the Tenement House Department of New York City revealed that over 350,000 windowless rooms existed in the city.[13]

One disaster finally drew attention to the deplorable living conditions in New York's tenement buildings. The riot that took place during the Civil War in July 1863 still ranks as the deadliest in U.S. history. In March 1863, the U.S. government had passed the Conscription Act, which established a lottery-type draft system for all males between the ages of 20 and 45. Men—or their families—could buy their way out of the draft by paying a $300 commutation fee, a considerable sum of money at the time and beyond the means of the poor and working class. On July 13, on the Lower East Side, a riot ensued shortly after New York City's first lottery drawing. The riot lasted four days, and when it was over, 100 people were dead and the city sustained $1.5 million in property damage.

The riots prompted many sympathetic newspaper stories describing the deplorable living conditions of the rioters. Americans were aghast and ashamed when they read about the plight of the working poor. Within three years, the first tenement housing laws were passed, and over the course of the next five decades, incremental improvements were made to the laws. Eventually, the tenement regulations culminated with the cornerstone achievement, *A Model Housing Law,* published in 1914, which advocated, among many other improvements, windows and ventilation for all bedrooms in all types of residences. Within a few years, major cities throughout the United States turned the recommendations of *A Model Housing Law* into code requirements.

Current building codes also require bedroom windows to be low enough to the floor (44 inches maximum) and wide enough (20 inches minimum) so a person can climb out in an emergency.[14] Unfortunately, many people suffered from smoke inhalation and died in fires before we earned the right to climb out of our windows to safety.

The sizes of the rooms in houses are governed by building code requirements. One room must be at least 120 square feet (generally this is the living or living/dining room), and the smallest habitable room must be at least 70 square feet in area. The ceiling height is governed by code, too, with 7 feet as the minimum, although 8 feet is the much more commonly used height.[15] With these requirements in force, no developer or landlord can construct habitable rooms the size of broom closets with ceilings so low one can barely stand. In the mid-19th century, penny-pinching tenement owners frequently constructed bedrooms measuring less than 50 square feet. Some rooms, particularly those in basements, required tenants to duck to avoid hitting beams and plumbing piping.

When we take showers, our shower stalls or tubs are enclosed with nonporous materials, such as ceramic tile, marble, fiberglass, or solid or laminated plastic. Until the early 20th century, no such requirement existed. Wood and plaster were commonly used around tubs, showers, toilets, and sinks, promoting dry rot, nests for insects and vermin, and the growth of mold, a serious respiratory hazard.

If a house is two stories, we go downstairs for breakfast. Our stair risers and treads are all equal in dimension so we will not stumble and fall down the stairs, as many people did before this common-sense safety regulation. Stairways also must have handrails. If a stairway is open on one or both sides, the open sides have handrails with balusters. In houses built before the mid-1990s, these balusters were spaced six inches apart. Because some children managed to get their heads stuck between the six-inch-spaced balusters and were seriously injured, the code requirement was changed to four inches as the spacing width for balusters.

The houses we live in and the buildings we work in are designed to stand not only in calm weather, but also in unusual conditions. In Florida, for example, current code provisions require that houses and buildings be able to withstand hurricane-force winds. These provisions are the result of lessons learned and incremental code improvements made in response to a century's worth of destructive hurricanes—such as the 1900 Galveston Hurricane, 1928 Okeechobee Hurricane, 1965 Hurricane Betsy, and 1992 Hurricane Andrew. (For more about these hurricanes, see Chapter 6.)

In California, hurricanes are not the problem. Instead, houses and other buildings are designed to withstand the violent lateral shaking caused by earthquakes. Little was done to improve building earthquake safety after the 1906 San Francisco Earthquake and Fire, although many improvements to deter and fight fires were made. Substantial improvements to resist earthquakes weren't made until after the 1933 Long Beach Earthquake, which destroyed many schools. Fortunately, the earthquake struck after school was over for the day. Additional improvements were made following the 1971 San Fernando and the 1994 Northridge earthquakes. (For more about earthquakes, see Chapter 5.)

With each earthquake, the earthquake-resistive strength of houses and other buildings has improved. During the past century, thousands of hurricane and earthquake victims paid dearly, resulting in the numerous life-preserving safety features that are hidden in the roofs, walls, and foundations of the buildings in which we live and work today.

After breakfast we leave our homes for work. We drive by front yard after front yard, unaware that all of them are set back the same minimum distance from the street. Generally, the distance is 20 or 25 feet. As far back as the aftermath of the Great Fire of London in 1666, cities have used street setbacks to control both the spread of fire and to limit density to promote community health and sanitation.

The Establishment of Zoning Regulations

For most of us, where we work is some distance away from where we live. This is because the immediate vicinity in which we live is very likely zoned to prohibit factories, industries, office buildings, commercial establishments, and most businesses. Dividing cities and suburbs up into zones for various uses is a relatively recent phenomenon.

There have been nuisance laws for centuries in Europe. Shortly after the Great Fire, London prohibited businesses such as tanneries, slaughter houses, and fat-rendering establishments from setting up shop in heavily residential areas due to their noxious odors. In the United States, Boston and San Francisco were the first cities to enact nuisance laws in the late 19th century. However, other than nuisance laws, there were no comprehensive regulations governing land use within cities.

The first city in the United States to establish comprehensive zoning regulations was New York City. Its 1916 Zoning Regulations were a groundbreaking and ground-dividing achievement. New York's zoning regulations have had an enormous and everlasting impact on life within major cities throughout the United States. Soon after New York enacted its zoning laws, other cities followed suit, dividing their jurisdictions along lines similar to those in New York. As might be expected by now, disaster played a significant role in the establishment of New York City's zoning regulations.

At the beginning of the 20th century, New York was the financial center of the United States, as it is today. With space limited on the island of Manhattan and with the city's prosperity ever rising, there was nowhere to build but up. So up it went. Tall, steel-framed buildings rose skyward, jutting straight up from the edges of sidewalks, creating massive canyonlike walls.

After the Great Chicago Fire of 1871, Chicago was the birthplace of tall buildings. However, by the end of the 1890s, New York had surpassed Chicago and boasted the tallest buildings in the world. These behemoths blocked out sunlight, and during hot, sweltering summer days, they severely curtailed air movement at street level. During the winter, the cliff-like walls of granite and terra cotta had the opposite effect. They created cold and windy tunnels. In both summer and winter, the quality of life at street level suffered considerably in the narrow and sunless chasms created by the vertical faces of tall buildings. New Yorkers grumbled and protested, but nothing was done to halt the incremental walling-in of New York City streets.

Then, in 1912, there was a fire. It was not a large fire, as fires go, but it completely destroyed the 7-story, 142-foot-tall office building at 120 Broadway. Built in 1870, the building was the home office of the Equitable Life Assurance Company. Shortly after the fire, Equitable was approached by Thomas Coleman DuPont of the DuPont dynasty of Delaware. Having developed a recent financial interest in New York real estate, DuPont convinced Equitable to form a partnership and rebuild at 120 Broadway. The term "rebuild" is a misnomer, because what DuPont had in mind was nothing like the 7-story building that was destroyed by the fire. He wanted to build the biggest office building in the world. Not the biggest in terms of height or prestige, but biggest in the only term that made any sense to DuPont: the biggest in rent-generating area. His objective was to squeeze the maximum amount of useable office space possible onto the 1-acre site. The result was the 1.2 million square foot Equitable Building. The 42-story-tall giant was nothing like its namesake. It rose straight up from the edge of the sidewalk, its 6-story base covering just about every square foot of the site. Above the sixth floor, the building continued skyward in an H-shaped configuration to a neck-craning height of 537 feet. A *New York Times* story written as construction began summarized the building's objective:

> The new Equitable building . . . was not constructed to create an architectural splurge or to stand as a monument to perpetuate anyone's name. The building was planned on the idea of an ocean liner, to carry a maximum cargo with the highest degree of efficiency, comfort and safety to its tenants at a minimum cost.[16]

Owners of neighboring buildings protested even as it was being built, but they had no recourse. New York had no planning or building regulations to prohibit the colossal and insensitive design. When it was completed in 1915, many other New Yorkers joined in with complaints.

The following year, New York City passed the first comprehensive zoning regulations in American history. The regulations established step-backs for tall buildings related to their height. Thereafter, New York skyscrapers stepped back as they ascended skyward. The Empire State Building and the Chrysler Building are stepped skyscrapers and notable examples of the zoning regulation's impact on the New York City skyline. There are, however, modern-day exceptions to this stepped-back approach. Perhaps the two most notable are the Seagram Building (1956) and the World Trade Center (1977—September 11, 2001). (For more on the World Trade Center see Chapter 8.) The Seagram Building is set back far enough from the street to allow it to ascend straight up like a modern skyscraper.

New York's zoning regulations also divided the city into use areas or zoning districts: residential, commercial, and manufacturing. Other major cities soon followed New York's lead, subdividing their cities into zoning districts.

Fire's Affect on Zoning Laws and Building Codes

Perhaps your office is in a skyscraper, located in the downtown of a large U.S. city. If so, it is located in a fire zone. All large cities are divided into fire zones. In general, all buildings within the central core of large cities must be constructed of noncombustible materials such as concrete and steel. As buildings get progressively farther away from the central business district, requirements become more lax until, finally, buildings can be built of any materials allowed by the building code. Almost all suburban houses fall into this last category—any building material permitted by the building code—which is a wordy way of saying wood-framed construction. Fire zones, as the name suggests, grew out of the ashes of fires.

Medieval London was filled cheek by jowl with half-timbered buildings. They overhung London's narrow, twisting streets, and they even stretched across the London Bridge. Half-timbered buildings made terrific kindling. In 1633, a fire destroyed most of them on the London Bridge. The rest were consumed by the Great Fire of 1666. After the Great Fire, London enacted the Rebuilding Act of 1667. Henceforth only buildings faced with brick or stone were allowed in central London. (For more on the Great London Fire, see Chapter 2.)

In 1871, downtown Chicago was destroyed by fire. Much of it had been built of wood. After the fire, Chicago implemented fire zones and prohibited the construction of wood-framed buildings downtown. After the 1906 Earthquake and Fire, San Francisco also saw the need to expand its fire district, moving wood-framed buildings farther away from downtown.

(There is more about the Great Chicago Fire in Chapter 2 and the San Francisco Earthquake and Fire in Chapter 5.)

Chances are that you enter your office building through a revolving door. Although you may not notice, there is an exit door near the revolving door and the exit door swings out.

Revolving doors have been around for years. Unfortunately, they have been around longer than the requirement for those exit doors adjacent to them. In 1942, during World War II, there was a terrible fire at the Coconut Grove nightclub in Boston that claimed 492 lives. In the panic to exit, many patrons met their deaths because they became trapped in the revolving door they had used to enter the building. Others died because exit doors in other parts of the building swung in instead of out. Within a year, Boston required exit doors to be built adjacent to revolving doors and for those doors to swing in the direction of egress.

Suppose you work on the tenth floor of an office building. You take the elevator up in the morning and down at the end of the day. You rarely use the stairs, but your building has them—at least two sets of stairs from every floor. The stairs are separated by a distance equal to at least one-half of the longest diagonal dimension of the building. The stairs are separated so you have two alternative exit paths in the event of an emergency. Disastrous fires taught us the importance of having two distinct ways out. If the exit path to one exit stair is blocked, we have another stair we can escape toward. The exit stairs are enclosed in stairwells or stair towers that are separated from all floors of the building by two-hour rated walls and fire doors, roughly meaning that it would take a fire two hours to burn through. The purpose of the two-hour fire rating is to give building occupants reasonable time to escape. At street level, the stairs exit directly to the exterior, although one of the stairs may exit through the lobby under certain conditions.

The main noncombustible structural components of our skyscraper office buildings are protected by fireproofing. During the 9/11 attack on the World Trade Center, portions of this all-important fireproofing were damaged by the airplanes' impacts. This exposed portions of the noncombustible steel structure to immense heat in the resulting fires. Although steel is noncombustible, it melts, but long before it melts, it loses strength through a process called yielding. The result of yielding steel in the World Trade Center attack led to devastation beyond anyone's wildest nightmare.

Your office building has many other safety features that are the result of lessons learned from past disasters. Dead-end corridors are limited in length to 20 feet. Corridor widths are also regulated. How fast corridor finish materials burn and how much smoke they generate are limited by code regulations. There are illuminated exit signs located in corridors and theaters, designed to guide the way to exits. In the event of a power failure, they remain illuminated via battery backup systems or UPS (uninterruptible power systems). There are doors that close automatically when smoke is detected. There are smoke detectors, fire suppression systems, emergency pull-stations, fire alarm systems, and protected safe areas of refuge within tall buildings just in case we cannot make it to an exit. All of these safety provisions are the result of lessons learned from past disasters.

Unfortunately, we often have to learn lessons more than once. The previously mentioned 1942 fire in Boston was not the first time people died because exit doors did not swing in the direction of egress. In 1903, over 600 people died in the Iroquois Theater Fire in Chicago. Many were crushed to death, stacked against exit doors that swung in. Chicago changed its code shortly thereafter, requiring all exits to swing out. It took a fire much closer to home before Boston changed its requirements.

WATER: ANOTHER SOURCE FOR DISASTER

On April 1, 1946, a large undersea earthquake occurred near the Aleutian Islands of Alaska. It caused a gigantic tsunami that spread out across the Pacific Ocean. Hours later, tidal waves reached Hawaii, causing surge run-ups of over 24 feet in Hilo on the big island, killing 159 people and causing $26 million in damage. By mid-August 1948, a tsunami early warning system was in place for Hawaii and the Pacific region. In 1964, another earthquake struck off the coast of Alaska. Again a tsunami raced out from the epicenter. Traveling south along the west coast of North America, it caused coastal flooding and damage in Alaska, Vancouver Island, Washington, Oregon, and as far south as Long Beach in Southern California. Crescent City in northern California was especially hard hit. Docks and buildings along the harbor were completely destroyed and 11 people lost their lives. Areas in the tsunami's path received little or no warning because they were not part of the

Hawaiian/Pacific tsunami warning system. In 1967, a warning system for Alaska, British Columbia, and the west coast of the United States was established.

On December 26, 2004, a magnitude 9.0 earthquake in the Indian Ocean caused the most devastating tsunami in recorded history, killing an estimated 180,000 people who were caught without warning. While there are tsunami warning systems for Japan, South America, French Polynesia, Hawaii, and the Pacific Ocean and the west coast of North America, as noted above, the Indian Ocean had no early warning system despite centuries of recorded devastating tsunamis dating as far back as 1524. The Indian Ocean Tsunamis of 1977 killed hundreds. In a January 2005 United Nations conference in Kobe, Japan, U.N. Secretary General Kofi Annan said:

> We must draw on every lesson we can to prevent tragedies like this occurring in the future. Prevention and early warning systems must become a priority.[17]

By mid-2006, the Indian Ocean had an operational tsunami warning system. Our prowess in planning and design is only as good as the lessons we have learned and our willingness to implement what we have learned.

IMPACT OF THE NATURAL ELEMENTS

There have been numerous disasters in history—too many, really. Throughout history disasters have been the result of fire, wind, water, and the shaking of the earth—the ancient Greek's four basic natural elements of the cosmos. The pages that follow trace the impact of disasters caused by these four elements on the built environment. Because disasters caused by fire have played a tremendous role in shaping cities and many planning and design requirements, fire is good place to start.

C *h a p t e r*

2

FIRE

Of the four elements that shape the world—water, air, earth, and fire—the pre-Socratic philosopher Heracleitus thought that fire was the most fundamental. Writing around 500 BC he argued:

> All things are an exchange for fire, and fire for all things; as goods are for gold, and gold for goods.[1]

He likened fire's flame, which is always in motion, to the fundamental cosmic process that is at work in everything: constant change. In Heracleitus's worldview, everything relies on everlasting fire "kindling in measure and going out in measure."[2] Heracleitus did not see fire as a destructive force. He saw it neither as good nor bad, but omnipresent, forever shaping and reshaping the world.

Today, few people, if any, share Heracleitus's worldview; most see fire as destructive. But Heracleitus was right about fire, at least as it pertains to shaping the built environment. Destructive as it may be, fire has been a fundamental force in determining the form of cities and the way we build within them.

All modern city building codes and zoning ordinances contain regulations to prevent fire and control its spread. So, in a book about planning for disaster, a discussion of fire's role in shaping cities and buildings is a good place to begin and there may be no better fire to begin with than the first Great Fire in recorded history: the Great Fire of Rome.

THE GREAT FIRE OF ROME

Crowded and chaotic Rome disgusted Nero, emperor of Rome from 54–68 AD. The city was a labyrinth of narrow, twisting streets, poorly constructed wooden tenements, and merchant stalls of lashed-together boards and sticks.

Nero had a plan for a new Rome with wider and straighter streets, regularly sized blocks, improved sanitation facilities, less crowded residential areas, and fire-resistant buildings. Nero's plan also included an enormous palace for himself, located in a gigantic park in the heart of Rome. Rumor had it that Nero planned to name the new Rome after himself. There was one thing standing in his way, however, and that was existing Rome.

Nero's preferred site for his palace was the most expensive neighborhood in Rome, the area near the Forum that contained the homes of Rome's most prominent citizens, the patricians, and many of Rome's senators. Understandably, the senators were not too keen to see Nero's plan implemented, so Nero's master plan sat on the shelf. Rome went along as it always had, its narrow streets growing ever more congested. Slipshod market stalls and shacks continued to be hastily erected. Some were so poorly built that they literally blew down in strong winds. Dozens of small fires broke out daily,[3] routinely burning down a market stall or a building before they were extinguished. Sunlight never fell upon the narrow streets closely lined with tenement buildings. Nearby marshlands filled regularly with polluted and stagnant water. Diseases plagued the city. For the majority of its citizens, living conditions in Rome were deplorable.

Sometime during the hot summer night of July 18, 64 AD, a fire started in the deserted marketplace near the Circus Maximus. Soon flames were leaping out of control, landing on parched roofs, burning down flimsy market stalls, one after another. Winds quickly spurred the fire beyond the Circus and, ravenously, it began devouring the city. In the *Annals of Imperial Rome,* the ancient Roman historian Cornelius Tacitus (c. 56–120) lamented:

> A disaster followed . . . more dreadful than any which have ever happened to this city by the violence of fire. It had its beginning in

that part of the circus which adjoins the Palatine and Caelian hills, where, amid the shops containing inflammable wares, the conflagration both broke out and instantly became so fierce and so rapid from the wind that it seized in its grasp the entire length of the circus. For here there were no houses fenced in by solid masonry, or temples surrounded by walls, or any other obstacle to interpose delay. . . . It outstripped all preventive measures; so rapid was the mischief and so completely at its mercy [was] the city . . . [with its] narrow winding passages and irregular streets, which characterized old Rome.[4]

The fire raged for nine days. Many helpless and exhausted Romans perished in the blaze. When the fire finally died out, 10 out of Rome's 14 districts were nothing but smoldering ash. (See Figure 2.1.) Although built mostly of stone and masonry, even the homes of the patricians were not spared. The fire torched their roofs and gutted the insides.

Rumors about the fire spread almost as quickly as the conflagration. Many of Rome's distressed and angry citizens claimed Nero had torched the city himself to clear the way for his new palace. Tacitus recounted a story that claimed Nero, who fancied himself an actor and musician, "had gone on his private stage and, comparing modern calamities with

FIGURE 2.1 *64 A.D. Burning of Rome. Emperor Nero was suspected of instigating the fire. Here he is shown triumphantly standing over the destroyed city.*
Artist: Robert Hubert (1733–1808), Musee des Beaux-Arts Andre Malraux, Le Havre, France.
Photo Credit: Giraudon/Art Resource, NY.

ancient, had sung of the destruction of Troy,"[5] accompanying himself on the lyre. Through centuries of retelling, the story has come down as "Nero fiddled as Rome burned."

There was, however, a foundation for the rumors. Nero was a ruthless and mentally unstable despot. His reign was punctuated with atrocious acts. In the year 54 AD, 16-year-old Nero Claudius Drusus Germanicus, the great grandson of Caesar Augustus, became the fifth emperor of Rome. To solidify his position, he poisoned his primary rival Britannicus, who was his younger stepbrother and son of the deceased emperor, Claudius. In 59 AD, Nero had his mother clubbed to death, and in 62 AD he exiled his wife Octavia and subsequently had her murdered. Nero, who never really liked governing, preferred more lecherous pastimes such as roaming the streets at night in search of women and boys, sometimes dressing up as a wild beast to better terrorize unsuspecting citizens. A man who could do all this was certainly capable of arson.

However, at the time the fire started, Nero was at home in nearby Antium, his birthplace. Upon hearing news of the fire, he quickly returned to Rome and personally organized and led the firefighters. First, he tried to save his own palace, but alas, it was lost in the fire. He then set up temporary shelters for the thousands left homeless and provided them with food and water. Nevertheless, the rumors persisted. If Nero did not personally start it, perhaps he had ordered it. Tacitus recounted:

> [N]o one dared to stop the . . . [fire], because of incessant menaces from a number of persons who forbade the extinguishing of the flames. . . . [O]thers openly hurled brands, and kept shouting that there was one who gave them authority, either seeking to plunder more freely, or obeying orders.[6]

To quell the rumors that he had ordered the torching, Nero blamed someone else, a small religious sect called the Christians. In pagan Rome, Christians were despised for their bizarre religious beliefs, which, rumors claimed, included the abhorrent act of ceremonial cannibalism. Blaming them for the fire would be believable and convenient—child's play for someone with Nero's grotesque talents.

Nero ordered the arrest of everyone who professed Christianity. Tacitus wrote that Christians who confessed their faith were quickly tried and convicted, "not so much of the crime of firing the city, as of hatred against mankind."[7] Many were burned to death, like human torches, "to serve as a nightly illumination, when daylight had expired."[8]

Nero built a new Rome. Its name, of course, was not changed. But it was a new Rome, nevertheless, built following much of Nero's master plan. Recall that Tacitus, in the quotation above, referred to the narrow and irregular streets of "old Rome" as the reason why the fire spread so quickly. Tacitus, who wrote some 40 years after the fire, lived in "new Rome."

New Rome had wider and straighter streets and standardized city blocks. This reduced congestion and improved the ability to move first responders quickly through the city in the event of an emergency. Wider streets gave greater separation from buildings on opposite sides creating firebreaks, making it more difficult for fire to jump from one side of a street to the other. Wider streets also allowed in more sunlight and fresh air.

After the fire, buildings in the center of Rome were required to be constructed of noncombustible stone and masonry up to a specified height. Stone walls were required at property lines. The ancient Roman historian Gaius Suetonius Tranquillus recounts in his history, *Lives of the Twelve Caesars*, that Nero

"devised a new form for the buildings of the city, and in front of the houses and apartments he erected porches, from the flat roofs of which fires could be fought; and these he put up at his own cost."[9]

To encourage rebuilding, a monetary reward program was established, based on a sliding scale that took into account the location of the property, an individual's status, and the length of time it took to rebuild. Debris from the fire was hauled to nearby lowlands and used to fill them in, thus eliminating areas for the accumulation of stagnant water that bred diseases. Water cisterns were strategically placed throughout the city, providing sources of fresh drinking water. In addition, the cisterns could be used to combat future fires. Thus, the new Rome that took shape out of the destruction of old Rome was a cleaner, safer, and healthier place to live.

Nero built his palace called Domus Aurea—Golden House. It was located within a 240-acre wooded park with its own lake, right in the middle of Rome, on the same land that once housed Rome's aristocracy. Suetonius said of Nero's ostentatious Golden House:

Its vestibule was large enough to contain a colossal statue of the emperor—a hundred and twenty feet high; and it was so extensive that it had a triple colonnade—a mile long. There was a pond too, like a sea, surrounded with buildings to represent cities. . . . In the rest of the house all parts were overlaid with gold and adorned with gems and mother-of-pearl. There were dining-rooms with fretted ceils of ivory, whose panels could turn and shower down flowers and were fitted with pipes for sprinkling the guests with perfumes. The main banquet hall was circular and constantly revolved day and night, like the heavens. . . . [Of his house, Nero] deigned to say . . . that he was at least beginning to be housed like a human being.[10]

The Golden House and its lush grounds were never completed. By the spring of 68 AD, the Senate was at long last fed up with Nero and had mustered enough support and courage to pronounce him a public enemy. On June 9, as soldiers arrived to arrest him, Nero took his own life.

Forty years after his death, parts of Nero's Golden House became the substructure for another emperor's extravagant building project, the Baths of Trajan, constructed in 109 AD. Historians believe that the walls of the main banquet hall that Suetonius mentioned in the quote above formed part of Trajan's bathhouse foundations. A strange mechanism and octagon-shaped room exist among the bath's foundation walls, suggesting that at one time the mechanism—possibly water powered—could have made the ceiling of the room revolve.

Principles of Disaster Planning That Arose from the Great Fire of Rome

The Great Fire of Rome illustrates three important principles about disaster planning that occur in subsequent disasters throughout history. First, Roman authorities did not take serious action to prevent fires until after the Great Fire forced their hand. As discussed in Chapter 1, this is a common phenomenon in disaster planning.

Second, although the disaster was caused by fire, the improvements that Rome made transcended fire safety. Increasing the separation of buildings to control the spread of fire also decreased population density, which relieved overcrowding and congestion. This had significant sanitation and health benefits. Using debris from the fire to fill in low-lying areas eliminated wet places prone to breeding diseases such as malaria, which had plagued old Rome. In addition, the changes improved the city's overall appearance, as noted by Tacitus's comment that "these changes which were liked for their utility, also added beauty to the new city."[11]

Third, the Great Fire of Rome illustrates that disasters play a significant role in shaping history. The Great Fire scattered and weakened Rome's aristocracy—the patricians—who never recovered. The fire marks the beginning of the end of aristocratic influence on matters of government in Rome; subsequent emperors became stronger and the aristocracy weaker. In addition, the fire sent Nero in search of a scapegoat and he found one in the Christians. After the Great Fire, the systematic persecution of Christians became official Roman policy, a doctrine that continued on and off for nearly the next three centuries and became a significant factor in the early history of Christianity.

In a different way, the following disaster, the Great Fire of London, also shaped history. In addition, it illustrates that lessons from disasters do not travel well. London had to learn on its own the lessons that fire had taught Rome centuries before.

THE GREAT FIRE OF LONDON

Today, many historical areas of London are characterized by well-proportioned, two-, three-, and four-story red brick buildings dating from the late 17th, 18th, and early 19th centuries. Closer examination reveals that their character and heights are similar and that they are proportionate to the width of the streets they front. Those dating from 1714 to 1820 are called Georgian architecture, a classical style of architecture that accommodated local building materials and regulations and reflected the reserved, understated tastes of Britain. The style derives its name from the three Kings of England—all named George—during whose reign the style became prevalent.

But it was not a king named George who was responsible for the style of these buildings, rather, a disaster was responsible. The Great Fire of 1666 cleared the ground, and the Rebuilding Act of 1667, passed only months afterward, established the regulations that brought about Georgian architecture.

Prior to the Great Fire of 1666, most of early 17th-century London was a medieval city located within medieval walls. It was a city of half-timber construction, the predominant building technique of Tudor England (1485–1603). Timber posts and beams—usually oak—were mortised and pegged together to form a wooden skeletal system. Diagonal timbers were often used to brace the structure, and it is these members that give half-timbered buildings their distinctive crisscross look. The areas between the wood skeleton were filled in with wattle and daub, which was a forerunner to lath and plaster. It consisted of a lattice work of spaced boards or wood stakes called wattles. To the wattles, a wet mixture of clay, straw, and animal dung, called daub, was applied. The wet daub stuck to the wattles and worked through and around them. When the daub dried, it locked into place. The surface was then whitewashed to better resist rain.

Timbers forming the roof were covered with spaced boards. Many half-timbered buildings had thatched roofs. London established a roof covering regulation in 1212 that banned the use of thatch, requiring, instead, the use of lead, wood, tile, or slate shingles. However, the regulation was rarely enforced, and because thatch was much less expensive, it was the roofing material of choice. There is an interesting story that dates from 1302 that illustrates how feebly the ban on thatch was enforced:

> One Thomas Bat being hailed before the Mayor on a charge of neglecting to put tiles instead of thatch on his houses offered to indemnify the city in case of any fire happening by reason of his thatch. The offer was accepted, on the understanding that the thatch was to be removed by a certain time. . . . The naiveté of Mr. Bat in offering and the city accepting, an indemnity in case of fire is truly remarkable. What would Mr. Bat have done, how far would his personal estates have gone, if a quarter of the city had been burned down by reason of his thatch?[12]

Multistory, half-timbered buildings employed jetties to increase the floor areas above the first floor. Jetties were floor-beam assemblies that cantilevered over a supporting timber-framed wall below. The wall above was constructed at the end of the cantilevered structure. The third floor often jettied out over the second. The result was two- and three-story buildings—some even taller—that hung out over narrow packed-earth or cobble-paved streets, giving medieval London streets their distinctive appearance. Narrow streets lined with jettied half-timber buildings with thatch roofs were very prone to fire. They were stacked tinder waiting for a match.

There were many fires, mostly small, caused by fireplace, oven, and cooking mishaps. Fireplace and oven fires were so common that it was against the law to leave a fireplace or oven burning overnight. In 1066, William the Conqueror enacted the "Cover-Fire" Law, requiring all fires to be extinguished at night to reduce the chance of fire. Our modern word "curfew" derives from this law.

Firefighting was primitive. It was done mostly with dowsing buckets, blankets, and beating sticks. Larger fires required cooperation in the form of bucket brigades. The primary source of water was the Thames River, and it was often some distance away. Other buildings often blocked access to the river. If the structure was too far gone to be saved, it was pulled down using grappling hooks and ropes in an attempt to prevent the fire from spreading to adjacent buildings. On occasion, buildings adjacent to the burning buildings were pulled down as well to form firebreaks. In the early 1600s the London Fire Brigade invented a large syringe-like, wagon-mounted contraption called a fire squirt, which was a fire hose with nozzle set atop a water tank mounted on a wagon. A manual pump pumped the water from the tank into and out of the nozzle of the hose. Its lack of maneuverability combined with its inadequate hose stream, however, made it ineffectual in fighting large fires.

In an attempt to quell the number of fires and limit their spread, an ordinance was enacted in 1607 stating that, for all new buildings and reconstructions on existing foundations, "the front and all the outer walls shall be built of brick or stone."[13] In addition, the ordinance prohibited the use of jetties. But, like so many previous laws regarding construction in London, it was rarely enforced. Worse, it had an unintended consequence. Because facing a building in brick or stone was considerably more expensive than doing so with wattle and daub, Londoners made do with their half-timbered buildings. Rather than replacing them, they patched them up the best they could and snuck in little additions here and there when needed.

In 1619, London passed its first Building Act. It contained provisions regarding the thickness of walls, story heights, windows, doors, and shop fronts. It reiterated the ban on thatched roofs and the requirement for exterior walls to be brick or stone. Londoners mostly ignored the act and continued building as they saw fit.

In 1625, a specification for bricks was established. It set standards for their quality, ingredients, and method of forming, drying, and firing. It established a standard brick size: 9 inches in length by $4\frac{3}{8}$ inches in thickness by $2\frac{1}{4}$ inches in height.

In 1630, another ordinance was issued that primarily summarized all the previous ordinances. It set an exemption for buildings on London Bridge. There were many buildings on London Bridge built in the half-timbered style, jutting out over the bridge and the Thames. None were faced in brick or stone because requiring them to be faced with these much heavier materials would have significantly overloaded the bridge, requiring an upgrade to the bridge structure itself:

> . . . [A]s concernteth the building with bricke or stone shall not extend to any buildings upon London Bridge which by reason of the situation thereof cannot with convenience be so built.[14]

In 1661, King Charles II (1630–1685) issued a proclamation reminding everyone of the building laws. His proclamation went unheeded. Building regulations require enforcement, and London had few means and little will to enforce them.

In 1665, London was struck by the Black Plague, which lasted until September of the following year. Thousands died every month, giving Londoners little reason to worry about anything other than the mounting death toll. As many as 30,000 Londoners died in the 1665–1666 plague.

Thomas Farynor was a baker who lived on Pudding Lane. Today, a marker identifies where his house once stood. Farynor was no ordinary baker; his employer was King Charles II. Around 10 PM on Saturday night, the 1st of September 1666, after the maid had gone to bed, Farynor grew tired of baking and retired upstairs. Unfortunately, he did not douse the oven fire, a violation of the Cover-Fire Law of 1066. A nearby stack of firewood caught fire, and by the time the maid awoke on the morning of September 2, the bakery was engulfed in flames. She woke up Farynor, his wife, and daughter. Escape downstairs through the flames was impossible, so the Farynor family climbed out an upstairs window and escaped across neighboring rooftops. The maid refused to go and became the first victim of the Great Fire of London.

Embers lit upon a nearby haystack and this, in turn, caught the neighboring Star Inn on fire. After that, it was St. Margaret's Church. Strong easterly winds pushed the fire onto Thames Street, lined with warehouses, which were filled with wooden crates, tallow, and lamp oil. Wooden wharves jutted out into the Thames like fingers of cribbed firewood. The well-fed fire grew and was soon unstoppable. Panicked residents could do nothing but flee its advance. The fire marched through medieval walled London, leveling it as it headed toward London Bridge.

Because there was no way to combat the flames directly, King Charles ordered the destruction of buildings in the fire's path. Hastily, buildings were pulled down.

Londoner Samuel Pepys (1633–1703) was the secretary to the Earl of Sandwich. Between the years 1660 and 1669, he kept a diary, which included entries that discussed audiences with King Charles. After his death, Pepys's diary was published and has become a rich source of information about life in London during the mid-17th century. Pepys's diary suggests that constructing firebreaks was his idea. On the day of the fire, Pepys ventured out to the Tower of London:

> . . . and there up to the King's closet in the Chapel, where people came about me, and I did give them an account [about the fire that] dismayed them all, and the word was carried to the King. So I was called for, and did tell the King and Duke of York what I saw; and that unless His Majesty did command houses to be pulled down, nothing could stop the fire. They seemed much troubled, and the King commanded me to go to my Lord Mayor [Bludworth] from him and command him to spare no houses.

> At last [I] met my Lord Mayor in Cannon Street, like a man spent, with a handkerchief about his neck. To the King's message he cried, like a fainting woman, "Lord, what can I do? I am spent: people will not obey me. I have been pulling down houses, but the fire overtakes us faster than we can do it." . . . so he left me, and I him, and walked home; seeing people all distracted, and no manner of means to quench the fire.[15]

To speed the work of constructing firebreaks, buildings were blown up with gunpowder. This created flying embers that started other fires. The fire raged for a total of five days. When it was finally extinguished, approximately 80 percent of London was destroyed. The Tower of London was spared as was the London Bridge, but most of the structures within the walled portion of the medieval city were gone, the smoldering ground punctuated by charred stone church towers. Stories were told that the ground was too hot to walk on for days.

All told, an area measuring roughly a half-mile wide by a mile-and-a-half long lay in ruins. Over 13,000 houses were destroyed, including the property deeds that defined their ownership and location of property lines. Eighty-seven churches were destroyed. Approximately 65,000 Londoners were left homeless. Medieval London was gone.

London Rebuilds

London was a clean slate, albeit a smoldering, rubble-filled one. London could rebuild as it was before or it could try something new. Perhaps no one was more dead set against rebuilding London as it had been than the architect, scientist, mathematician, Oxford professor of astronomy, and cofounder of the Royal Society of London, Christopher Wren (1633–1703).

Wren first took a stab at architecture in 1662–1663, designing and building a model of a classical-styled building for Oxford University called Sheldonian Theatre. He enjoyed the experience immensely, and soon turned all his attention and considerable talents away from science to architecture.

When the Black Plague struck in 1665, Oxford University closed. With school closed and the plague in full bloom, Wren took the opportunity to visit France to study architecture. As a confidant of King Charles and a member of the Royal Society, he was granted the assignment to study how best to repair St. Paul's Cathedral, London's most significant church. It had suffered terribly from neglect and vandalism.

It was not the St. Paul's we know today. The old medieval St. Paul's was on a different site and in a sad state of repair. In one form or another, St. Paul's had stood atop Ludgate Hill since the year 604. Saxons had built the first cathedral there, a wooden structure that burned down in 675. The second St. Paul's was built in 962, using stone for the walls, but a wood-framed roof. A fire destroyed most of it in 1087. Construction of the third St. Paul's—that today is called the "Old St. Paul's—started shortly thereafter. Work progressed very slowly and suffered a setback in 1135 or 1136 when another fire damaged portions of it. It was finally completed in 1240. London had grown considerably during this time, so soon work began to lengthen it, which was completed in 1311. Soaring 489 feet in height, its spire was among the tallest in Europe.

Old St. Paul's suffered during the 16th century, as Protestants and Catholics argued bitterly. In 1549, a mob of Protestants destroyed much of the cathedral's interior. In 1561, the spire was struck by lightning and toppled to the ground. Both Catholics and Protestants saw it as a sign of God's displeasure, and it was not replaced.

In the 1630s, the architect Inigo Jones (1573–1652) made repairs and changes to Old St. Paul's. Considered England's first classical architect, Jones had visited Italy and studied the works of the Renaissance architect Andrea Palladio. Jones substituted classical pilasters for the medieval buttresses that reinforced the nave, and added a Corinthian-styled portico at the west end. Old St. Paul's was mistreated again during the Puritan revolution. The central tower was in such poor repair that scaffolding was added to hold up the tower.

In July 1665, Wren left for Paris to study the modern buildings of the continent with hopes of meeting the architect Jules Hardouin Mansart (1646–1708) and the great Italian Baroque artist and architect Gianlorenzo Bernini (1598–1680). Wren returned to London in the spring of 1666, a full-fledged proponent of modern architecture, or what we call today classical or traditional architecture. He presented his scheme to the Royal Commission assigned to oversee Old St. Paul's reconstruction. Wren's proposed reconstruction included an enormous domed space over the central crossing, featuring evenly spaced classical columns in a ring around the base of the dome. It was unlike anything in England at the time, clearly inspired by Michelangelo's dome of St. Peter's in Rome and Jacques Lemercier's dome of the Sorbonne in Paris.

By the end of August 1666, after much discussion, Wren's scheme was approved by the Commission. Only a week later, the Great Fire made the scheme useless because Old St. Paul's was destroyed in the fire.

FIGURE 2.2 *View of Old St. Paul's Cathedral burning in the 1666 Great Fire of London. Artist: Hollar Wenceslaus (1607–1677), Guildhall Art Gallery, London, Great Britain. Photo Credit: HIP/Art Resource, NY.*

(See Figure 2.2.) John Evelyn, a member of the Royal Society, wrote in his diary about the destruction of St. Paul's:

> [T]he stones of [St.] Paules flew like grenados, the Lead melting down the streetes in a streame, and the very pavements of them glowing with fiery rednesse, so as nor horse nor man was able to tread on them.[16]

The debris from the Great Fire was hardly cold when Christopher Wren stood before King Charles II on September 10, 1666, to present a master plan for a new London. His drawing bore little resemblance to old London. It was much more like the Piazza del Popolo in Rome or the Place de France proposed for Paris during the reign of the French King Henri IV. Although the Place de France was never built, engravings of the Place existed and Wren probably saw them during his stay in Paris.

Gone were London's narrow and irregular medieval winding streets. Wren's plan replaced them with straight streets in new alignments. The streets were of three different widths, depending on their importance. The widest streets were the boulevards that radiated from a civic center that contained the Post Office, the Mint, the Excise Office, and other important government buildings, none of which existed at the locations that Wren proposed. New churches were situated on prominent street corners. One of the radiating streets led directly to a new St. Paul's, surrounded by a park. Wren's London was rational, geometric, and grand, with a mathematician's eye for beauty—all in keeping with the Age of Reason, as Wren was one of its staunchest adherents.

It was also completely unworkable.

King Charles agreed that rebuilding the city based on the old model would be a mistake. But implementing Wren's plan would require the government to seize large portions of the city, lay out the city anew, and, in some equitable way, compensate the owners whose property had been confiscated and then somehow fairly dole out the property again. This would take considerable sums of money, time, and untold disagreements, none of which the Crown could afford. The Great Fire had slowed London's economy to a near standstill. London's citizens were already returning to their burnt properties, salvaging boards and bricks, and preparing to rebuild. The city would be haphazardly reconstructed in its ashes, long before all the logistics could be figured out to implement such a sweeping master plan as Wren proposed.

On September 13, just a few days after Wren's presentation, King Charles issued a proclamation that guaranteed two things:

1. London would not be rebuilt following its medieval model, and
2. improvements would be practical ones that respected the property rights of all its citizens. The second guarantee ensured that Wren's master plan would never be implemented.

The proclamation was an interim measure and it bought time for planning a more comprehensive rebuilding program. It required all new buildings to be faced in brick or stone, and it mandated the widening of narrow streets so that fire could not jump across as easily. It stated that an extensive survey would be conducted to establish exact property lines. The owners of portions of properties confiscated to make wider streets would be fairly compensated. It provided tax benefits for those who rebuilt following the new laws.

The proclamation was followed five months later with the Rebuilding Act of 1667, issued on February 8. The act started with an explanation of its purpose:

> Forasmuch as the City of London, being the imperial seat of his Majesty's kingdoms, and renowned for trade and commerce throughout the world; by reason of a most dreadful fire lately happening

therein, was for the most part . . . burnt down and destroyed within the compass of a few days, and now lies buried in its own ruins for . . . [its] restoration . . . better regulation, uniformity and gracefulness of new Buildings . . . and to the end that great and outrageous fires . . . may be reasonably prevented . . . by the matter and form of such building . . . be it therefore enacted . . . that . . . no building or house for habitation . . . may . . . be erected . . . [that does not comply with] the rules and orders of . . . this present act hereafter specified.[17]

The Rebuilding Act included many provisions that were reiterations of previous acts that had been ignored and not enforced. The difference this time was the magnitude of the situation. London had to rebuild thousands of houses and buildings and dozens of churches. The act included provisions for enforcement of its rules and punishments for those who did not comply. It called for the Lord Mayor of London to appoint building officials whose responsibility it was to inspect and enforce the Rebuilding Act. The act required that building officials be qualified for their position—not just political appointments:

> . . . the lord mayor, aldermen and common council . . . shall . . . nominate and appoint . . . discreet and intelligent . . . persons in the art of building, to be surveyors or supervisors to see the said rules and scantlings well and truly observed. . . . [A]ll the said surveyors or supervisors [shall take] an oath upon the holy evangelists, for the true and impartial execution of their office.[18]

Enforcement procedures included a hearing before the Lord Mayor or justices, duly appointed for the task of enforcement of the act. The hearings included testimony from witnesses, the building official, and the defendant. At least two witnesses against the defendant were required for a verdict of guilty. A fine was levied against those found guilty. The amount of the fine varied and covered the cost of demolition of the noncomplying structure. If the convicted offender did not pay the fine, he was sent to jail without bail until the fine was paid.

Streets were required to be paved. Control was removed from local districts to centralized control by the city, which was given power of enforcement and taxation for street improvements. Spouting gutters were no longer permitted. Gutters had to drain into downspouts that ran from the roof level to the paved streets below and be directed to flow into channels (gutters) running in the streets.

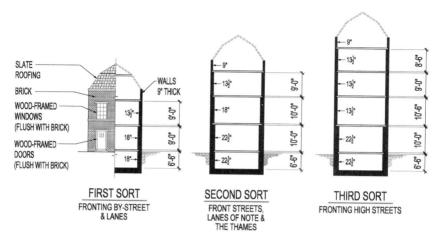

SLATE ROOFING
BRICK
WOOD-FRAMED WINDOWS (FLUSH WITH BRICK)
WOOD-FRAMED DOORS (FLUSH WITH BRICK)
WALLS 9" THICK

FIRST SORT
FRONTING BY-STREET & LANES

SECOND SORT
FRONT STREETS, LANES OF NOTE & THE THAMES

THIRD SORT
FRONTING HIGH STREETS

FIGURE 2.3 *Sorts of Houses permitted by the London Rebuilding Act of 1667.*

Within central London, noncombustible stone or brick facing was required on all exterior façades. Only doors and windows were permitted to be constructed of wood. Half-timbered construction was prohibited, as was jettied construction. Houses were required to conform to one of four standardized "sorts." The "First Sort" was houses fronting on minor by-streets or lanes. First Sort houses were permitted to be two stories in height. The houses' story heights and wall thicknesses were established by the Rebuilding Act. (See Figure 2.3.)

The Second Sort was houses that fronted the Thames and streets and lanes of note. These houses were permitted to be three stories in height. The Third Sort was houses fronting high streets (prominent streets) and these could be four stories in height. Wall thicknesses and room heights were established for these sorts as well. The Fourth Sort was mansions and they could not exceed four stories in height. No ceiling heights or wall thicknesses were prescribed for this sort, the feeling being that only competent architects would design mansions.

Party walls between houses were required to straddle the common property line and be of equal thickness on both sides. The first builder had to construct the entire wall's thickness and leave pockets to receive the floor framing for the future house. When the second house was built, its owner had to pay one-half the cost of the party wall to the previous builder plus interest, thus sharing in the expense of building the wall.

It is these standards—the establishment of allowable building heights, materials, and their permitted arrangements—combined with the vast number of new houses required to replace all those lost in the fire, that so dramatically affected the overall appearance of new London. The requirements set the design conditions that affected the general character and proportions of the Georgian-styled buildings that would come during the following century.

To avoid spring flooding of wharves and stockpiles of hay, coal, and other goods, London required all wharves to be raised three feet. A sewage commission was established and commissioners were given power to set sewage rates and construct sewage systems. Dangerous and offensive trades were prohibited on high streets, which included enterprises such as tanneries and smoke-belching factories. Open areas along the Thames were created to allow access to the river for firefighting purposes.

The existing street pattern was retained. Two new processional routes were created, King Street and Queen Street, that ran from the Thames to Guildhall. Some existing streets were widened, including Fleet Street, Ludgate Hill, St. Paul's Churchyard, Cheapside, Cornhill, Newgate Market, and others. To pay for the street-widening program, a tax of 12 pence per ton was levied on all coal imports.

A new St. Paul's Cathedral was constructed, although not on the same site as Old St. Paul's. Christopher Wren designed it, along with 51 other churches. St. Paul's Cathedral, built between 1675 and 1710, is a triumphant blend of classical and Baroque architecture. Its dome is considered by architectural historians to be one of the most perfect in the world. It is a magnificent testament of the tenacity, courage, political will, and artistic and scientific spirit of its time. And it is a tribute to the architectural genius of its creator, Christopher Wren. Thousands of visitors each year stand beneath its dome and look up into its soaring, majestic splendor. Few realize that its very existence is the result of a centuries-old disaster of colossal proportions.

Lessons Learned from the Great Fire of London

The Great Fire of London illustrates many points about disaster planning. First, London had to learn the lessons of fire on its own, the hard way. London is not unique in this regard. For example, many major cities in the United States could have realized and implemented fire regulations based on lessons learned by other cities. They chose not to, and so they learned the lessons on their own. Disasters in one American city did not lead to improvements in others until the advent of model codes in the early 20th century.

Second, conditions for London's disaster built up gradually through years of neglect.

Third, only after the Great Fire were significant steps taken to *improve and enforce* fire prevention standards. Although London had laws that could have controlled the spread of fire prior to the Great Fire, the city did not enforce them. Laws that are not enforced are little better than no laws at all.

Fourth, some of the improvements that London made went beyond mere fire safety. Raising the wharves, improving drainage from rooftops, restricting certain enterprises from high streets, and building a sewage system improved the general health and well-being of its citizens, but were not fundamentally necessary to control fire.

Fifth, restricting heights of houses in relationship to the widths of streets did more than just provide firebreaks. It also allowed more healthful sunlight to penetrate to street level.

Sixth, cities are organic, and like organisms, they must change slowly, incrementally, and practically. After a disaster, radical whole-sale changes are unlikely to gain wide support because dramatic changes would be disruptive to too many. Evolution teaches that organisms that change, or mutate, drastically do not survive. Wren's plan, as rational and elegant as it was, could not be implemented. To do so would have caused incalculable delay and hardship for virtu-ally all Londoners when most were distraught from the ravages of the fire.

This last lesson has significant repercussions as Americans deal with rebuilding New Orleans after Hurricane Katrina. Many crit-ics called for wholesale changes to New Orleans after Katrina—in effect, a new New Orleans. Such suggestions fly in the face of les-sons learned from past disasters and modern city planning. Wren was not a modern city planner. His approach was more attuned to absolutism, typical of a self-assured genius from the Age of Reason, who thought that one man could solve all problems. Today, most city planners know better. Planning today involves establishing an outline of sound development principles that is dynamic, not the creation of a finished, fixed-form end product. In a way, the Rebuilding Act of 1667 was more in tune with a modern approach to planning than Wren's master plan. Sweeping changes, as Wren proposed, are not realistic. Wren, however, was not the last to offer up unworkable master plans.

In 1905, only months before San Francisco's devastating earthquake and fire, the Chicago architect-turned-planner Daniel H. Burnham prepared a master plan for a new San Francisco, literally modeling San Francisco, the Paris of the West, on the real Paris. On April 18, 1906, an earthquake and fire destroyed over half of San Francisco. Chapter 5 discusses the earthquake and fire, and San Francisco's decision to not implement Burnham's plan.

In 2005, Katrina flooded 80 percent of New Orleans. In January 2006, a comprehensive master plan for rebuilding the city was presented to New Orleanians in a town hall meeting. The master plan proposed many changes to New Orleans, including the reconfiguration and consolidation of New Orleans's generations-old neighborhoods and the relocation of many of New Orleans residents to areas of higher ground. It received angry condemnation from many New Orleanians, who did not want to be moved. By May 2006, the plan was replaced with a much less ambitious approach that did not threaten the existence of New Orleans's neighborhoods.

THE GREAT CHICAGO FIRE

In 1830, Chicago was a settlement of about 100 people along the swampy shores of Lake Michigan and the Cecagou River (Chicago River), as the Native Americans called it, named after the onion-like tubers that grew along its banks. On March 4, 1837, Chicago was incorporated as a city. Ideally situated to take advantage of America's westward migration, Chicago grew rapidly in the 1840s. Over the next 40 years, it became a bustling inland port city with a population of 300,000.

Buildings went up quickly during the 1840s because of a new, fast, and easy form of construction called balloon framing. Chicago was its birthplace. In balloon framing, 2-inch-thick pieces of wood, called studs, were used to frame the walls. The studs continued uninterrupted from the foundation to the roof. (See Figure 2.4.)

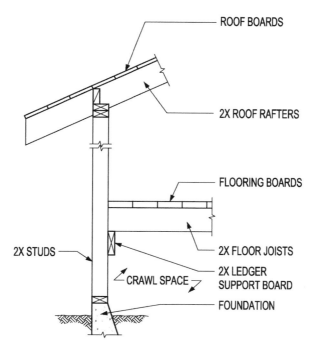

FIGURE 2.4 *Typical Balloon Framing.*

The building's floor and roof joists framed into the walls, supported on boards, called ledger boards, that were nailed to the studs. Generally, the exterior of balloon-framed buildings were covered with horizontal boards. Nails were used in balloon framing, not the mortise and tendon joints commonly used at the time in timber construction.

Nails had been around for centuries, but due to their expense, they were used sparingly. By the 1840s, nails were mass produced and, consequently, their cost plummeted, making them the preferred fastener. Milled lumber, in combination with cheap nails, made balloon-framed buildings inexpensive and easy to construct. The services of an architect or a skilled craftsman were not necessary to design and construct a balloon-framed building. Unskilled laborers could hammer together a balloon-framed building in days, sometimes in a single day, making it the perfect construction technique for a city that was growing by leaps and bounds.

There is a problem with balloon framing, however, and it has to do with fire. Balloon-framed buildings have void spaces between every stud.

These pockets form rectangular shafts—in effect, wood-lined chimneys—running from the foundation of the building up to the roof. Flames can easily burn upward inside balloon-framed walls, quickly turning a small fire into a raging, building-consuming inferno.

By 1850, Chicago's population had grown to approximately 30,000 people. The city covered an area of 9.3 square miles, with a population density of about 3,200 people per square mile. Most buildings were constructed of wood, and most of these were balloon framed. By 1860, the population had more than tripled to over 100,000, its area not quite doubling to 17.5 square miles. The population density nearly doubled to 6,200 people per square mile.[19]

While most of the buildings constructed during the 1850s were balloon framed, some had brick-bearing walls with wood-framed floors and roofs. The more pretentious of these were faced with a limestone material called Athenian marble. Cast-iron fronts started to become popular in the late 1850s. Three sides of these buildings were wood framed or had brick-bearing walls, but the front was cast iron, which permitted large, framed openings for windows and storefronts.

Fires were common in Chicago during the 1850s and 1860s. The results were disastrous at times, destroying entire buildings and sometimes spreading to adjacent buildings. Although Chicago had no building department per se, attempts were made to control the spread of fire. A few fire-resistant buildings were constructed, with demand coming from the particular needs of their owners, rather than from any mandated or concerted effort to require fire-resistant construction. The U.S. Post Office and Custom House, which housed official records, is one example. Built in 1855, the three-story building employed stone-bearing walls for the first floor and brick-bearing walls for the upper two. Its floors and roof were framed with noncombustible wrought iron. At the time, the building was considered fireproof.

One of Chicago's most prestigious buildings was the three-story Chicago Court House and City Hall, designed by Chicago architect John Mills Van Osdel, who started the first architectural office in Chicago in 1844. The Court House, which housed the city's legal and real estate records, was the pride of the city. It was originally built in 1853 as a two-story building. After the streets around it were raised as part of a citywide effort to improve drainage, a third story was added in 1858, and two wings were added after the Civil War. The building was faced with Athenian marble, which was believed to be fireproof. The façade was rendered in a Greek revival style, a popular architectural motif at the time. Perched above the building's roof was a cupola housing the city's fire bell.

By 1870, the population of Chicago was nearly 300,000 with an area of approximately 35.2 square miles and a population density of 8,500 per square mile.[20] It was crowded, busy, and filled with wood-framed buildings, interspersed sparingly with stone-, brick-, Athenian marble-, and cast-iron-faced buildings. Chicago's population was growing quickly, increasing between 1870 and October 1871 by 10 percent to 334,270.

Just about everyone has heard the following story and many can sing the song—such is the lore and appeal of disasters long after they have passed. On Sunday night, October 8, 1871, after everyone had gone to bed, Catherine O'Leary, of 558 South DeKoven Street, took a kerosene lantern and headed out back to her shed to milk her cow, Naomi. Naomi kicked the lantern over, flames exploded in the dry straw, and Mrs. O'Leary yelled, as we all know, "It will be a hot time in the ole town tonight!"

The composer of the song is unknown and exactly how the Great Chicago Fire really started is not known either. There are other suspects besides O'Leary and her cow. A transient named Daniel Sullivan may have accidentally started it, or perhaps it began with burning embers from a chimney. In the 1990s, astronomers suggested that an asteroid may have broken up over Chicago, starting the fire. In 1997, 126 years after the fire, the City Council of Chicago officially exonerated Mrs. O'Leary and her cow, without a definitive answer to the question of how it started. Nevertheless, the myth persists.

Regardless of how it started, the fire changed Chicago forever. Historian Ross Miller wrote in his book *The Great Chicago Fire:*

> The fire was the modern city's great generative event. On the most basic level it was a palpable demarcation between Chicago's past—frontier boom town—and its future.[21]

The Great Chicago Fire was also a demarcation line for all American cities. It is "The Fire" that fundamentally changed the way Americans build. It ushered in the first comprehensive American building code, and it cleared the ground for building in a new direction—skyward. It stands at the cusp between unconfident American architecture, dependent upon Europe for its tastes, and confident American architecture that responds to contemporary American needs, aspirations, and sensibilities. It is the demarcation line between traditional architecture and modern architecture.

Starting in the southwest corner of the city, on DeKoven Street, the fire burned diagonally through downtown Chicago toward Lake Michigan, leaving behind a trail of charred balloon-framed houses and buildings. Horace White, the editor-in-chief of *The Chicago Tribune*, wrote an eyewitness account:

> The dogs of hell were upon the housetops . . . bounding from one to another. The fire was moving northward like ocean surf on a sand beach. . . . A column of flame would shoot up from a burning building, catch the force of the wind, and strike the next one, which in turn would perform the same direful office for its neighbor.[22]

There were hopes that downtown could be spared because of the number of stone and masonry buildings located there. (See Figure 2.5.) The Custom House, for example, was supposedly fireproof. Although its

FIGURE 2.5 *Ruins After 1871 Great Chicago Fire. The view looks across the ruins of the Field, Leiter, and Co. store toward the standing walls of the First National Bank at State and Washington Streets. Note in the foreground the destroyed cast irons columns and other iron remains.* © *Bettman/CORBIS.*

walls were stone and brick, its wrought-iron floor and roof framing were not encased with masonry or any other fire-resistant material. When heated, the wrought iron lost its strength and the building collapsed.

When architect Van Osdel realized that the fire could not be contained, he snatched drawings and papers from his office and hurried to the basement. He dug a deep hole, put them in, and covered them back up with sand and damp clay.[23] Van Osdel's drawings and papers survived the fire, however, his Athenian marble-faced Court House did not. Its façade softened and melted away in the flames. Its wood-framed cupola caught fire and the fire bell fell, coming to rest in the basement, among the city's burned papers.

Chicago's firefighters fought the fire gallantly for two full days. As frantic Londoners had done two centuries earlier, Chicagoans blew up buildings in the fire's path to form firebreaks. This proved futile and only worsened the spread of the fire. It was finally stopped by the shoreline of Lake Michigan with a little help from light rain. In the early morning of October 10, it was over.

Afterward, when the devastation was tallied, 300 Chicagoans had lost their lives, 100,000 residents were homeless, and approximately 20,000 buildings were destroyed, including most of downtown. Officials estimated the loss at $200 million, a colossal sum at the time.

The Great Chicago Fire taught us many lessons about fire. The two most important were: (1) balloon-framed wood buildings burn rapidly and their use should be restricted in downtown areas, and (2) stone or masonry walls alone do not make a building fireproof. Floor and roof framing must also be fire resistant. Although wrought iron is technically noncombustible, floors and roofs framed with it can and do fail in fires because wrought iron loses strength at fire temperatures. It loses strength at temperatures much lower than steel, a relatively new and more expensive building material at the time. After the Great Fire, the use of wrought iron slowly phased out. By the mid-1880s, steel had become the building framing material of choice in downtown Chicago.

After the fire, Van Osdel dug up his drawings. When he found them undamaged, he came to an interesting, although not unique, realization: Earth could prevent fire from burning combustible materials. There were already building materials made of earth such as stone, brick, and terra cotta, with terra cotta being the lightest in weight of the three. Van Osdel surmised: Why not use terra cotta to protect structural framing members from fire? Or, better yet, why not use terra cotta as a structural material? In 1873, Van Osdel designed the Kendal Building (later called the Chicago Real Estate Exchange, demolished in 1940). It was the first fireproof building constructed in Chicago. Van Osdel used terra cotta to form the Kendal Building walls and floor arches.

Chicagoans wasted no time rebuilding. On October 10, the day the fire ended, the Chicago Chamber of Commerce issued a call encouraging everyone to rebuild immediately. Rumors spread quickly that wood buildings would soon be prohibited in downtown. A rebuilding frenzy was on. Quality was not as important as speed and quantity. Within a month, over 5,000 houses were either rebuilt or were under construction. Real estate speculators, banking on the rumor that wood buildings would be banned, saw an opportunity to profit. Real estate values in downtown Chicago escalated. It is no coincidence that the first building finished after the fire was a real estate office. Plans of buildings lost in the fire were dusted off and reused. Blocks and blocks of buildings were hastily rebuilt. Within a year after the fire, over 42,000 feet—8 miles!—of street frontage had been replaced, much of it no safer than what the fire had destroyed.

America's First Building Code Is Established

In 1873, the nation plummeted into an economic depression. Chicago was hit particularly hard. Rebuilding ground to a near halt. The depression lasted approximately two years and gave city authorities a chance to plan and get ahead of the real estate speculators and developers. On June 15, 1875, Chicago passed an ordinance creating a Department of Buildings for the city of Chicago. The ordinance established basic criteria for the construction and remodel of all buildings and structures within its jurisdiction. It has since come to be recognized as America's first building code.[24]

After the depression, Chicago began building again. The building spree was back on, but this time with regulations. In downtown Chicago, the exterior walls of buildings were required to be of noncombustible materials, except that small sheds, shelters, and privies were permitted to be sided with wood. Wood was permitted for building framing, but only if it was protected by noncombustible materials.

In 1881, an updated version of the building ordinance was included in the *Municipal Code of Chicago*. The next year saw a record 3,113 buildings built in Chicago.[25] By this time, Chicago architects were beginning to experiment with skeleton-framed tall buildings, the forerunners to modern skyscrapers. In effect, these architects were the prophets of modern architecture. They used post-fire downtown Chicago as their experimental laboratory. Dubbed the Chicago School, they made advancements in foundation design and building framing. They experimented with artistic expressions of building façades based on materials and function. For these architects, architectural expression was not a matter of historical style. Style grew out of use of materials, utilitarian needs, and the sensibilities of the building's owner. The primary leaders of the Chicago School were William Le Baron Jenney, Dankmar Adler, Louis H. Sullivan, John Root, and Daniel H. Burnham.

The Home Insurance Building is regarded by architectural historians to be the first true skeletal-framed building. Architectural historian Carl W. Condit wrote that the Home Insurance Building was the first

> major step in the conversion of a building from a crustacean with its armor of stone to a vertebrate clothed only in a light skin. . . . It was the major progenitor of the true skyscraper, the first adequate solution to the problem of large-scale urban construction.[26]

William Le Baron Jenney began designing the Home Insurance Building in 1883. Construction was completed in 1885. It was nine stories in height, with two additional stories added in 1891. It was not a true steel-framed building but a hybrid, framed with a combination of cast-iron round columns, wrought-iron box columns, and steel I beams, forming an iron and steel skeleton that was bolted together using steel angles and plates. The exterior framing of the lower story was fire protected by heavy granite-bearing walls, but above that, lighter brick and sandstone were used for fireproofing. The brick, sandstone, and the building's array of large windows were supported at each story on angles connected to the building frame. The technique of hanging a building's façade on its structural frame is called curtain wall construction. The technique used by Jenney was fundamentally the same as the technique used today to support the façades of skyscrapers.

Soon other Chicago architects were employing Jenney's techniques on other buildings, with various improvements and refinements. The Home Insurance Building's façade was far from satisfactory. Jenney, more the engineer than artist, did not seem to know whether to accentuate the building's height or mask it. Consequently, he accomplished neither. The building's façade was a confused mixture of horizontal and vertical elements combined with chaotic ornamentation. It was left to another Chicago architect, Louis Sullivan, who possessed a more refined artistic sense, to finally hit upon the solution. Sullivan explained it in an 1896 *Lippincott's Magazine* article entitled, "The Tall Office Building Artistically Considered":

> What is the chief characteristic of the tall office building? [A]t once we answer, it is lofty. . . . It must be tall, every inch of it tall. The force and power of altitude must be in it, the glory and pride of exaltation must be in it. It must be every inch a proud and soaring thing, rising in sheer exultation [such] that from bottom to top it is a unit without a single dissenting line.[27]

In the article, Sullivan simultaneously described the classical skyscraper and three of his grandest achievements, the Wainwright Building in St. Louis, Missouri (1892), the Chicago Stock Exchange Building, in Chicago, Illinois (1894), and the Guaranty Building in Buffalo, New York (1896).

The modern skyscraper is an American phenomenon. By the end of the 19th century, its continued development moved from Chicago to New York, but its seed originally grew from the fertile ashes of the Great Chicago Fire.

3

CODES

Modern building codes contain mandated requirements for the design and construction of buildings. They provide criteria for the selection of building materials and the design of building structural systems. They establish requirements for the installation of building materials and systems. The purpose of building codes is to protect the public by establishing minimum standards for the health and life safety of buildings. In building code parlance, "health and life safety" is a catchall phrase that encompasses all materials and systems of a building that reduce the risk of accident and injury. These include building structural systems; emergency exiting systems; sanitation, lighting, and ventilation systems; and fire protection, controls, and alarm systems.

Building codes are built on disasters. They are the result of calamitous events that caused enough loss of life, devastation, hardship, fear, and outrage that citizens and governing officials took steps to prevent the disasters from reoccurring. In a sense, codes are driven by the same mentality that causes the farmer to finally shut the barn door after the cow has left. It is not until after the undesirable event has happened that we take steps to prevent it.

Codes are reactive, pragmatic, and subject to change when the next calamitous event illustrates a particular shortcoming. Through trial and error, building codes have helped improve the safety of the built environment.

Building codes are as old as recorded history. Their historical progress can be told as a story of disaster after disaster. The earliest building code dates from around 1750 BC. The specific disasters that caused it to be written are unknown, but reading the code suggests the answer: Poorly constructed buildings must have tragically fallen down and killed their inhabitants. In addition, the code suggests it was written in response to unscrupulous builders taking advantage of owners and overcharging for their services. It is called Hammurabi's Code, and it was written in ancient Babylonia during the reign of King Hammurabi, approximately 1795 to 1750 BC. It is a list of 282 laws governing most aspects of social interaction, including construction. The laws were posted in villages on large blocks of stone so the citizens could read and obey them. Laws 228 through 233 cover the construction of houses:

228: If a builder build a house for some one and complete it, he shall give him a fee of two shekels in money for each sar [12 square feet] of surface.

229: If a builder build a house for some one, and does not construct it properly, and the house which he built fall in and kill its owner, then that builder shall be put to death.

230: If it kill the son of the owner the son of that builder shall be put to death.

231: If it kill a slave of the owner, then he shall pay slave for slave to the owner of the house.

232: If it ruin goods, he shall make compensation for all that has been ruined, and inasmuch as he did not construct properly this house which he built and it fell, he shall re-erect the house from his own means.

233: If a builder build a house for some one, even though he has not yet completed it; if then the walls seem toppling, the builder must make the walls solid from his own means.[1]

As is readily apparent, Hammurabi's Code was keen on punishment, but contained no preventive guidelines or standards for construction or inspection.

By the 4th century BC, Athens had requirements for the dressing and setting of stones, and required architects to inspect buildings that were under construction to confirm that the stones were properly prepared, set square and plumb, and had the required number of interlocking iron dowels. In the 1st century BC, the streets of Rome had become too crowded with people, horses, and carts, and the city experienced frequent health problems due to poor sanitation. To limit density, the Roman Republic set a maximum limit of 18 inches for the thickness of masonry walls. The requirement had the affect of limiting the height of buildings, which in turn reduced density and congestion along its twisted, narrow streets. In 6 AD, Caesar Augustus, Rome's first emperor, improved the law, limiting the height of buildings to 70 feet.

In 27 AD, during the reign of Rome's second emperor, Tiberius Caesar, the deadly collapse of a large amphitheater created an enormous public outcry for safer buildings. A Roman entrepreneur named Atilius had constructed an amphitheater in Fidena, located on the outskirts of Rome. Ancient Roman historian Cornelius Tacitus recounted the story:

> Atilius . . . having undertaken to build an amphitheatre at Fidena for the exhibition of a show of gladiators, failed to lay a solid foundation [and] to frame the wooden superstructure with beams of sufficient strength; for he had neither an abundance of wealth, nor zeal for public popularity, but he had simply sought the work for sordid gain.[2]

During an event, the amphitheater suddenly collapsed. Approximately 50,000 spectators were killed or injured. The Roman citizenry was outraged. The Senate quickly banished Atilius and passed a decree establishing a minimum personal net worth of 400,000 sesterces, which were large bronze coins, on developers who would undertake the construction of large public projects. The Senate also established the requirement for official inspections of the foundations and super-structures of public buildings to confirm their strength and fitness.

The Senate's decree addressed only the construction of large public projects, not housing. Tenement buildings and shops in Rome continued to be shoddily constructed and packed closely together. As previously mentioned, the Great Fire of Rome destroyed 70 percent of the city in 64 AD.

LONDON'S EARLIEST BUILDING CODE

London was frequently plagued by fire during the Middle Ages. Because most buildings were wood with thatched roofs, a fire in one frequently spread to others. There were major fires in 675 and 1087 and again in 1135 or 1136. During the latter fire, the old wooden London Bridge was destroyed, as was part of St. Paul's church.

The oldest known building code in the English-speaking world is London's Assize of Buildings. Tradition dates it from 1189, under the administration of Henry Fitz Ailwin, London's first mayor. Assize is an archaic English word that means decree. The purpose of the Assize was to control the spread of fire and to establish procedures to adjudicate noncriminal disputes among neighbors arising from living too close together in cramped conditions. The Assize advocated, but did not mandate, the use of stone for building walls, explaining the following:

> In this way the house [built of stone] will remain safe and protected against any conflagration that reaches it and thereby many houses may be saved and preserved, unharmed and unviolated by the flames.[3]

Rather than requiring stone outright, it instead granted privileges to those who used it. Roofs of houses built with stone were allowed to drain onto neighbors' properties, whereas those that did not were required to have roofs with gutters that discharged rainwater onto the owners' properties.

Ovens and chimneys were not permitted next to wood walls, "whereby the fire might easily cause a disaster."[4] Chimneys had to be constructed of stone or lined with noncombustible tiles or plaster, "and not of timber, under penalty of it being torn down."[5] During the summer, barrels or tubs of water were required in front of houses for fighting fires. Roofs were required to be lead, tile, or stone: "If any other exists, it may be pulled down forthwith by the constables."[6]

The Assize also settled nuisance complaints among neighbors for such things as the following:

- Disputes over ownership and locations of property lines
- Responsibility for party walls, drainage, gutters, and the control of rain runoff
- Acceptable distances between indoor cesspits and property lines
- Blockage of windows and natural light by new construction

Most Londoners lived in small wooden houses or multistory tenement houses built very closely together. Because many houses had existed for generations without deeds, exactly who owned party walls between houses was often unknown. If one neighbor stacked firewood against the party wall, families on both sides were potentially threatened. If someone wanted to make changes, such as add a window or an additional room or story, it affected the neighbors. Roofs frequently drained onto neighboring properties. Rainwater cascaded from the ends of gutters, sometimes falling two or three stories before splashing onto a neighbor's property, unpaved street, or passersby.

There were no requirements for the proper construction of privies or cesspits. Some privies were behind and away from the house, but close to a neighboring house or window. Some Londoners chose to construct cesspits within their homes. Cesspits were dug beneath floorboards into which commodes emptied or bedpans were dumped. Waste shafts were constructed of wood. There are anecdotal stories about floorboards rotting away and astonished victims falling in.

The Assize established a committee of 13 people: the mayor and 12 appointed citizens. They listened to disputes, frequently visited the sites of contention, and rendered judgments. During the earlier years of the Assize, there was no requirement that the assizors have any knowledge of the building trades. But, by the beginning of the 14th century, the assizors were tradesmen such as masons, carpenters, and the like.

The following entry is from the Assize records of 1301–1431 kept by the London Record Society. It illustrates a typical case brought before the Assize for resolution:

> Friday, 8 June 1313. John de Preston . . . plaintiff appears against William Spot and Muriel his wife and Margery la Fundour, defendants., complaining that the cesspit of the privy they have made in their house in the parish of St. Lawrence Jewry adjoins too closely the plaintiff's tenement and so undermines it that his house and timbers are ruined. The defendants do not come [to the Assize hearing]. Judgment after view[ing the situation was] that within 40 days . . . the cesspit complained of be well and firmly blocked up and another made 3 ft. from the plaintiff's land.[7]

The Assize rendered judgments for many centuries, making only piecemeal and marginal improvements in living conditions within medieval London. It did not make major planning decisions that improved the overall layout and sanitation of the city. It was a reactive body, rendering opinions and decisions on a case by case basis. London grew as always, without any prescribed planning. The Assize notwithstanding, fire was a constant threat. There was a major fire in 1212 that destroyed much of London and killed an estimated 3,000 people. For the next few centuries, Londoners referred to this fire as the Great Fire. That changed after the Great Fire of 1666.

Early Building Regulations in American Colonies

In the American colonies, many cities were enacting their own building regulations. In the 1630s, Boston ratified regulations prohibiting the use of thatch for roofing and wood for chimneys. In 1647, New York created the Department of Surveyor of Buildings that had the power to "condemn all improprieties and disorder in buildings, fences, palisades, posts, and rails."[8] The following year it banned thatch roofs and wood and plaster chimneys. In 1653, Boston had the first of its great fires, which destroyed one-third of the town. Later that year, Boston bought its first fire engine. In 1676, a fire started by a single candle in a tailor's shop burned down 50 wooden buildings. So in 1678, Boston added to its building laws, requiring slate or clay tile for roofs and stone or brick for walls.

In 1761, the colonial government of New York created the first fire district, requiring that all houses in specified areas of the city have exterior walls of stone or brick and roofs of tile or slate. In 1872, another great fire burned Boston, destroying 776 buildings and killing 13. The fire led to the appointment of a board of fire commissioners.

By the end of the 18th century and the beginning of the 19th, fires were so common in New York City that, according to historical lore, founding father Alexander Hamilton (1755–1804) is said to have remarked that "one could not be twenty-four hours in New York without hearing an alarm of fire."[9]

Between 1800 and 1860, New York City's population and density grew by over 1,300 percent, from roughly 60,000 with a density of 2,955 people per square mile to 800,000 and a density of 39,351 per square mile. Conditions in the city were congested, unhealthy, and unsafe—and growing more so with every passing year. New York City experienced major fires in 1804, 1811, 1835, 1839, 1845, and 1860, and countless minor fires. The 1835 fire consumed some 650 buildings, including most of Wall Street, and the 1845 fire destroyed 300 buildings. A tenement building caught fire in 1860, killing 20 people. It sparked outrage about the unsafe living conditions in tenement buildings and led to an 1862 law requiring fire escapes for all new and existing tenements, making it one of the earliest retroactive building regulations. The 1862 law also created the position of "Superintendent of Buildings" to enforce the city's building laws. In 1863, the Draft Riots (as discussed in Chapter 1) refocused attention on the deplorable living conditions in tenement houses in New York, and changes were made again to New York's building regulations.

Prior to the 1870s, laws governing the design and construction of buildings were limited in scope and comprehensiveness. To call them building codes in the modern sense is a stretch. They were generally unrelated laws, enacted in response to a particular disaster in hopes of preventing it from happening again. Requirements for strengths of materials, fire ratings, exiting, lighting, ventilation, foundations, framing systems, and roof coverings were often not addressed. When compiled, the laws and regulations did not necessarily form a cohesive strategy for improving the fire and life safety of buildings.

Construction Regulation begins in the United States

The first comprehensive set of construction regulations in the United States—a building code—was Chicago's 1875 series of ordinances that grew out of lessons learned from its Great Fire. The ordinances created a wide range of standards for the design and construction of buildings. They established a building department with the role of interpretation and enforcement of the building ordinances. The paragraphs of the ordinances were related and dependent on one another, creating a logical, comprehensive, and consistent strategy for regulating the fire and life safety of buildings. *The Municipal Code of Chicago*, in 1881, included a compilation of Chicago's building ordinances and the laws of Illinois as they related to the city of Chicago. Its "Article IX Buildings" presented detailed requirements for the design and construction of buildings based on their use and story height. Two paragraphs of the code are worth quoting because they established the basic fire safety strategy for Chicago's tall buildings:

> [Paragraph] 1002. Any elevator building [meaning a tall building] may be constructed of wood, externally protected by an envelope of incombustible material. . . . [A]ll window frames and sash in superstructure shall be of iron.[10]
>
> [Paragraph] 1044. All buildings having an area exceeding 10,000 superficial feet [square feet], and more than 40 feet high; also, all buildings having an area exceeding 6,000 superficial feet, and being more than 56 feet high, shall have all their floors deadened with mortar or its equivalent, spread at least one inch thick.[11]

It was with these requirements that Chicago's architects of the 1880s—the so-called Chicago School—had to comply as they developed and experimented with tall buildings. Tall buildings could be framed with wood, iron, or steel, or any combination thereof, provided the exterior building envelope was faced with noncombustible materials, the windows had steel frames and sash, and the structural framing was covered, or encased, with at least a 1-inch-thick coating of noncombustible mortar.

The National Fire Protection Association

In 1895, a concerned group of insurance men met in Boston. They were members of the Underwriters Bureau of New England and they met to discuss ways of controlling losses—their losses—due to fire. In particular, they discussed a relatively new invention, the fire sprinkler head.

Fire sprinkler systems had been around for quite some time. The first was invented in England by John Carey in 1806, but was nothing like the fire sprinkler systems of today or, for that matter, like the fire sprinkler systems that the Underwriters discussed in their 1895 meeting. Carey's system relied on a device that, when heated to fire temperature, caused water to run through perforated pipes installed overhead. Unfortunately, Carey's system did not always work, and when it did, it did not always put the fire out.

The first modern fire sprinkler system was invented in the United States by Frederick Grinnell in 1881. It used solid pipe and a device called a fire sprinkler head. Grinnell experimented and improved his invention, and by the 1890s his fire sprinkler head looked and functioned very much like the fire sprinkler heads used today.

For insurance underwriters, the fire sprinkler system was like manna from heaven. When designed and installed correctly, it extinguished fires quickly, drastically reducing fire damage and consequently the amount of money the insurance underwriters had to pay out in claims. The problem was that the system was not always designed or installed correctly, which often led to devastating consequences for both building owners and insurance underwriters. The Bureau decided that standardized design and installation procedures could help tremendously in limiting their losses. They established a committee to study the matter and make recommendations. In 1896, the committee published suggested standards in a report entitled, *The Report of Committee on Automatic Sprinkler Protection.* That same year, the Underwriters Bureau of New England and the New York Board of Fire Underwriters met and formed a new association called the National Fire Protection Association (NFPA). The NFPA adopted the fire sprinkler standards proposed in the committee report and the report became known as *NFPA 13: Installation of Sprinkler Systems,* which is one of the oldest codes still in use. In 1897, the NFPA stated its purpose:

> To bring together the experience of different sections and different bodies of underwriters, to come to a mutual understanding, and, if possible, an agreement on general principles governing fire protection, to harmonize and adjust our differences so that we may go before the public with uniform rules and conditions which may appeal to their judgment is the object of this Association.[12]

Between the year of its inception, 1896, and 1903, the NFPA formed numerous committees and investigated various aspects of fire safety and prevention. In addition to fire sprinklers, its committees studied the use of fire doors, fire hoses and hydrants, portable fire extinguishers, steel fire shutters, fire pumps, fire department equipment, municipal fire alarm systems, and many other materials and systems for the purpose of establishing guidelines and standards for their installation and use. The NFPA's committee reports were not laws per se, and the NFPA had no enforcement capabilities. The NFPA's member organizations could only encourage the adoption and use of the standards by their insurees. The only clout insurers had was the cost of insurance premiums.

The NFPA's reports were model standards that could be followed or adopted if some code enforcement authority, such as a state or city, chose to do so. But, at the beginning of the 20th century, the idea of model codes that could be used by multiple municipalities or states nationwide was just in its infancy. Their advantages were not yet fully appreciated.

Instead, by the beginning of the 20th century, major cities in the United States had their own building codes. Their requirements varied considerably, even when there was no particular reason to do so. For identical conditions, material and exiting requirements, allowable floor loads, wall thicknesses, and many other code requirements differed. The result was confusion among design professionals and a resulting sacrifice in building safety. Worse, because smaller cities did not have the expertise or resources necessary to develop a code of their own, some did without or had only piecemeal regulations at best. This all played havoc with public safety. It also made it difficult for insurance underwriters and multicity business enterprises to predict and control their losses.

Another important area that lacked standards was firefighting. Fire hoses, fire extinguishers, hose couplings, fire hydrants, and other equipment essential to firefighting varied among fire departments from city to city.

The country needed a thoughtfully considered, comprehensive, and standardized approach for both building design safety and the selection and use of firefighting equipment. The NFPA was on the right track. Our modern-day requirements are mostly standardized from state to state through the use of model codes. Unfortunately, at the time, there was no urgency for standardization, so little was done. Having come this far in our discussion, we might guess what happened next: It took a disaster to spur us into action. Actually, it took two.

THE IROQUOIS THEATER FIRE

December 30, 1903, was a cold, wintry day in Chicago. An excited audience of mostly women and children packed into the new Iroquois Theater to see a holiday matinee performance of the comedy

"Mr. Bluebeard Jr." The Iroquois Theater, located on West Randolph Street between State and Dearborn Streets, had opened only a month earlier. It was wonderfully elegant, a "virtual temple of beauty," as it was described at the time. Indeed, its front façade was templelike—a quirky combination of a Roman Triumphal Arch nestled inside a skin-deep Classical Doric Greek Temple—a typical Beaux Arts Classicism motif that was very popular at the time. Its interior was richly finished in marble and mahogany, and its auditorium included a total of 1,724 plush velvet seats.

The theater was equipped with an asbestos curtain that could be manually lowered to seal off the proscenium opening, separating the auditorium seating from the stage. The stage was wonderfully lit by scores of overhead carbon arc lamps that could be turned on and off and dimmed with shutters to create a variety of lighting moods. Additional stage lighting was installed along the edge of the proscenium opening. The hoods of the arc lamps contained openings about 2 inches in diameter to exhaust hot carbon gas. The arc lamps burned at a temperature of about 4,000 degrees Fahrenheit.[13]

As required by the city's *Municipal Code,* there was a rooftop ventilator over the stage with shutters that could be manually opened to vent out smoke in the event of a fire. The theater had more than the required number of exits. The *Municipal Code* required at least three egress openings, clearly marked with the word "exit" over them. There was no requirement for the illumination of these exits. Exit doors were required to swing outward. However, the Iroquois had other doors that led to the exterior that swung inward.

Like all buildings in downtown Chicago after the Great Fire, the four-story Iroquois Theater was so-called fireproof. To better understand this, let's take a look at what it means to be "fireproof." *Webster's Dictionary* defines "fireproof" as "virtually impossible to set fire to or destroy by fire." In 1903 code parlance, however, it meant something quite different. Chicago's *Municipal Code* explained the meaning of fireproof this way:

> [Paragraph] 1119. All auditorium floors in theatres shall be fire-proofed, either by deafening the same with at least one inch of mortar, or have the under side of joists lathed with iron and plaster with at least one heavy coat of mortar.[14]

In effect, the code requirement meant that floors of theaters could be framed with iron or steel, provided the iron or steel was protected by 1 inch of mortar. It also meant that theater floors could be constructed of wood joists, so long as the underside of the wood joists were covered with metal lath and coated with plaster. Note the similarity to the requirements for tall buildings as prescribed in paragraph 1044 of the *Municipal Code* quoted earlier. The two framing systems described in paragraph 1119 are hardly fireproof. What they are is "fire resistant," meaning that they retard the passage of heat, thus slowing down the burning process and giving people in a burning building more time to escape. Although the term "fireproofing" is still used today to describe the materials used to coat or encase structural framing members to retard heat, buildings fireproofed in this manner are not fireproof. On September 11, 2001, nearly a century after the Iroquois Theater Fire, this fact was made horrifyingly clear by the World Trade Center disaster.

Chicago's *Municipal Code* required all theater buildings to "have a water stand pipe . . . placed on the stage . . . or in its immediate vicinity."[15] It also required that a "hose shall be attached to such stand pipe."[16] Fire extinguishers were required and, for theaters accommodating 1,000 patrons or more, theater owners were required "to employ one or more competent, experienced firemen, approved by the fire marshal, to be on duty at such theater during the whole it is open to the public. . . . [The person] shall be in uniform and shall see that all fire apparatus required is in its proper place and in efficient and ready working order."[17]

During the performance that day, a uniformed theater employee, who was a retired Chicago fireman, was posted near the stage. His fire extinguisher was two tubes of Kilfyre, which was a tube-shaped chemical fire extinguisher that worked by deploying a chemical powder that blanketed a fire, thus starving the fire of oxygen and extinguishing it. Kilfyre extinguishers worked best when fires were both small and low to the ground.

Because the theater had only been opened for a few weeks, ushers had not yet been trained on emergency evacuation procedures, nor had pikes been installed. Pikes are long, hooked poles used to pull down scenery in the event of fire. Although required to be connected, fire hoses were not yet connected to standpipes. To prevent nonpaying patrons from sneaking in, the theater owners installed deadbolt latches on the inside of many of the theater's doors.

The matinee was packed, with 1,900 people crammed into the 1,724 seats, small children sitting on their parents' laps. Shortly into the second act, the musical number "In the Pale Moonlight" called for the arc lamps to shine through gauze to create the illusion of moonlight. A hot arc lamp set the gauze on fire. Within seconds, adjacent scenery and rigging caught on fire. The stage fireman quickly tried to pull the burning scenery down by hand but was only partially successful. Without a pike, he could not reach high enough. Next he pointed his Kilfyre up at the blaze and fired. The powder shot up toward the fire, then fell away. He fired a second time, and again no affect. The fireman yelled out for someone to close the asbestos curtain. However, the falling curtain's progress was halted by the proscenium border lights that interfered with the curtain's track. The curtain stuck partway down. A few patrons were already heading for the exits in the auditorium and at the rear of the balcony. Someone, an usher perhaps, opened the roof ventilator over the stage. The opened ventilator and the opened doors high up in the balcony created a draft under the half-closed fire curtain. In his *Annual Report* of 1903, the Chicago Fire Marshall described what happened next:

> A great, rolling sheet of flame burst . . . suddenly from the stage, and reach[ed] up towards the dome of the auditorium and the upper galleries, in the natural line of draft. Numbers perished instantly by suffocation, many being found still in their seats.[18]

The lights went out and terrified patrons rushed out of the auditorium and into unlit hallways toward unlit exits. Untrained ushers watched in helpless horror. Those in the balcony rushed down unlit stairs only to be confronted by a traffic jam of panicked patrons exiting from the main floor. When exit doors were reached, the patrons pushed on the doors but could not open them. Many doors opened inward and required unfastening a deadbolt in order to open them. Terror-stricken patrons fumbled in the dark to unlatch the doors as others stacked up behind. The doors could not be opened. In the dark, bodies piled up behind the doors. The living crawled over the dead, trying to make their way out. Many died from smoke inhalation, others were crushed in the stampede. With exits blocked, others jumped to their deaths out windows. Within 15 minutes, 575 were dead and 27 more died later from

FIGURE 3.1 *Ruins of Iroquois Theater, Chicago, Illinois, December 30, 1903. Photo of charred seats and portion of the stage.* © Bettmann/CORBIS.

their injuries. Firemen arrived within minutes after the fire started, but the damage was already done. (See Figure 3.1.) It took less than a half hour to extinguish what was left of the blaze.

The Iroquois Theater building suffered only minor damage. Its fire-resistant walls, floors, and roof structure worked well in confining the fire to the auditorium and stage areas. Most of the finishes and furnishings within these two areas were destroyed, though, and the loss of life was astonishing. Within less than a year, the theater was repaired and reopened, although under a different name—the Colonial Theater, which was demolished in 1925.

More people died in the Iroquois Theater Fire than in the Great Chicago Fire, and this shocked both Chicago and the nation. Within a week, an investigation was under way. Until the cause was determined, the mayor ordered the closing of all of Chicago's assembly buildings including theaters, social halls, and churches—170 buildings in all.

In 1904, the NFPA formed a "Theater Construction and Protection" committee to study theater safety and to make recommendations. After the fire, new safety provisions were implemented in Chicago and existing laws were better enforced. Additional regulations were enacted regarding the types of fire extinguishers that were required for assembly buildings. Corners of exit corridors were prohibited from having 90-degree bends because in the panic some patrons had become trapped in exit corners.

New provisions required that exit doors and all other doors that could be used for exiting had to swing in the direction of egress. Exit doors could not be locked or have door hardware that required special knowledge to operate. Illuminated exit lighting systems were required to mark exit ways, even during power failures. Laws regarding fire hoses and emergency water standpipes were better enforced. Ropes and rigging used in theaters had to be fireproof. A steel curtain was required to protect proscenium openings. As these new requirements were being determined, a fire in another city again focused national attention on fire safety.

THE GREAT BALTIMORE FIRE

Like so many fires, the Great Baltimore Fire was probably the result of a careless accident. On February 7, 1904, it is believed that a passerby dropped a cigar or cigarette butt onto the city sidewalk in front of the John Hurst & Company Building on German Street (now Redwood Street). The butt slipped through a crack in the sidewalk and into the building's basement, which was filled with open boxes of blankets and flammable goods. Because it was Sunday morning, the building was empty, and by the time the fire department arrived at 11:00 AM, the fire had already ascended the building's wooden elevator shaft and black smoke billowed from the upper floors. Firefighters were inside when the roof exploded, sending a hail of glowing embers down onto adjacent buildings, landing on rooftops and breaking through windows. Baltimore's Great Fire had begun.

Strong winds whipped the fire northeast, toward City Hall. Within the next hour, every firefighter and horse-drawn fire engine in Baltimore was battling the blaze, but they could not stop the fire's march. By noon, Baltimore's fire chief called in reinforcements from Washington, D.C. When D.C.'s first firefighters arrived, they attempted to connect their hoses to Baltimore's fire hydrants, but their hose couplings did not fit. So they wrapped canvas around the hose/hydrant connections. With hoses leaking and reduced water pressure, they pointed their hoses at the flames. The fire continued to grow, fed by wood-framed building after wood-framed building. As more D.C. firefighters arrived, they discovered the same thing as the first group of firefighters—their hoses did not fit the fire hydrants either.

By 5 PM, the fire was still spreading and the firefighters were growing desperate. As Chicagoans had tried decades earlier the firefighters decided to clear buildings from the path of the advancing flames by blowing them up. Tons of explosives were hauled in and stacked in the John Duer & Son Building on Charles Street. The explosion shook the building ferociously, but it remained standing, at least until the fire consumed it. The next building they attempted to blow up was the Schwab Bros. Building farther down Charles Street. It, too, shuddered violently but remained standing. Other buildings were tried, but all the dynamiting managed to do was make matters worse. The fire was closing in on City Hall.

Around 8 PM the wind changed, and with it the direction of the fire. The fire veered eastward. After midnight the wind picked up and changed again. Now the wind was steering the fire southeast toward the Baltimore River and the wooden docks and piers.

By Monday morning, additional fire engines from D.C., Philadelphia, New York City, and Wilmington, and from the Pennsylvania towns of York, Chester, Harrisburg, and Altoona had arrived. Gallantly, the firefighters tried to stop the fire, but by 8 AM the docks fell to the flames.

The firefighters took a last stand along Jones Falls in hopes of saving east Baltimore. Pumping water from the falls, 37 fire engines and scores of firefighters created a wall of water. By 3 PM, the fire was out. (See Figure 3.2.)

Recounting the size of the Great Baltimore Fire makes the following statistic seem unbelievable: Only two lives were lost in the conflagration, a homeless person and one firefighter who died from his injuries a few days later. The damage, however, was appalling. The fire consumed 1,526 buildings on more than 70 blocks, and about 2,500 businesses were burned out, including 20 banks, leaving approximately 35,000 people without jobs.

Baltimore Rebuilds

Immediately after the fire in 1904, Baltimore began rebuilding and reshaping its downtown. Baltimore's mayor Robert McLane was dead set against letting the fire mark Baltimore's decline as a great city. Instead, he pushed the city forward, turning the fire from a disaster into a landmark of progress. Narrow streets were widened to reduce the potential spread

FIGURE 3.2 *Burned Out Buildings in Baltimore, Maryland, 1904. Photo looking south on Liberty Street near where the fire started.* © *Underwood & Underwood/CORBIS.*

of fire and increase the feeling of spaciousness. Baltimore's sewer system was upgraded. Overhead electrical lines were removed and run underground. Within two years nearly all of downtown was rebuilt. The Great Fire had spawned a renaissance, turning downtown Baltimore into a safer, more vibrant, and more beautiful city.

February 7, 2004, marked the 100-year anniversary of the Great Baltimore Fire. During the city's anniversary ceremony, descendants of firefighters told stories about their family members. Throughout their lives, many of the firefighters considered the Great Fire their personal failure and tragedy. Mayor Martin O'Malley did not agree. In his speech he reminded Baltimore of the true legacy of the Great Fire and the true purpose of the ceremony:

> This celebration is not about devastation, but the resurrection of the city and the triumph of the indomitable human spirit.[19]

The fire has left another legacy, also. Throughout the United States, firefighting equipment is more standardized and buildings are safer because of the Great Fire of Baltimore.

The *National Building Code*

The Great Baltimore Fire played a significant role in the history of building codes. Coming on the heels of the Iroquois Theater disaster only five weeks earlier, it propelled public and private organizations into action. In 1904, the NFPA changed its membership rules to allow other industries and organizations to become members. The New York City Fire Department became the first fire department member in 1905.

In 1905, the National Board of Fire Underwriters published the first model building code, entitled *Building Code: Recommended by the National Board of Fire Underwriters*. Soon, code officials and city authorities were referring to it as the *National Building Code*. Within ten years, it went through three editions with more than 20,000 copies in print.[20] A fourth updated edition was published in 1915. In the forward of the 1905 and 1915 editions, its authors wrote:

> In the belief that safe and good construction of buildings should be universally recognized as the utmost importance this Building Code . . . is based on broad principles which have been sufficiently amplified to provide for varying local conditions. Thousands of human lives and millions of dollars' worth of property have been sacrificed by the criminal folly of erecting unsafe or defective buildings. So long as those in authority permit such buildings to be erected, neither life nor property can be safe.[21]

When the National Board of Fire Underwriters originally formed in 1866, it represented just 75 insurance companies, although there were hundreds of companies scattered throughout the United States. The purpose of the organization was to establish uniform insurance rates for different areas of the country. Competition among insurance companies was intense, forcing insurance companies to base the cost of their premiums on short-term costs and cut-throat market tactics, often leaving them unable to pay out claims associated with large disasters.

At the time of the Great Chicago Fire in 1871, about 200 insurance companies were operating in Chicago. The Great Fire drove 68 of them into bankruptcy. The following year, the Great Boston Fire bankrupted another 32 companies.

The National Board had little success in establishing uniform rates due to the ever-rising number of companies that entered the insurance business. In 1877, it changed its strategy. Rather than try to control insurance rates, it turned its attention to disaster prevention and began collecting statistics, studying the causes of disasters, and establishing procedures and standards to prevent disasters. For example, prior to the Great Baltimore Fire, the National Board had collected considerable data regarding fire hoses and fire hydrants and found that there were over 600 different sizes and variations of them in use throughout the country.

Prior to the Baltimore fire, the National Board of Fire Underwriters and the NFPA were strong advocates for standardizing fire hoses and hydrants, but their recommendations fell mostly on deaf ears. After the Baltimore fire, cities and fire departments began listening, and in 1905 the NFPA published model standards for fire hoses, nozzle connections, and fire hydrants. Cities immediately started standardizing hydrants and firefighting equipment.

The NFPA's model standards and the National Board of Fire Underwriter's model code dramatically improved the effectiveness of firefighting and building fire and life safety. They also paved the way for the development of other model codes.

In 1915, another code organization formed—the Building Officials & Code Administrators International, Inc. (BOCA), located in Country Club Hills, Illinois. Shortly thereafter, it published its model code, called the *National Building Code*. To avoid confusion with the National Board of Fire Underwriters' code, BOCA's code soon came to be known as the *BOCA Code*.

In 1922, the International Conference of Building Officials (ICBO) formed in Whittier, California. It published its model code, called the *Uniform Building Code* (UBC). In 1940, yet another model code organization formed—the Southern Building Code Congress International (SBCCI), located in Birmingham, Alabama—and published its model code, the *Southern Standard Building Code*. The name was later changed to the *Standard Building Code* (SBC).

Unfortunately, cities and states did not start adopting these model codes immediately; it took decades to accomplish standardization. Consequently, lessons learned from a disaster by one municipality had to be relearned by another. For example, the inward-swinging exit door problem that led to such disastrous results in the 1903 Iroquois Theater Fire in Chicago was repeated decades later in the 1942 Coconut Grove Fire in Boston (see Chapter 1). Writing in 1929, the engineer and author W. C. Huntington lamented:

> Each city has its own building code to which the buildings of that city must conform. There is great lack of uniformity in these codes even where there is no reason for variation. For identical conditions . . . items vary through a wide range. This results . . . in a . . . sacrifice of safety and leads to confusion among architects and engineers whose practice is not confined to one city.[22]

From the end of World War II to the end of the 1990s, most state and city codes were based on one of these three model codes—the UBC, the BOCA Code, or the SBC. During the 1990s, these three organizations began working together and combined their codes into one model code called the *International Building Code*, the IBC. The IBC has since become the primary model code of the United States.

NEW YORK CITY'S TRIANGLE SHIRTWAIST FIRE

By the early 1900s, hundreds of little factories existed in buildings throughout New York City that were originally designed for other purposes. Tenement apartments were converted into factories, which coexisted with tenants occupying other apartments within the same building.

Loft buildings were also converted to factories. Loft buildings were office buildings, generally with commercial shops on the ground floor and offices and sales rooms above. Upper-story spaces within these buildings were often made into factories. The peaked-roof loft portions of these buildings were especially popular; factories could be shoe-horned into lofts that were otherwise unusable for office space, thus increasing a building's usable and rentable space.

These factories often manufactured garments or other flammable articles. The factory floors were messy, with cuttings and fragments of cloth littering the floorboards. Oil and grease drippings from the machines soaked into the floors. Light bulbs were often unprotected by globes.

The exterior walls of the buildings were generally brick or stone, but the floor and roof framing were often wood, unprotected by any fire-resistant materials. Stairways were also unprotected and often open at every floor. Stairs were narrow, generally only 3 feet wide, sometimes less. Some buildings had elevators, others did not. Exit doors often opened inwards.

Wooden partitions were used to divide the factory space that was generally overcrowded with machinery and employees. The primary objective was to squeeze as many workers and machines into the space as possible. Safety concerns ran a distant second. Fire prevention was generally limited to fire pails. Fire escapes, which were poorly maintained, were frequently vertical ladders, although some had steeply inclined stairs. They were often flimsily constructed and dropped into rear yards with no exit, and were sometimes blocked by stacked boxes or piles of other materials stored in the way. To make safety matters even worse, workers were often locked in until shifts were over. Smoking was permitted and very common.

On Saturday, March 25, 1911, hundreds of young women and girls were in the Triangle Shirtwaist garment factory, busily working overtime. The Triangle Shirtwaist Company occupied the eighth through tenth floors of the Asch Building on the corner of Greene Street and Washington Place in lower Manhattan. The Asch Building was 150 feet tall, faced with masonry, and framed with wood floors and roof. It had two sets of stairs and one elevator. Fire escapes were located in the rear. At the eighth through tenth floors, the doors leading to both stairs were locked to prevent theft and to keep workers from leaving until the shift was over.

At quitting time, as the tired women prepared to leave, a voice yelled "Fire!" and bedlam ensued. Perhaps the fire was started by a cigarette or a spark from one of the machines—no one knows. Regardless, by the time the fire department raced the six blocks from the fire station to the building—an elapsed time of about ten minutes— many women had already jumped to their deaths. In desperation, others were still hurling themselves from window ledges while some pounded on the locked doors. The elevator went down once, packed with women, but never returned. Some made it to the fire escapes, but due to years of neglect, they did not extend properly and instead twisted under the weight.

Desperately, firefighters tried to catch the jumpers in life nets. Other firefighters raised the fire ladders, but the ladders reached only to the sixth floor. Benjamin Levy worked in a nearby building, and when he saw the fire he raced to help, recounting:

> I rushed downstairs, and when I reached the sidewalk the girls were already jumping from the windows. None of them moved after they struck the sidewalk. Several men ran up with a net which they got somewhere, and I seized one side of it to help them hold it. It was about ten feet square and we managed to catch about fifteen girls. I don't believe we saved over one or two however. The fall was so great that they bounced to the sidewalk after striking the net. Bodies were falling all around us, and two or three of the men with me were knocked down. The girls just leaped wildly out of the windows and turned over and over before reaching the sidewalk.[23]

When it was over, 141 were dead, most of them young women and teenage girls. Within the next few days, 7 more died from their injuries. (See Figure 3.3.)

The Triangle Shirtwaist Fire became a catalyst for workplace reform. Within months, the State of New York appointed a factory investigation commission to investigate factory safety and make recommendations to improve safety. The fire spurred the International Ladies Garment Workers Union (ILGWU) to protest and fight for better working conditions and improvements in worker safety. The ILGWU was joined in its efforts by other reformist groups and concerned citizens and politicians.

One such politician was New York Assemblyman Al Smith. Smith listened to and sympathized with the reformers, and soon he joined their cause. For the next seven years, he pushed forward legislation for social programs that included the reduction of working hours for women and children, pensions for widows, and workers' compensation. His efforts paid off. In 1918, he was elected governor of New York State.

FIGURE 3.3 *Triangle Shirtwaist Fire of 1911, New York City. Fire fighters put out the catastrophic fire that killed 146 garment factory workers. © Underwood & Underwood/ CORBIS.*

The Triangle Shirtwaist Fire precipitated changes in New York City's building code as well. In 1915, New York issued its *New Code of Ordinances*. The New Code mandated that fire escapes were required from all buildings three stories and taller, and it required their proper installation and upkeep. It also prohibited the blocking of access to fire escapes, as was done by the Triangle Shirtwaist Company in the Asch Building:

> No person shall at any time place any encumbrance of any kind whatsoever before or upon any fire-escape, balcony or ladder. . . . In constructing all balcony fire-escapes the manufacturer thereof shall securely fasten thereto, in a conspicuous place, a cast-iron plate having suitable raised letter on the same, to read as follows: "Notice: Any person placing any encumbrance on this balcony is liable to a penalty of $10 and imprisonment for 10 days."[24]

The Triangle Shirtwaist Fire focused attention on the hundreds of other unsafe factories scattered throughout the city, located in various buildings and areas of the city never intended to house such activities. It raised an important question for many concerned New Yorkers: Is it possible for a factory to move into my neighborhood and possibly right into my own apartment building? In 1911, the answer to that question was, "Yes," but within five years the answer changed.

New York City Establishes a Zoning Resolution

In 1916, New York City enacted its pioneering Zoning Resolution, which established use requirements for different areas or zones within the city. The city was divided into use zones with letter designations: R for residential, C for commercial, and M for manufacturing or industrial uses. The zones were hierarchical, with R zones the most restrictive and M zones least restrictive. Only residences were permitted in R zones, whereas commercial and residential uses were permitted in C zones, and all uses were permitted in M zones.

The Zoning Resolution also created street or property line setback requirements for buildings and constraints of the percentage of the lot that could be built on, which were called "lot coverage" requirements. For tall buildings, it set up a system of step-backs, requiring tall buildings to step back progressively farther from property lines as the height increased. No longer could tall buildings fill their entire site and continue straight up from the edges of sidewalks as the Equitable Life Assurance Building had done, as discussed in Chapter 1.

The Zoning Resolution of 1916 forever changed the face of New York City. Today, tall buildings throughout New York owe their shapes to the city's pioneering zoning laws. Famous tall buildings such as the 1930s Chrysler and Empire State Buildings step back as they do because of the zoning regulations. Even the 1958 Seagram Building, which rises 38 stories straight up, is set back far enough from the street to have permitted its architect, Mies van der Rohe, to design the first iconoclastic international-styled skyscraper.

Within a short time, other American cities copied or adapted New York City's regulations. Since then, life and buildings in and around American cities have not been the same.

4

OVERCROWDING

The disaster of overcrowding is unlike any of the disasters we have discussed thus far. It is a slow-burning fuse. It is the by-product of decades of poor planning or no planning at all. It is purely man-made.

During the 19th century, living conditions for the poor and working class in large cities were appalling. Overcrowded and unsanitary tenement buildings were little more than fetid Petri dishes for disease, causing untold misery, health problems, and deaths. Overcrowded tenements produced inhumane environments ripe for crime, immoral behavior, and social unrest. Eventually the problem became so acute that various groups decided to do something about it. Their attempts had long-lasting consequences on the built environment.

By the end of the 19th century, three independent groups, or movements—the Garden City Movement, the City Beautiful Movement, and the Tenement Reform Movement—had begun grappling with the problem of overcrowded living conditions among the poor and working class. The groups advocated different solutions to the problem. While none of their solutions put an end to overcrowding and the problems of housing the poor and working class, all three movements contributed greatly to shaping the built environment.

THE GARDEN CITY

By the end of the 19th century, the industrial revolution and its resulting congestion and filth had overwhelmed London. For nearly a century, peasants had flocked to the city. Most lived in tenement buildings, where conditions were abysmal. The repercussions of the 1798 Windows Tax had taken its toll. Although repealed in 1851, thousands of windowless tenement apartments existed throughout the poor and working-class neighborhoods of London. To make matters worse, in 1840, a new street was cut through the heavily populated Irish worker parish of St. Giles, displacing approximately 5,000 people. With no other place to go, the workers moved into adjacent tenements, making them all the more overcrowded. As mentioned in Chapter 1, physician Southwood Smith went before the Select Committee of the House of Commons that year to discuss the living conditions in London, telling the committee that no more attention was paid to the health of those living in tenements than "is paid to the health of pigs." Conditions were not much better by the end of the century.

At the beginning of the 19th century, London's population was approximately 1 million. By the end of the century, it had grown to 6 million people. London's big building boom occurred during the 1870–1880s. Men, women, and children toiled from sunrise to sunset in the unregulated, unsafe, and unhealthy factory work environments, creations of the industrial age. Day after day, black smoke from chimneys relentlessly coated buildings, streets, clothes, faces, and lungs. Interspersed with factories were smaller, yet no less filthy, industries—blacksmiths, liveries, slaughterhouses, tanneries, and fat-renderers—that added their own particular filth and noxious odors to the soot.

Contagious diseases ran wild. Estimates are that for every Londoner who died of old age, eight died from disease. Among the lower working class, life expectancy was less than 20 years. Laborers and their families slept at night tightly packed together in dirty tenements. To accommodate the constant influx of new peasants from the countryside, tenement apartments frequently housed multiple generations of families. Rooms and basements were sublet. Privacy was virtually nonexistent. Common decency often succumbed to the squalid conditions. Depravity and unwholesome marriages resulted, with abandoned children living in the streets. With little recourse, necessity turned many orphans to lives of crime.

Sanitary conditions were abhorrent. By the middle of the 19th century, London figuratively, if not literally, floated on a toxic sea of centuries-old cesspits. Beneath floorboards and adjacent to basement apartments, abandoned and active cesspools oozed their fetid gruel through masonry walls, undermined foundations, collapsed floors, and leached into groundwater. Indoor plumbing was virtually nonexistent. Communal wells located on neighborhood street corners were the only source of water for many working-class Londoners. Water for cooking, drinking, and bathing was drawn from these communal wells. Hand-operated pumps lifted contaminated groundwater to street level, where it was carried home in buckets. Contagious diseases spread like wildfire.

London's rudimentary storm drainage and sewer system discharged directly into the Thames. Many parts of London smelled as foul as they looked. One story of the era describes a day when Queen Victoria and Prince Albert wanted to take a pleasure cruise on the Thames. Shortly after they started their voyage, they turned back due to the stench.

Cholera was perhaps the most life-threatening illness. Four major outbreaks occurred in London during the 19th century. The 1848–1849 epidemic was particularly severe, killing approximately 60,000. In the mid-19th century, most people believed that cholera was spread through pollution in the air, not by water. In 1854, the pioneering epidemiologist Dr. John Snow proved that cholera spread via contaminated water. On August 31, an outbreak of Asiatic cholera broke out in the Soho district of London. Within three days, nearly 130 people died, and within two weeks, over 500 died. Dr. Snow managed to trace the outbreak to a particular hand pump, and he convinced authorities to remove the pump handle so no one could draw water from the well beneath the pump. The number of cholera cases soon subsided. Dr. Snow suggested that steps be taken to clearly separate sources of groundwater from cesspits, but London officials were slow to react and implemented few changes. By the end of the 19th century, cholera had killed an estimated 140,000 Londoners.

Ebenezer Howard, who had little formal education and left school at age 15, thought he had a solution to London's problems. In 1871, at the age of 21, Howard had moved from England to Nebraska to become a farmer. He quickly failed at farming and moved to Chicago, where he took a job as a court reporter. He returned to London in 1876. Howard was a prolific reader and was always on the lookout for inspirations for new inventions. He kept a workshop and always had projects in various states of development. Eventually, his interests turned to solving London's ills. With no training in architecture or planning, other than what he had read and seen, Howard proposed a solution to the city's problem of overcrowding. His idea was not to improve the congested living conditions in London, but to stop it from growing and getting worse.

In 1898, he presented his radical plan in a book entitled *To-Morrow: A Peaceful Path to Real Reform*. His book offered ideas about city planning that would eventually change the shape of cities worldwide. Howard suggested the creation of a new kind of place to live, the suburban town.

The Rise of the Suburban Town

In 1898, there were basically only two places to live in England, the town—or city—and the country. Howard likened the town and country to magnets that pulled people in opposite directions, toward one life style or another, both with their own set of advantages and disadvantages. Howard suggested that towns had the following potpourri of advantages and disadvantages:

- *Advantages:* Social opportunities, numerous places of amusement and distractions from work, high wages, numerous opportunities for changes in employment, well-lit streets
- *Disadvantages:* Closing out of nature, high rents and prices for goods, excessive work hours, armies of unemployed, fog, drought, poor drainage and sewage, foul air, murky sky, slums, palaces of sin, disease

The countryside, as well, had its own hodgepodge of advantages and disadvantages:

- *Advantages:* Beauty of nature, woods, fresh air, low rents, abundance of water, bright sunshine
- *Disadvantages:* Lack of society, idle hands out of work, land lying idle, long work hours with low wages, lack of amusement, no public spirit

Howard proposed constructing a third place for living, with the advantages of both and the disadvantages of neither. He called it the town-country, and listed its advantages as the following:

- Beauty of nature, social opportunity, fields and parks with easy access, low rents, high wages, low cost of goods, plenty to do, no sweating, pure air and water, good drainage, bright homes and gardens, no smoke, no slums, freedom, and cooperation

In his book, Howard proposed the question: "The People, where will they go?" Howard's answer: If given a choice, they will be attracted to the town-country.

Howard called his town-country villages "Garden Cities." To promote his idea, he founded the Garden Cities Association in 1899. The association still exists today, and is called the Town and Country Planning Association. It is the oldest environmental-related charity in England. To further promote the Garden City idea, he renamed the second edition of his book, published in 1902, *Garden Cities of To-Morrow*.

Garden Cities promised planned communities with just the right blend of city and nature. Howard's idea was to restrict their sizes to around 30,000 people to avoid developing the city slum conditions associated with overcrowding. Garden Cities would be arranged in clusters around larger cities separated by green belts.

The proposed arrangement of streets and land use within the Garden City was radically different from typical large cities. Streets radiated out from the city's center. The Garden City had well-defined use districts or zones, completely unlike any other cities at the time. These zones restricted various land uses to their appropriate designated zone within the Garden City.

As the name suggests, at the center of the Garden City was a garden or central park. Howard was aware of Frederick Law Olmsted's New York Central Park, which was constructed between 1857 and 1861. Also, he witnessed Chicago's rebuilding of downtown after the Great Fire. He was aware of Olmsted's 1870 master plan for a landscaped park along Lake Michigan near the outskirts of Chicago in an area called Jackson Park. The park was never built because Chicago, understandably, changed its priorities after the Great Fire. Olmsted's master plan was resurrected 20 years later, however. With modifications and improvements, it became the fairgrounds for the Columbian Exposition of 1893. By the mid-1890s, the Chicago World's Fair was world famous as a city-planning marvel. At the time, many believed it held the answer for improving cities throughout the United States.

Radiating from the Garden City's central park, Howard proposed wide streets or boulevards that extended to the city's perimeter (technically its circumference). Howard's Garden City was laid out as a series of concentric rings, each ring having different land uses. Howard imagined the garden park core to be approximately five acres, well watered and maintained, surrounded by public buildings in a parklike setting. Buildings included the town hall, theater, library, hospital, museums, and art galleries. The next ring out was dedicated to recreation, outdoor playgrounds, and, for inclement weather, indoor recreational areas with plenty of glass for natural lighting, what Howard called a "crystal palace," no doubt inspired by the glass and cast-iron-framed Crystal Palace of the 1851 London World's Fair. Howard envisioned the Crystal Palace as a series of glass and steel buildings that included shops selling manufactured goods and restaurants.

The next ring out was the residential area, as he describes below:

> Passing out of the Crystal Palace on our way to the outer ring of the town . . . we find a ring of very excellently built houses, each standing in its own ample grounds; and, as we continue our walk, we observe that the houses are for the most part built either in concentric rings, facing the various avenues (as the circular roads are termed), or fronting the boulevards and roads which all converge to the centre of the town.[1]

Howard envisioned standardized lot sizes for the houses, large enough to accommodate the house, tree-lined streets in front, and gardens in back. While the geometry and land use of the Garden City was rigidly controlled by the municipal authorities for the greater health and well-being of the city, Howard saw the architectural styles of the houses varying with "the fullest measure of individual taste and preference."[2]

The next ring out was a wide ring with public schools, playgrounds, gardens, and churches of all denominations. The outermost ring contained all of the town's factories, workshops, warehouses, power plants, lumber and coal yards, dairies, produce markets, and rail yards. The arrangement placed these activities away from the inner city streets and closer to points of shipping by railroad. It also kept industry, which Howard called the "smoke fiend," away from the rest of the city.

In his lifetime, Howard saw two of his Garden Cities built. The first was Letchworth and the second Welwyn. Letchworth was constructed in 1903, 30 miles north of London. Welwyn, about 20 miles north of London, was built after World War I, in 1920.

After World War II, many more cities in England were constructed on Howard's Garden City principles, including new towns like Stevenage in Hertfordsire and the largest, Milton Keynes, in Buckinghamshire.

But the true legacy of the Garden City was its influence on other planners. Frederick Law Olmsted, Jr. was much influenced by the Garden City Movement and incorporated it into the U.S. City Beautiful Movement. Also, its concept of partitioning a city into different single-use zones had a tremendous impact on 20th-century city planning.

Howard's description of the typical houses of the Garden City sound very familiar. Individual houses, each on its own little piece of land, fronted on tree-lined streets, with backyards, have become the quintessential American suburban dream. After World War II, suburbs based on many of Howard's principles grew like weeds around major cities throughout the United States. Today, approximately one-half of all Americans live in the suburbs in houses similar to those in Howard's Garden City.

THE TENEMENT REFORM MOVEMENT

Between the end of the Civil War and 1900, America changed. It quickly moved from an agrarian society to an urban one. In 40 years the population more than doubled from 31 to 76 million. By 1900, approximately 40 percent of the population lived in cities. Cities such as New York, Boston, and Chicago grew quickly and became more and more overcrowded. Poverty, crime, and the newly identified condition of urban blight had become major problems.

By the end of the 19th century, the most densely populated corner of the world was in New York City. It was the southeast corner of the island of Manhattan, called the Lower East Side. An estimated 240,000 people per square mile lived there in severely cramped and unsanitary conditions.[3]

The Lower East Side was originally developed as single-family row houses in the late 18th century by two landowners, James Delancey and Henrick Rutgers. Comprehensive city planning was nonexistent at the time, and Delancey and Rutgers obviously did not coordinate their efforts. Delancey laid out his section of land in rectangular blocks with long streets running north/south, and Rutgers used rectangular blocks with long streets running east/west. The nonaligning block patterns confusingly intersect at what is today Division Street and Seward Park.

New York City was a modestly sized city when Delancey and Rutgers laid out their city blocks with typical individual lots measuring 25 feet wide by 100 feet deep. They sold or leased the individual lots to developers, who built comfortable and modestly spacious single-family row houses.

By the 1840s, New York was a large city. Irish immigrants escaping the Great Famine and German immigrants fleeing the German Revolution arrived in droves. During the 1840s, New York's population grew from 312,000 to 515,000. The following decade brought even greater growth. By 1860, New York's population was over 813,000, a 260 percent increase in 20 years. Most of the new arrivals lived on the Lower East Side.

To accommodate the influx, row houses were converted to tenements or were torn down to clear the way for large tenement buildings. Quickly, lots that were originally sized for one family were converted to four- and five-story buildings housing 20 families or more. By the mid-1860s there were approximately 15,000 tenement buildings in New York City, and most were on the Lower East Side.

A notorious example was Gotham Court. Located on Cherry Street, it was five stories in height and contained 120 separate apartments. Each apartment contained two rooms, totaling just over 260 square feet. Apartments did not have toilets or running water. Communal toilets, sinks, and showers were located in the basement.

In 1864, an extensive survey was done of the tenements on the Lower East Side. (The reason for the survey will become clear shortly.) At the request of the newly formed New York City Council of Hygiene, Dr. Ezra R. Pulling visited numerous tenements, including Gotham Court. He prepared an extensive report of the terrible living conditions he found. Regarding Gotham Court, he wrote:

> In the basement of this building are the privies, through which the Croton-water is permitted to run for a short time occasionally; but this is evidently insufficient to cleanse them, for their emanations render the first story exceedingly offensive, and may be perceived

as a distinct odor as high as the third floors. The contents of the privies are discharged into subterranean drains or sewers, which run through each alley and communicate with the external atmosphere by a series of grated openings through which fetid exhalations are continually arising.[4]

In his report, Dr. Pulling estimated that on average seven people lived in each apartment, giving each individual a living space of approximately 37 square feet, not much more than a closet. Dr. Pulling reported that he found swarms of vermin and cases of typhus and measles.

He found apartments that were not used as apartments. Instead, they were small workshops—garment factories filled with seamstresses making army uniforms (the Civil War was still in progress). Dr. Pulling's interviews of tenants and subsequent research revealed the appalling fact that in a 32-month period, which was the average length of time that residents stayed, one out of five had died. The toll was even higher among infants. Dr. Pulling wrote, "It may be safely assumed that 30 percent of those born here do not survive a twelvemonth."[5] Dr. Pulling concluded that the abhorrent conditions of Gotham Court was not an aberration:

> On the whole, perhaps this section of Gotham Court presents about an average specimen of tenant houses in the lower part of the city. . . . There are some which are more roomy, have better ventilation, and are kept cleaner, but there are many which are in far worse condition and exhibit a much higher rate of mortality than this.[6]

By the 1860s, the Lower East Side of Manhattan was a tightly packed powder keg of filth, vermin, disease, and the desperation that living in such conditions brings. All that was needed was a small spark to set it off.

Riot Leads to Tenement Housing Reforms

The spark was the Enrollment Act of Conscription of 1863. On March 3, President Abraham Lincoln enacted a draft. An additional 300,000 young men were needed to fight in what seemed like an endless war to many citizens.

On Saturday, July 11, the first names of New Yorkers were called, and on Monday, July 13, more were called. Mobs of mostly poor immigrant workers from the Lower East Side soon formed and began burning local draft offices and then police stations. The violence escalated as more and more rioters joined in. Soon, 50,000 rioters were burning, looting, and assaulting everyone that crossed their paths. The New York Police Department, woefully outnumbered, could not control it. The riot lasted four days. Finally, federal troops were summoned, and eventually the riot was quelled on July 15. But, before it was over, 100 people had been killed and an estimated $1.5 million in property destroyed.

The riot brought public attention to the deplorable living conditions of the Lower East Side for the first time. The journalist N. P. Willis, who visited the destroyed areas of the riot, wrote:

> The . . . closely backed houses where the mobs originated seemed to be literally hives of sickness and vice. It was . . . difficult to believe that so much misery, disease, and wretchedness could be huddled together and hidden by high walls, unvisited and unthought of so near our own abodes. . . . What numbers of these poorer classes are deformed, what numbers are made hideous by self-neglect and infirmity! Alas, human faces look so hideous with hope and self-respect all gone, and familiar forms and features are made so frightful by sin, squalor, and debasement! To walk the streets as we walked them in those hours of conflagration and riot was like witnessing the day of judgment, with every wicked thing revealed, every sin and sorrow blazingly glared upon, every hidden abomination laid before hell's expectant fire.[7]

A movement was now afoot: a tenement house reform movement. A group of New York's leading citizens concerned about the city's unsanitary conditions began to meet. They called themselves the Citizens Association, and by April 1864 they had formed the Council of Hygiene and Public Health, which included a group of physicians. The Council began to survey the living conditions on the Lower East Side, a result of which was Dr. Pulling's report of Gotham

Court. In 1900, Lawrence Veiller, an expert on tenement conditions, commented:

> Not . . . till the first-fruits of thirty years of municipal neglect had been gathered in the terrible "draft riots" of 1863, did the community become aroused to the dangers of the evils which surrounded them. When in those troublous times, during our Civil War, the tenements poured forth the mobs that held fearful sway in the city, during the outbreak of violence in the month of July, then, for the first time, did the general public realize what it meant to permit human beings to be reared under the conditions which had so long prevailed in the tenement houses in New York City.[8]

Based on the Council of Hygiene and Public Health surveys and reports, the New York City Metropolitan Board of Health was established in 1866. The following year saw the enactment of the first tenement housing laws in the United States. The law required that every sleeping room have a window or at least a ventilating transom window of at least three square feet. Fire escapes were mandated. Ventilation for common hallways was prescribed. Stairs were required to have balusters. Buildings were required to have one toilet for every 20 residents, and the toilets had to be connected to plumbed sewers. The use of cesspits was banned. Basement apartments were banned, unless specifically permitted by the Board of Health. Minimum room ceiling heights were defined, setbacks from other buildings were established, and rubbish containers were mandated, as well as other sanitation requirements.

The 1867 tenement housing laws were the first start. In 1879, a new tenement house law was enacted. The area of the lot permitted to be occupied by a new tenement house was limited to 65 percent. The concept is called lot coverage, and it has been used ever since to control density. The act increased the window area of sleeping rooms from 3 square feet to 12, and the windows had to open directly to a public street or yard.

Shortly after the implementation of the act, a newspaper called the *Sanitary Engineer* set up a competition. A $500 prize was offered for the best tenement housing design. The winning design quickly came to be called the "dumb-bell" plan because of its shape. As Figure 4.1 shows, the middle of the building tapered in like the handles of a dumb-bell.

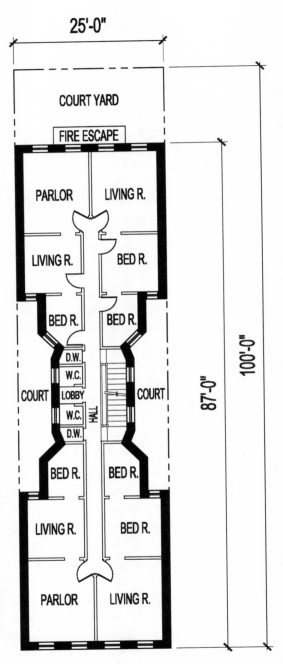

FIGURE 4.1 *Tenement Housing Dumbbell Plan.*

An article appeared in the *New York Times* on March 16, 1879, that summarized the shortcomings of the dumb-bell plan, as well as those of the first and second runners up:

> If the prize plans are the best offered, which we hardly believe, they merely demonstrate that the problem is insoluble. The three which have received the highest prices offer a very slightly better arrangement than hundreds of tenement houses now do. . . . The only access to air, apart from the front, is through the courts in the small spaces between the houses. To add to their ill effects each suite on the second story has apparently that old nuisance, a dark bedroom which, under the present arrangement, is a prolific source of fever and disease. . . . [I]f one of our crowded wards were built up after any one of these prize designs, the evils of our present tenement house system would be increased tenfold.[9]

Nevertheless, shortly thereafter, hundreds of such tenements were built. The dumb-bell design permitted a way to meet the letter, although not the spirit, of the tenement housing laws. It filled the lot as much as the laws permitted and it was cheap to construct. Veiller commented on the dumb-bell plan:

> This is the type of tenement house which today is the curse of our city. Many people have pointed out that what was considered a model tenement in 1879 is in 1900 considered one of the worst types of tenement houses ever constructed.[10]

In 1887, the tenement housing laws were amended and then again in 1895. Among other requirements, the 1887 amendments increased the number of toilets to one for every 15 residents instead of one for every 20. In addition, tenement building hallways had to have windows opening directly to the outside air. The 1895 amendments prohibited the covering of air shafts with roofs. It required the ceilings of basement apartments be at least 2 feet above grade, thereby providing some natural lighting and ventilation to basement apartments.

New York's tenement housing problem was not unique to New York City. Chicago, Boston, Buffalo, Cincinnati, Pittsburgh, Washington, D.C.,

Jersey City, and Hartford all had tenement housing problems to varying degrees. Various laws were passed to control the planning, design, and construction of tenement houses, including:

- 1867: New York City enacted provisions to improve daylighting and natural ventilation. Provisions required a space of 10 feet between one-story buildings, 15 feet between two-story buildings, 20 feet for three-stories, and 25 feet for buildings over three-stories in height.
- 1889: The State of Illinois enacted a law requiring all tenement houses to meet minimum lighting, ventilation, drainage, and plumbing standards. Tenement housing plans had to be submitted to local Health Commissioners for approval.
- 1892: Boston enacted statutes that set height limits for buildings based on type of construction. Building heights were limited to two and a half times the width of the street. Side yard setback requirements were enacted. Two separate exits were required from second floors and all floors above. All tenement rooms had to have at least one window that opened to an air space at least one-tenth the width of the room. All newly constructed tenement buildings had to be of fireproof construction throughout. This last requirement proved impractical and was changed in 1899 to require only noncombustible materials for external walls and party walls.
- 1893: Buffalo enacted a set of ordinances to regulate the design, erection, and maintenance of tenement houses after an outbreak of cholera in the summer of 1892.
- 1895: Hartford enacted requirements for fire escapes. The following year it created the department and title of Building Inspector.
- 1896: Chicago enacted requirements for the ventilation, light, drainage, and plumbing of buildings based on Illinois's 1889 law.
- 1897: Hartford's Board of Health passed plumbing rules that included the requirement of registration for all plumbers.
- 1898: Chicago's City Council enacted building and health ordinances modeled after the housing laws of New York and Boston.

- 1901: New York City passed the Tenement House Act that established health and fire safety regulations for Tenement Buildings.
- 1914: *A Model Housing Law* was published. It established model code requirements for all houses, not just tenement houses. Quickly, cities throughout the United States began enacting housing laws based on the model code.
- 1917: The State of Michigan implemented a Housing Code, requiring all towns with populations of 10,000 or more to follow the state code's requirements for all dwellings. Minnesota, California, and Indiana also enacted housing laws.

In the preface to the second edition of *A Model Housing Law*, published in 1920, author Lawrence Veiller proudly wrote of his work:

> When the Model Housing Law was published in 1914 it was a pioneer effort. There were practically no housing laws of any kind in the country.[11]

The laws listed above did not solve all the housing problems. Indeed, housing the urban poor and lower working class is still an unresolved problem today. Nevertheless, they were important steps and did improve living conditions for many tenement residents.

From today's perspective, many of these laws were a mix of city planning and building regulations. At the time they were enacted, there was no clear distinction between regulations that governed planning on a general or large scale and those governing the detailed design of buildings. This distinction was yet to come, and by the end of the 19th century, it was still over a decade away. The need for cities to govern how they grew and how the land within their jurisdictions should be used was becoming more and more apparent.

THE CITY BEAUTIFUL MOVEMENT

When Howard published his book in 1898, city planning was in its infancy. There were hardly more than a handful of city planners worldwide, and all were self-trained. In the United States, the three most prominent ones were the landscape architect Frederick Law Olmsted (1822–1903), the architect-turned-city-planner Daniel H. Burnham (1846–1912), and Olmsted's son, Frederick Jr., (1870–1957) who took over the daily operations of his father's landscape design practice in 1894.

In 1893, the United States celebrated the 401st anniversary of Columbus discovering America with the Columbian Exposition held in Chicago. Although Chicago was the birthplace of the tall building—later to be dubbed the skyscraper—the fair buildings broke ranks with the experimental and innovative building form being developed by the Chicago School. Instead, the fair's designers fashioned the buildings on the Beaux-Arts Classicism style, popular in the eastern United States and Europe. The style derived its name from the L'Ecole des Beaux Arts School of Architecture in Paris where the style was taught. The style borrowed heavily from ancient Greek and Roman architecture, combining their classical forms in various eclectic mixtures. Chicago architect Daniel H. Burnham was appointed Director of Construction, and he selected and led the fair's design team, which was made up mostly of East Coast architects. While Burnham was a self-taught architect, many on his design team had attended L'Ecole des Beaux Arts. Burnham became a convert from the Chicago School to the Beaux Arts School. The team established Beaux Arts Classicism guidelines for all fair architecture.

Frederick Law Olmsted designed the fairgrounds, which included lush landscaping, ornate fountains, and canals reminiscent of Venice, Italy. The overall result was a composition of classical-looking buildings set in a lushly landscaped water park, forming a shimmering ideal city—a White City, as it was dubbed, because all the buildings were painted white. (See Figure 4.2.)

The White City was a beautiful city, free of poverty, crime, and alcohol. Families came from all around the country and the world to visit the Fair. They left very much impressed by the clean, wholesome, and poverty-free White City. *Harper's New Monthly Magazine* reported:

> The fair! The fair! Never had the name such significance before. Fairest of all the Worlds' present sights it is. A city of palaces set in spaces of emerald, reflected in shining lengths of water which stretch in undulating lines under flat arches of marble bridges and along banks planted with consummate skill.[12]

FIGURE 4.2 *Chicago Illinois, View c. 1893 looking towards the Beaux Arts Classicism Administration Building. Richard Morris Hunt, architect. Historic architecture and Landscape Image Collection, Ryerson and Burnham Archives, The Art Institute of Chicago, Reproduction. © The Art Institute of Chicago.*

The White City was not a real city and its buildings were not even real buildings. With the exception of the Hall of Fine Arts, the buildings were constructed of steel and wood and covered with a relatively new invention called staff, which was a mixture of burlap and plaster.

The Chicago World's Fair was an amazing success. It propelled Daniel Burnham to the world stage, as both architect and city planner. Emboldened and self-assured, Burnham met with Frank Lloyd Wright after the fair and made Wright an offer that Wright refused. The fair had so lifted Burnham in the eyes of his architectural colleagues that other architects in Chicago called him "Uncle Dan," Wright included. In his autobiography, Wright wrote about his meeting with Burnham:

> Sitting there, handsome, jovial, splendidly convincing was "Uncle Dan." To be brief, he would take care of my wife and children if I would go to Paris—four years for the [L'Ecole des] Beaux Arts. Then Rome—two years. . . . "The Fair, Frank, is going to have a great influence in our country. The American people have seen the Classics on a grand scale for the first time. You've seen the success of

the Fair and it should mean something to you too. . . . I can see all America constructed along the lines of the Fair, in noble dignified classic style. The great men of the day all feel that way about it—all of them."[13]

Wright turned down Burnham's offer and went on to become one of the three leading architects of the 20th century, the other two being Le Corbusier and Mies van der Rohe. At the time, however, the prominent architect was Burnham. After the fair, Burnham's office received many commissions.

Others shared Burnham's ideas about city planning. As mentioned before, Frederick Law Olmsted and his son Frederick Jr. were proponents. The architects Charles F. McKim and Cass Gilbert were supporters, as were various groups made up of socially minded middle- and upper-class citizens. Supporters included America's aristocracy, familiar names like Vanderbilt, Morgan, Astor, and Whitney. They all held in common the same fear: the disastrous deterioration of society due to the unchecked spread of inner city poverty and congestion. Overcrowded slums, they believed, were the breeding grounds of crime and immorality. Something had to be done to stop the spread. They had taken journalist Jacobs Riis's words to heart when he wrote in his 1890 book, *How the Other Half Lives*, that in the tenements of inner city slums

> . . . all the influences make for evil; because they are the hotbeds of the epidemics that carry death to rich and poor alike; the nurseries of pauperism and crime . . . [and] above all, they touch the family life with deadly moral contagion. . . . That we own it . . . does not excuse it, even though it gives it claim upon our utmost patience and tenderest charity.[14]

The City Beautiful Movement's solution to the problem was simple—too simple, really: Clean up inner cities and make them beautiful through glorious architecture rendered on a grand scale. Beaux Arts Classicism was the perfect style for it—grand, elegant, and disciplined—just what was needed to add beauty and order to chaotic inner cities. It was architecture as a social tool, used to control behavior, alleviate poverty, curb immorality, and elevate society.

The City Beautiful Movement Heads to Washington

In 1901, Washington, D.C., became the first city to test the ideas of the City Beautiful Movement. The year 1900 was the centennial year of Washington, D.C., as the nation's capital. The American Institute of Architects (AIA) held its annual meeting there with the theme "The Beautification of the Nation's Capitol."

The original master plan for Washington, D.C., which was developed over a century earlier by architect and city planner Pierre Charles L'Enfant, was never finished. The area of the current National Mall was incomplete in 1900—not much more than pasture land. Railroad tracks encroached upon the mall. L'Enfant had envisioned a formal mall lined with great and important buildings. The mall of 1900 was anything but.

During the 1900 AIA convention, papers and master plans were delivered by leading designers, including Frederick Law Olmsted Jr., and Cass Gilbert. Senator James McMillan, Chairman of the Senate Committee on the District of Columbia, took a keen interest in the presentations and soon formed a subcommittee to study how to improve Washington, D.C. Daniel Burnham, Frederick Law Olmsted Jr., and Charles McKim were appointed to the subcommittee. The subcommittee went abroad to study European architecture and city planning. When they returned, they unveiled their master plan.

The plan was to create a greenbelt of parks and boulevards around the city. The mall would be carpeted in grass and planted with rows of elm trees along the sides, and it would be lined with public galleries and museums. The White House axis would extend to the Potomac River, the Capitol axis to the Washington Monument and beyond to a new memorial to President Lincoln. Beyond the Lincoln Memorial would be a bridge to Arlington Cemetery. The plan included a Beaux Arts railway station—Union Station—with a Romanesque triumphal arch. The master plan was called the McMillan Plan, and the city quickly went to work implementing it. The City Beautiful McMillan Plan led to the Washington, D.C., we know today.

Other cities saw what Washington, D.C., was doing and they wanted Beaux Arts architecture, too. Soon, the City Beautiful Movement was in full swing. New York City began building the Beaux Arts Penn and Grand Central stations in 1903. The Movement quickly became international.

In 1904, Burnham began developing a City Beautiful master plan for Manila in the Philippines. In 1905, Burnham finished a Beaux Arts master plan for the city of San Francisco. In 1909, he developed one for his hometown of Chicago. Beautification projects were under way in Cleveland and Columbus, Ohio, and in Denver, Colorado, and Madison, Wisconsin.

The City Beautiful Movement, however, did not eliminate poverty. Like the Garden City Movement, it did not solve the economic issues that caused poverty. In reality, the City Beautiful Movement was about the look of poverty. It was about keeping it out of sight. Yet the problem still existed hidden beyond the precisely ordered lines of City Beautiful architecture.

Eventually, the ideas of the Garden City Movement and the City Beautiful Movement merged. Together their ideas solved the problem of poverty by making it all but invisible to just about everyone except those trapped in it. By employing the ideas of the City Beautiful Movement in city centers and Garden City's idea of single-family-use districts in the suburbs, poverty could virtually disappear for middle- and upper-class families. It would exist outside of the normal workaday world of most Americans. In her 1961 book *The Death and Life of Great American Cities*, which has become a city planning classic, Jane Jacobs wrote:

> The idea behind the [City Beautiful] centers was not questioned, and it has never had more force than it does today. The idea of sorting out certain cultural or public functions and decontaminating their relationship with the workaday city dovetailed nicely with the Garden City teachings. The conceptions have harmoniously merged.[15]

Today, middle- and upper-class Americans who live in the suburbs drive or take public transportation to work every weekday. Watching the freeway ahead or reading their morning newspapers, they whiz by overcrowded areas of intractable poverty that exist within every major city of the United States. They pay the areas no mind. They work each day in clean and well-maintained downtown buildings. They return home each day the same way they came. They spend their weekends in the suburbs, while tall buildings downtown stand empty. All the while, lives are lived unseen in congested enclaves of poverty, out of sight and out of the minds of most Americans.

For a few days in August 2005, though, poverty rose to the surface. In disbelief, we watched New Orleans's poor neighborhoods struggle in the aftermath of Hurricane Katrina. We saw generational poverty trapped on rooftops, waving desperately for help. We were not used to it. So alien is poverty to us that we likened what we saw to a third-world country. Certainly our government would help, we thought. As we know, however, help was slow in coming.

5

EARTHQUAKE

The ancient Greek philosopher Parmenides believed that the earth did not move. Motion was impossible because "all is full of what is,"[1] and nothing can exist outside of what is. Because the world was full, empty space did not exist. How could it? It would have to exist outside of what exists, and that is logically impossible. Parmenides called what lay beyond existence the "void." To move, an object would have to move outside of existence into the void and yet somehow still exist, which, again, is logically impossible. So Parmenides believed nothing moved.

Parmenides's thought process sounds strange from a 21st-century perspective. However, around 500 BC when Parmenides lived, the existence of atoms had not yet been logically inferred. In Parmenides's worldview, the four elements—earth, fire, water, and air—were continuous and filled everything. Consequently, the earth did not move because it could not move, regardless of what our senses told us.

Parmenides was wrong, of course, on two counts. First, substances are not continuous and they do not fill up existence in the way he thought. Everything is made of atoms, as Leucippus and his student Democritus reasoned years after Parmenides. Second, the earth does move. It not only spins on its axis as it travels around the sun, but the earth's crust constantly moves in a process called plate tectonics. Rocks at different temperatures, strengths, and depths move over, under, and pass one another, slowly remaking the earth's surface.

In the areas where this process is most active, breaks or fault lines occur. For example, the earth beneath California has many active fault lines. Sometimes stress within the plates of rock builds up along fault lines. When the plates suddenly move, tremendous energy is released in the form of earthquakes.

Earthquakes have been destroying buildings and cities for millennia. In the *Iliad,* Homer tells that an earthquake destroyed the Ilium (ancient Troy) of King Priam. Archeologists equate the Ilium in Homer's poem to the ancient Troy VI site in Turkey. Indeed, an archeological excavation of Troy VI suggests that the city was destroyed by an earthquake in 1275 BC.

The Chinese recorded an earthquake in 1177 BC. The earliest known earthquake in Europe dates from 580 BC. The earliest known earthquakes in the Americas occurred during the 14th century in Mexico and Peru. During the 17th century, eyewitness accounts of many earthquakes were recorded.

In early times, the cause of earthquakes was not understood. How to construct buildings to resist earthquake damage was also unknown. Earthquakes shook buildings and cities to the ground. Afterwards, the shaken survivors, knowing no better, picked up boards, stacked stones, and rebuilt again as they always had.

In the United States, California is especially prone to earthquakes. The heavily populated areas along the west coast from San Diego to San Francisco have experienced literally thousands in the past 200 years. Most amounted to nothing, but dozens caused people to take note and record them in newspapers and diaries. A few rose to the level of disasters, causing severe damage and loss of lives. It is just a matter of time before the next one strikes.

Not surprisingly, earthquakes have had a major impact in shaping the cities, buildings, and history of California. Perhaps no other city's history is more linked to earthquakes than San Francisco. Although the 1906 Great Earthquake and Fire is San Francisco's most famous earthquake, it was not its first.

THE SAN FRANCISCO EARTHQUAKES OF 1865 AND 1868

The Spaniards who settled California and built missions and forts up and down the coast often felt earthquakes. In 1808, the commander of the Presidio in San Francisco wrote to the Spanish Governor in Monterey, California, reporting the damage to adobe walls caused by a series of earthquakes during June and July. Four years later, another earthquake collapsed the Presidio chapel and also caused a small tidal wave, which flooded portions of San Francisco along the bay. There also were other quakes in 1827, 1829, and 1839.

Gold was discovered at Sutter's Mill on January 24, 1848, approximately 100 miles east of San Francisco. At the time, San Francisco was a quiet little town with a population of around 800 people. That soon changed. By mid-1849, San Francisco was a boom town as miners from around the world arrived, many by ship. They bought food and clothing and they gambled and drank. Most moved on to the gold fields, but many stayed. By the end of 1849, San Francisco's population had grown to 25,000.

Dozens of earthquakes were reported over the next two decades. Most amounted to nothing more than unsettling nuisances. On Sunday afternoon, October 8, 1865, however, a large earthquake shook the city. It broke windows and cracked and toppled brick walls. Buildings collapsed. City Hall was badly damaged, shaking so violently that its fire bell rang. Buildings and streets constructed on top of bay fill caved in or sunk. *The Daily Alta California* reported:

> Scarcely a house in the city . . . does not show some mark of visitation, in cracked walls, open joints. . . . [M]any of the old heavy brick structures are so shaken up and twisted as to be dangerous to the occupants. . . . [T]he low made ground in the southern portion of the city . . . exhibited lively signs of caving in. . . . A lot on the southwest corner of Seventh and Howard streets, sunk 14 feet. . . . [W]here Saturday was a dry bank of sand, today a flock of ducks are disporting themselves in a pond of water.[2]

Mark Twain lived in San Francisco at the time. Fifteen years later, he gave his account of the earthquake in his book *Roughing It:*

> I enjoyed my first earthquake. [T]here came a really terrific shock; the ground seemed to roll under me in waves, interrupted by a violent joggling up and down, and there was a heavy grinding noise as of brick houses rubbing together. . . . I saw a sight! The entire front of a tall four-story brick building in Third street sprung outward like a door and fell sprawling across the street, raising a dust like a great volume of smoke![3]

Today we know that the 1865 Earthquake occurred on the San Andreas Fault. Its magnitude was approximately 6.3 on the Richter scale, and its epicenter was located about 50 miles south of San Francisco in the Santa Cruz mountains. At the time, however, no one really understood the cause of earthquakes, and no one knew how to measure their intensity. All anyone knew was that earthquakes happened suddenly, without warning, and for no apparent reason. Understandably, earthquakes had many San Franciscans worried.

In 1868, geologist Dr. John A. Veatch (1808–1870) published an article in the March 31 edition of *Mining & Scientific Press* entitled "Earthquakes in San Francisco, and Especially on Their Direction." In the article, he argued that earthquakes occur along "earthquake lines," and that San Franciscans should not worry so much about them because

> San Francisco is removed considerably from the central disturbance of either the coastline or submarine line of earthquakes; that the intensity of the shocks will therefore be always greatly mitigated; and that the fury of the heaviest shocks will be expanded on the sea waves 30 or 40 miles from the shore; and therefore the shore is probably safe from any shock of very great destructive violence.[4]

Whether Veatch's article quelled many fears is unknown. What is known is that on October 21, 1868, an event took place that called into question the conclusion Veatch had drawn in his article.

At 7:53 AM, San Francisco shook violently for approximately one minute. Buildings shook, store shelves emptied and tipped over, windows broke, and masonry walls cracked and fell. Entire buildings were destroyed. A second earthquake struck at 9:33 AM, causing even more damage. The next day, *The San Francisco Morning Call* reported:

> Yesterday morning San Francisco was visited by the most severe earthquake the city ever experienced. . . . The oscillations were from east to west, and were very violent. Men, women, and children rushed into the streets—some in a state of semi-nudity—and all in the wildest state of excitement. Many acted as if they thought the Day of Judgment had come.[5]

The 1868 Earthquake occurred closer to San Francisco than the 1865 Earthquake, along the Hayward fault. It was also more intense, with an estimated magnitude of 7.0. Again, many buildings were damaged; City Hall was severely damaged, as was the Custom House, the Gas Works, and the City and County Hospital.

The 1865 and 1868 Earthquakes revealed that some types of buildings performed better than others in earthquakes. In general, one- and two-story buildings constructed of wood faired well. Many of these were balloon framed. These buildings were nailed together and, as the buildings shook, the hundreds of nails that fastened board siding to studs worked back and forth, dissipating the earthquake's energy and converting it into harmless heat. Those built of stone and brick were much more brittle—much less elastic—and consequently suffered more damage. Tall brick buildings that were four stories and more suffered the most.

There were many brick walls in downtown San Francisco. Most suffered some degree of damage and many fell. Although brick walls are weak in resisting horizontal loads—that is, shaking back and forth—they are noncombustible, and this made them useful in controlling another type of disaster—fire—which also had been a great problem for San Francisco.

San Francisco's Other Great Disaster—Fire

Prior to the 1865 and 1868 Earthquakes, fire was San Francisco's greatest worry and the primary cause of disasters. The San Francisco of the 1860s was a relatively new city. Much of it had been destroyed over and over by fires. By the 1860s, San Francisco had already experienced six Great Fires and one was yet to come.

The first fire occurred in 1849 on the day before Christmas. At the time, San Francisco had no fire department. The fire started in a large gambling house on Kearny Street. Citizens banned together and finally stopped the fire by blowing up and tearing down buildings in the fire's path. On Christmas Day, San Francisco established its first volunteer fire department.

San Franciscans wasted no time rebuilding. It was the gold rush after all, and there was plenty of money to be made. Wooden San Francisco was rebuilt in a month. Five months later, on May 4, 1850, another fire destroyed virtually the same area of the city. Again, San Francisco rebuilt, and again, mostly out of wood. Reconstruction was almost complete when another fire broke out on June 14, 1850. San Franciscans rebuilt, but this time they dug more wells and constructed reservoirs. They also established more volunteer fire departments.

Another fire occurred on September 17, 1850. Again, San Francisco rebuilt. This time many of the buildings were constructed with brick walls and iron doors and window shutters. On May 4, 1851, however, a terribly destructive fire burned down approximately three-quarters of the city. The fire spread quickly from building to building, traveling underneath the raised wooden boardwalks. Citizens scrambled for safety within the new brick and iron buildings only to be trapped. The heat of the flames outside expanded the closed iron doors and window shutters making it impossible to escape. Again, San Francisco wasted no time rebuilding. Ten days after the fire, one-fifth of the area that was destroyed was already rebuilt.

June 22, 1851, marked the end of old San Francisco, however, when a sixth fire completely destroyed ten blocks of downtown and seriously damaged six more. City Hall, which had escaped damage from the previous five fires, was destroyed. Resilient San Franciscans again rebuilt, but this time they used brick to construct firewalls and placed water tanks on many roofs.

Rebuilding in Response to Earthquakes and Fires

While brick fire walls helped control the spread of fire, they crumbled during the 1865 and 1868 Earthquakes. Brick walls throughout the downtown area cracked, and many fell into piles of rubble. It is ironic, but the very materials that helped San Francisco resist the ravages of fire were the very materials that were the most life-threatening during the earthquakes and resulted in the most destruction.

The day after the 1868 Earthquake, the editorial staff of the *San Francisco Morning Call* offered a suggestion to reduce damage to buildings caused by earthquakes:

> As we said three years ago [after the 1865 earthquake], we now say: the city authorities should prohibit the erection of buildings of more than thirty-five feet in height. They should also prohibit the erection of "fire-walls," and the other man-traps in the shape of cornices, brackets, and other "filigree" ornaments on buildings, which are not only offensive to good taste, but do endanger life. The lives lost yesterday are not chargeable to the earthquake, but to the vanity, greed and meanness of those who erected the buildings.[6]

During the 1868 Earthquake, some buildings sank. These buildings were built on poorly compacted earth used to fill in portions of the bay. Buildings were then built on top of the unstable dirt, called "made ground." Much of the land south of Market Street was made ground and still is today. During the earthquake, the made ground liquefied and settled due to the quick back-and-forth motion of the earthquake. The process is called liquefaction. During the earthquake, the area around Sixth and Howard Streets liquefied and "great volumes of water were forced up into the air, in some instances as high as fifty feet."[7]

Immediately after the earthquake, San Francisco began to rebuild, but city officials did not heed the suggestion of the *Morning Call* editors. Virtually nothing was done to mitigate the damage that might result from future earthquakes, with one notable exception: The area south of Market Street did not rebuild as quickly. Understandably, people were a bit apprehensive to live or work there. Rents plummeted and some owners found it nearly impossible to lease their buildings. Desperate, some tore down their old buildings and built new ones on wooden piles driven deep down into the bay mud. Although the foundations were more expensive, they relieved many people's fears. Soon, buildings were filling up south of Market, so San Francisco filled in more of the bay.

A small number of scientists began to study earthquakes. In 1887, the first two seismographs were installed, one at the University of California–Berkeley and the other at the Lick Observatory at Mount Hamilton, California. Geologists from the U.S. Geological Survey began studying earthquakes, compiling historic data from past earthquakes.

Little was known about how and where earthquakes occur, and no one was working on how to mitigate the damage they caused, but all that would change after the next great disaster to hit San Francisco.

THE GREAT SAN FRANCISCO EARTHQUAKE AND FIRE

By the early 1900s, San Francisco was a center of world trade and finance, nearly equal in stature to New York City, London, and Paris. It was the largest city on the West Coast and the ninth largest in the United States with a population of around 350,000. San Francisco had plans to grow even bigger.

To do so, it needed a secure and never-ending source of water. San Francisco thought it found it in a valley near Yosemite named Hetch Hetchy, as the Miwok Native Americans called it. San Francisco's plan was to dam the Tuolumne River that flowed through the Hetch Hetchy valley, flood the valley, and turn it into a lake. Because the land was part of Yosemite National Park created by Congress in 1890, San Francisco needed federal approval. San Francisco did not get it. Twice during the early 1900s, President Theodore Roosevelt's administration denied the city permission to dam the river.

Unlike many large East Coast cities at the beginning of the 20th century, 90 percent of the buildings in San Francisco were constructed of wood. Like many western boom towns, San Francisco had grown quickly and without much long-range planning. Cross streets did not align along Market Street. The bay was haphazardly filled in when more land was needed. Many streets south of Market were nothing more than alleys. Often they were named after the prostitutes that frequented them, that bred crime, and licentious behavior. Buildings in San Francisco ran the gauntlet from wood shacks to decorated Victorian houses to four- and five-story brick buildings with austere brick and terra cotta cornices.

Few of the buildings were properly adorned in the popular ornamentation of Beaux Arts Classicism that was the rage among architects and elites of the East Coast. San Francisco's lack of a plan for growth and its general overall western-town look bothered many leading San Franciscan businessmen and officials. Believing that the city—themselves included—could benefit if San Francisco's image was more on par with other world-class cities, they decided to improve the city's appearance. In January 1904, a committee was formed called the "Association for the Improvement and Adornment of San Francisco." Its president was former mayor James D. Phelan. The committee's objective was to beautify the streets, public buildings, parks, and squares of San Francisco. In September 1904, the committee hired the architect, city planner, and prominent leader of the City Beautiful Movement, Daniel H. Burnham, to study San Francisco and prepare a master plan. One year later, in September 1905, Burnham's master plan was complete. Burnham envisioned a San Francisco like Paris of Napoleon III. Burnham's San Francisco had great boulevards radiating out from the intersection of Market Street and Van Ness Avenue. The Panhandle of Golden Gate Park would extend to Market Street. Burnham explained:

> The Panhandle is to meet Market street at Van Ness avenue, and the crossing of these three great thoroughfares naturally indicated the center of the city. Accordingly, this junction is to be a spacious concourse, from which wide thoroughfares will radiate in all directions. At this junction there should be constructed a semicircular *Place* having for its center the intersection of the axis of the Panhandle and Van Ness avenue.[8]

Burnham suggested that buildings around the Place should reflect the best architecture of the day and, consequently, the classical "column should be freely used as the governing motif."[9] He proposed that the city purchase property around existing Civic Hall Square and "on this space there should be constructed an arcade or colonnade of regular cornice height terminated by pavilions" and that this "treatment would, in some measure, extend the architectural effect of the Civic Center [the Place] around the City Hall and impose a sense of order."[10]

Although Burnham's master plan was consistent with the master plan he had prepared for Washington, D.C., three years before, San Francisco was not Washington, D.C. Washington, D.C., was, in many respects, a Renaissance city originally laid out by Pierre Charles L' Enfant. San Francisco was a western town that had grown big quickly and more or less organically. Like Wren's plan for London 240 years earlier, Burnham's master plan was unworkable for San Francisco as it then existed. So Burnham's plan sat on the shelf—at least for six months.

On Wednesday April 18, 1906, at 5:13 AM, the earth beneath San Francisco began to shake. It shook and shook and shook for 48 frightening seconds. San Franciscan Charles Keeler described it:

> [T]he deeps of the earth, far down under the foundations of the city, began to rumble and vibrate. The earth tremors increased in violence . . . there was a sickening sensation as if everything were toppling. Plaster poured from ceilings . . . heavy furniture moved about banged upon the floor; and then the brick walls gave way. . . . Tall structures, ribbed and rocked with steel, swayed like trees in a wind-storm, but stood triumphant at the end with scarce a brick or stone displaced.[11]

The earthquake was extremely powerful, much greater than the 1865 and 1868 Earthquakes, measuring an estimated 7.9 on the Richter scale.

The severe shaking and falling debris sent many terrified citizens, still in their nightclothes, rushing outside into the streets. When the shaking was over, they returned to their houses to cook breakfast and start their days.

In many areas south of Market Street, however, the situation was quite different. Built on fill, many houses tilted or collapsed, crushing victims inside. Fires started from overturned stoves and broken chimneys. Water and gas lines buried in liquefied bay mud broke and escaping gas started more fires. At one point, there were 52 separate fires burning in San Francisco with virtually no water to fight them.

By mid-afternoon, desperate authorities began dynamiting buildings to create firebreaks. The results were similar to those of the Great Fires of Chicago and Baltimore. Buildings were blown up in groups of three, often spewing flaming lumber that started more fires. The explosions continued throughout the day and into the night. A woman, known only as Philura, who witnessed the fire and dynamiting from her window, later wrote:

> It was an earth-racked night of terror. We watched the leaping and hissing flames in the city below us, and heard the crashing of buildings. By dynamiting buildings, the firemen hoped to check the conflagration. Much dynamite was used, many buildings blown to atoms, but all was in vain.[12]

FIGURE 5.1 *The City Hall building in San Francisco after the 1906 earthquake. © CORBIS. Photographer: A. Blumberg Date Photographed: 1906 Location Information: San Francisco, California, USA.*

The fire burned for three days. When it ended on Friday, approximately 80 percent of the city was gone. (See Figure 5.1.) Together, the earthquake and fire destroyed approximately 28,000 buildings and left 250,000 people homeless. San Franciscans slept in tents in Golden Gate Park and on John Daly's hill south of San Francisco. Estimates vary widely, but today it is believed that as many as 3,000 people were killed.

San Francisco Arises . . . Again

At the time, the San Francisco Earthquake and Fire was the largest disaster in U.S. history. Immediately, some wrote San Francisco off. The writer Will Irwin wrote about the disaster and San Francisco in the past tense, titling his article, "The City That Was." But, San Franciscans, like they always had done, began rebuilding immediately. By Sunday, plumbers were in the streets repairing water, gas, and sewer lines. Debris from the earthquake and fire was hauled to the bay and dumped in. Reconstruction was under way.

On April 21, three days after the earthquake, California governor George C. Pardee established the first government-commissioned scientific committee to investigate earthquakes. University of California—Berkeley professor Andrew C. Lawson was named Chairman, and on May 31, the "State Earthquake Investigation Committee" made its first report to the Governor. Its final report was published in 1908, which included photographs and information regarding the buildings destroyed by the earthquake, descriptions and maps of the geology of northern California, and detailed information on the earth's movement along the San Andreas Fault. The final report is still heralded today as a benchmark document for the investigation and study of earthquakes.

For some in San Francisco, the earthquake and fire brought new possibilities. Former mayor James D. Phelan of the "Association for the Improvement and Adornment of San Francisco" claimed that the disaster was "a magnificent opportunity for beautifying San Francisco."[13] Phelan contacted Burnham, who was traveling in Europe at the time. Burnham cut his visit short and came to San Francisco. On May 21, Mayor Eugene E. Schmitz approved a scaled-down version of Burnham's master plan, and soon a study was under way to determine how best to implement it.

Immediately, the public voiced dissention. Businessmen and average citizens alike threatened to sue the city if it took their property in order to widen streets and construct new boulevards. *The San Francisco Chronicle* called Burnham's master plan a "cobweb." Too reminiscent of the grand Renaissance plans of days gone by, the *Chronicle* concluded: "We may allow visions of the beautiful to dance before our eyes, but we must not permit them to control our actions."[14]

The public's objections notwithstanding, work on the master plan continued, and in October 1906, a report was published containing recommendations on how best to implement the practical portions of Burnham's master plan. On September 28, Mayor Schmitz wrote a preface to the study. In it he claimed that the implementation plan was

> in line with what I have been planning since the fire and if adopted by the people will make San Francisco, what we expect her to be, one of the best and most progressive cities on this continent. The plans have my hearty endorsement and I sincerely hope they will be realized at a very early date.[15]

Ultimately, San Francisco did not implement Burnham's master plan, although a portion of it was resurrected. As the debate about the master plan continued, the city was already rebuilding.

Disaster Spells Opportunity for San Francisco's Chinatown

One area not waiting for any master plan was San Francisco's Chinatown. Like Phelan, the Chinese saw opportunities in the earthquake and fire. However, what they had in mind was quite different. Chinatown was the oldest, most densely populated, and most dilapidated part of the city. Its old, rundown Victorian buildings, some with hardly a foundation, were mostly destroyed by the earthquake and fire.

Chinatown was also mostly male. In 1882, the U.S. Congress passed the Chinese Exclusion Act that drastically reduced the number of Chinese who could legally come into the United States. Men came, hoping to bring their families later, especially their children. Many came illegally. Besides burning Chinatown to the ground, the fire also consumed government buildings, including most immigration records.

The Chinese quickly took advantage of the two opportunities handed them by the fire. Many declared themselves legal immigrants, and with no paperwork to prove otherwise, they began bringing their children to America, including many who they only pretended were their children.

With old Chinatown destroyed, community leaders decided to make new Chinatown an attraction rather than an eyesore. Rather than rebuild in the old Victorian style, they hired non-Chinese architects to help them design an entirely new whimsical and Americanized interpretation of Chinese architecture. Street-level shops and restaurants catering to non-Chinese San Franciscans and tourists were fashioned to look like pagodas, which were religious buildings in China. Floors above were designed as apartments. Thus, San Francisco's Chinatown transformed. Today, San Francisco's Chinatown, visited by hundreds of thousands of tourists every year, owes its shape and character to the 1906 Earthquake and Fire.

San Francisco Revises Its Building Ordinances

Shortly after the disaster, the City and County of San Francisco repealed its previous building ordinances. The most recent version had been published in February 1903, and one prior to that in 1895–1896. The *Building Law of the City and County of San Francisco 1906* established new regulations for "the construction, erection, enlargement, raising, alteration, repair, removal maintenance, use, and height of buildings; regulating character and use of materials in and for buildings."[16] It also expanded the boundary of the city's downtown fire district. Height limitations were established for buildings, limiting the maximum height of buildings to one and one-half times the width of the street on which the building fronted. For example, a building fronting a street 100 feet in width could be 150 feet tall, whereas one fronting a street 70 feet in width could only be 105 feet in height.

San Francisco's 1906 *Building Law* established design criteria for resisting the horizontal forces associated with earthquakes without using the word "earthquake." Although it was the fire that destroyed San Francisco, it was earthquakes that really scared people. Immediately after the earthquake and fire, real estate agents, businessmen, and growth proponents—called "boosters"—went to work quelling people's fears about earthquakes. Everyone understood fires, as countless cities had experienced them, but earthquakes were another matter. Boosters were afraid that people would not come to visit or live in San Francisco because of the earthquake potential. Consequently, building damage caused by the earthquake was downplayed. The "E" word was used as little as possible. *Building Law* requirements for resistance to horizontal loads caused by earthquakes was dealt with in terms of "wind bracing":

> In buildings over one hundred feet high, or where the height exceeds three times the least horizontal dimension . . . the steel frame shall be designed to resist a wind force of 30 pounds per square foot acting in any direction upon the entire exposed surface.[17]

Wind bracing is important, of course, but it was the earthquake that brought both the destruction and the code provision. Wind bracing requirements had already made their way into Chicago's and New York City's building codes years earlier. San Francisco adopted a code provision from these cities and applied it to earthquakes. In 1906, engineers did not understand earthquake forces well enough to calculate the difference between horizontal loads caused by wind pushing on a building compared to an earthquake shaking it. This was noted by John D. Galloway, chairman of San Francisco's Building Law Subcommittee, when he wrote:

> There are no means of calculating the stresses in a building due to an earthquake, but, judging from the behavior of buildings such as the Shreve Building or the Claus Spreckels Building [two tall

steel-framed SF buildings that survived the earthquake], I would say that if a building is properly designed for a wind pressure of 30 pounds per square foot on its superficial area, that it would be sufficient to withstand an earthquake . . . [equal to the 1906 earthquake].[18]

At first glance, the code requirement for wind bracing sounded reasonable and fair, but it contained a subtle bias. Masonry buildings were unaffected by the new requirements. They did not have steel frames and they were generally less than four stories in height. Although masonry buildings had suffered the most damage in the quake, not steel buildings, the new regulations only affected tall steel buildings. Recall Charles Keeler's eyewitness account quoted earlier: "Tall structures, ribbed and rocked with steel, swayed like trees in a wind-storm, but stood triumphant at the end."

The requirement was illogical in another way. The earth does not shake differently depending on street widths. Earthquake forces on buildings fronting wide streets are the same as those on narrow streets. But, under the guise of safety, the code set different maximum heights for these two conditions. Engineers, architects, and real estate developers complained.

While engineers agreed it was a good idea to take into account horizontal loads caused by wind or earthquakes, the 30 pounds per square foot number seemed arbitrary. Why not 20 pounds or 15? Others argued that it made no sense to compare earthquake loads to wind loads, and instead suggested different values for both. Also, why were there no requirements for masonry buildings? San Francisco's Committee on Fire and Earthquake Damage reported:

> [It is] one of the most obvious lessons of the earthquake, that brick walls or walls of brick faced with stone, when without an interior frame of steel, are hopelessly inadequate.[19]

The masonry industry claimed that the masonry buildings that failed did so because they were not properly constructed and that there was nothing inherently unsafe with masonry construction. They advocated proper mortar mixes, wetting bricks, and ensuring all bonding surfaces were properly covered with mortar.

To a large degree, the *Building Law* was motivated by considerations other than earthquakes such as aesthetics, daylighting at street level, and the general fear and dislike of tall buildings by the public and politicians. Design and real estate professionals were persistent, however, and within a year, San Francisco repealed its building height limitation requirements, while retaining the other provisions of the *Building Law.*

Burnham's master plan did not all go to waste. In 1912, San Franciscans voted for an $8.8 million bond measure to purchase land and construct a new Civic Center. A new City Hall was constructed very near the location that Burnham had selected for the Place before the earthquake and fire. Designed by architect John Bakewell Jr., and Arthur Brown Jr., it was carried out in the Beaux Art style of the City Beautiful Movement. The Hall's main entry sits under a giant Greek temple façade with Doric pillars, flanked on both sides by Doric colonnades. Above the pediment of the temple soars a French Renaissance dome that rises 308 feet above ground level, making San Francisco's City Hall 16 feet taller than the U.S. Capitol.

San Francisco Finally Gets a Dam

After the earthquake, San Francisco again appealed to the Department of the Interior to dam Hetch Hetchy. A seven-year battle ensued, but eventually Congress, sympathetic to San Francisco in the wake of its devastating earthquake and fire, agreed. In 1913, it passed the Raker Act, which permitted the flooding of Hetch Hetchy, and in 1923, the O'Shaughnessy Dam was completed. Hetch Hetchy filled with water and changed from pristine valley to man-made lake. The damming of Hetch Hetchy forever changed the Bay Area, too. Today Hetch Hetchy provides drinking water for 2.4 million San Francisco Bay Area residents. Without it, the Bay Area could never have sustained its growth over the past 80 years.

THE 1925 SANTA BARBARA EARTHQUAKE

In the early 1920s, the U.S. Coast and Geodetic Survey resurveyed California to determine if any additional movement in the earth's crust had occurred since the 1908 report prepared by the State Earthquake Investigation Committee. Using survey data and benchmarks established in 1880, the new survey came to the astonishing and alarming conclusion that there had been a 24-foot shift between the west and east sides of the

San Andreas Fault in the area of Santa Barbara County. New maps and earthquake data were published in 1923, and earthquake scientists began spreading the news, calling for more studies and improvements in building standards. To assist in the efforts, they recruited architects, engineers, and code officials in support of the cause. Real estate and business groups, however, wanted to hear nothing of it. From the point of view of California boosters, discussing earthquakes was nothing but bad publicity.

As Santa Barbarians slept during the early hours of June 28, 1925, a series of small tremors were recorded by the city's water department pressure gauge. At 6:44 AM, a violent jolt from an estimated 6.3 magnitude earthquake woke everyone and sent virtually every chimney in Santa Barbara crashing to the ground. Other than their chimneys, most one- and two-story houses rode out the earthquake well, but the commercial buildings in downtown Santa Barbara did not fair as well. Dozens of masonry commercial buildings collapsed, including the partial collapse of several hotels. The Sheffield Reservoir, located within the city, broke, flooding a large portion of the city as the water rushed to the ocean. Falling rubble killed 13 people. The Santa Barbara earthquake was the most severe and devastating earthquake in California since 1906. The business manager of the *Santa Barbara Press* wrote:

> The whole earth rose and seemed to shake itself with the motion of a spaniel fresh from the water . . . and a minute later, State Street, the principal business avenue of the city, was a mass of ruins and wreckage.[20]

Earthquake scientists immediately redoubled their efforts and clamored for more earthquake preparedness. Again, they called for more earthquake research and better building standards. Again, their efforts were hampered by the boosters. One such booster was businessman, California Institute of Technology (Caltech) trustee, and financial benefactor Henry M. Robinson. In a letter to the administration of Caltech, he complained about two Caltech scientists who had been vocal about earthquake preparedness:

> I wonder if you have any idea how much damage this loose talk of these two men is doing to the [property] values in Southern California . . . if we . . . cannot stop their talk about the earthquake problem I for one am going to see what I can do about the whole seismological game.[21]

The boosters managed to stave off changes and improvements in building standards, at least temporarily. In 1927, the *Uniform Building Code* (UBC) became the first model code in the United States to include earthquake design criteria. Curiously, the section that discussed earthquake design, Section 2311, was omitted from the code's table of contents. Nevertheless, the section was included at the end of the chapter that discussed various building design load requirements, Chapter 23. Section 2311 directed the reader to the code's Appendix, which the code stated was not a legal part of the code. The Appendix contained the following statement:

> The following [earthquake design] provisions are suggested for inclusion in the Code by cities located within an area subject to earthquake shocks. The design of buildings for earthquake shocks is a moot question but the following provisions will provide adequate additional strength when applied in the design of buildings or structures.[22]

Note the use of the term "moot question," meaning that, at the time, the design of buildings to resist earthquake forces was still open to discussion and debate. Note, too, that because the earthquake provisions were in the Appendix, they were not technically a part of the code. It was up to individual cities to adopt provisions within the Appendix as they saw fit. Even after the devastation of the 1906 San Francisco Earthquake and the 1925 Santa Barbara Earthquake, the opinion of the boosters still held considerable influence.

Immediately following the above statement, the Appendix went on to establish the first comprehensive earthquake design criteria for heavy timber, masonry, concrete, and steel buildings over one story in height. It required that "all buildings shall be firmly bonded and tied together as to their parts and each one as a whole in such manner that the structure will act as a unit" during an earthquake.[23] It established earthquake force (horizontal or lateral) resistance criteria based on the strength of the soil that supported the building foundation. For soils with bearing pressures of less than 4,000 pounds per square foot (psf), the earthquake force (horizontal or lateral force) that the building had to resist was equal to 10 percent of the weight of the building plus its live load. In code parlance, "live load" is equal to the weight of a building's contents, including people, furniture, equipment, etc. If the soil-bearing pressure was 4,000 psf or greater (meaning it was very good soil), the building had to resist a somewhat smaller earthquake force equal to 7.5 percent of the weight of the building plus live load.

With much of its downtown destroyed, Santa Barbara turned the 1925 Earthquake disaster into opportunity. Santa Barbara adopted the earthquake provisions of the 1927 UBC. In addition, it established architectural standards for new buildings constructed along State Street, and created an architectural review board to enforce the standards. Today, Santa Barbara is dominated by a style of architecture reminiscent of the Spanish heritage of Southern California. Some call the style Spanish-Moorish, others Spanish Baroque, Spanish Revival, Spanish Mediterranean, Mission Revival, California Mission, or Spanish Eclectic. Regardless of the name, the main features of the style are easy to recognize: low-pitched roofs that have little or no overhanging eaves; roofs that are covered with barrel-shaped red clay tile and arches that occur over windows, doors, and porch entries; and exterior walls that are stucco and painted off-white or a faint yellowy cream. Although the style did not originate after the earthquake—it is the historical style of much of Southern California—the earthquake guaranteed its continuance and has since contributed to making Santa Barbara a popular tourist destination.

THE 1933 LONG BEACH EARTHQUAKE

It was 5:55 PM on March 10, 1933. School was over for the day. Families throughout Southern California were preparing or sitting down to dinner when the earthquake struck. Arthur G. Porter, who lived in Anaheim (about 15 miles from Long Beach), recounted:

> Myrtle was busy in the kitchen,—Mylet was sitting at the table in the dining room, and I was seated on the davenport. When the quake hit we all scrambled to get out the back door; I tried several times before I could get up off the sofa, and then as we stood (or rather attempted to stand) near the rear kitchen door, our garage appeared to be shaking just as it were on the end of a rug shaken by hand"[24]

An old man, on his way home after shopping, pulled a child's wagon full of groceries along a Long Beach sidewalk. As the old man passed the storefront of a laundry, he heard what sounded like an explosion, like something had blown up inside. He watched in astonishment as the entire front wall of the building fell into the street, just missing him. Heart racing, he hurried home.[25]

In Santa Ana, another man was not so lucky. He was walking in front of the Richelieu Hotel when the earth shook. A large piece of the hotel's terra cotta cornice broke off, hitting and instantly killing him. Another hotel in Santa Ana, the Rossmore, shook so violently that a man and a woman inside ran for their lives and made it outside only to be crushed by falling bricks.[26]

When it was over, 120 people had died, 70 K-12 schools were destroyed and another 120 were seriously damaged. Later estimates placed the earthquake at a magnitude of 6.3 and located it on the Newport-Inglewood Fault, its epicenter just south of the Orange County community of Huntington Beach. Had the earthquake struck only a few hours earlier, the schools would have been fully occupied and thousands of children could have been killed or injured.

Parents and other concerned citizens were extremely alarmed by what might have happened if school had been in session. They wanted immediate action. This time, the boosters offered little resistance. It was the Great Depression, and the days of the California real estate boom were long past.

On April 10, exactly one month after the earthquake, the Field Act was signed into law. Named after Sacramento Assemblyman Charles Field, who introduced the bill, the Field Act gave the State Division of Architecture the power to review school designs prior to construction and inspect them during construction. The act also authorized the Division of Architecture to hire structural engineers to inspect existing school buildings to make sure they were safe.

Next, on May 27, 1933, the Riley Act was passed. It required all local jurisdictions in California to establish building departments and inspect new construction. It also required that all new buildings be designed to withstand a minimum horizontal force of 2/100ths (0.02) times the acceleration of gravity due to an earthquake.

In 1935, the ICBO issued a new edition of the *Uniform Building Code*. For the first time, a model building code included a formula for calculating earthquake forces that buildings must resist:

> In determining the horizontal [earthquake] force to be resisted, the following formula shall be used:

$$F = CW$$

> Where "F" equals the horizontal force in pounds. "W" equals the total dead load plus one-half (1/2) the total . . . live load . . . [and] "C" equals a numerical constant.[27]

The constant or coefficient "C" varied depending on two conditions:

1. Whether the soil-bearing pressure was less than or equal to 2,000 psf or whether it was greater than 2,000 psf
2. In which seismic zone the building was located

The code included a map of the 11 western states and divided them into three different earthquake areas, which the code called zones of "approximately equal seismic probability."[28] The zones were numbered, with Zone 1 being the least seismically active and Zone 3 the most. If a building was located in Zone 1 and built on soil with a bearing pressure greater than 2,000 psf, C was equal to 0.02. If, however, a building was located in Zone 3 (the city of Long Beach was placed in Zone 3) and its foundation rested on the same soil conditions, C was equal to 0.08, a value four times higher than for Zone 1.

Interestingly, the earthquake requirements in the 1935 UBC appeared in the Appendix and, like the 1927 UBC, were not legally part of the code unless specifically adopted. Due to the Riley Act, buildings throughout California had to be designed to resist earthquake forces, but for jurisdictions in other states, adoption of the code's earthquake design requirements was discretionary.

Again, like the 1927 UBC, the 1935 UBC prefaced its earthquake provisions with the caveat that "the design of buildings for earthquake shocks is a moot question," meaning that the design of buildings to resist earthquake forces was still open to debate. It was not until after World War II, in the 1946 UBC, that the ICBO finally dropped this statement from its code.

In 1935, Caltech professor and seismologist Charles Richter developed his famous earthquake intensity scale called the Richter scale, which provided a standardized means for comparing the strengths of earthquakes. Richter's approach was to determine the magnitude of an earthquake by comparing the wave measurements of different earthquakes as recorded by seismographs. He used a logarithmic scale of whole and decimal numbers. Each whole number magnitude is ten times greater than the preceding number. Theoretically, there is no upper limit, but earthquake magnitudes most commonly are in the range of less than one to just over nine, with the less intense magnitude earthquakes far outnumbering the large ones. Earthquakes with Richter magnitudes of 2.0 or less are considered micro-earthquakes. There are thousands of them annually. Earthquakes with magnitudes of 8.0 or higher are great quakes. On average, we experience about one of these per year somewhere throughout the world.

The Richter scale does not measure or express damage done by earthquakes. However, there is an obvious correlation between the Richter magnitude and the degree of damage done by an earthquake: the larger an earthquake's magnitude, the greater the likelihood and severity of the damage.

THE LOMA PRIETA EARTHQUAKE

On the evening of October 17, 1989, millions of baseball fans were settling down to watch the World Series on TV. Tens of thousands were in San Francisco's Candlestick Park to cheer on their favorite team. Dubbed the Battle of the Bay, the 1989 World Series pitted two Bay Area hometown teams against each other—the Oakland As and the San Francisco Giants. The game had just gotten under way, when at 5:04 PM, Candlestick Park shook violently along with the rest of the Bay Area.

Immediately, baseball was the last thing on anyone's mind. Fans headed for the exits. In office buildings throughout the Bay Area, electricity went dead. In the Marina District of San Francisco, much of it built on fill from the 1906 Earthquake, gas lines broke and houses caught on fire.

A section of the upper deck of the Bay Bridge collapsed. A portion of the East Bay double-decker feeder freeway to the Bay Bridge, known as the Cypress Structure, pancaked. The double-decker Embarcadero Freeway near the piers along the San Francisco waterfront was severely damaged.

There were 63 deaths and over 3,500 injuries. There would have been more, but rush-hour traffic on the freeways was unusually light. Many commuters were already watching the game at home or in Candlestick Park.

With a magnitude of 7.1, the Loma Prieta Earthquake, named after the Loma Prieta Peak in the Santa Cruz Mountains where it was centered, lasted only 15 seconds. But those 15 seconds forever changed transportation in the Bay Area.

The Bay Bridge was closed for a month while the California Department of Transportation (Caltrans) made immediate repairs. In addition, Caltrans began to study the overall seismic safety of the Bay Bridge. Studies eventually concluded that the Bay Bridge needed major repair. The portion of the bridge between the East Bay and Treasure Island that was built on wooden piers into the bay mud was particularly vulnerable to failure due to liquefaction. Finally, after more than a decade of squabbling about its design and various state budget crises, a new bridge between Treasure Island and the East Bay is currently under construction. Estimates are the bridge will be completed in 2011, 22 years after the earthquake.

Once the rubble of the elevated Cypress Structure in Oakland was cleared away, neighbors on both sides of the street could see one another across the street, and they liked what they saw. They organized, applied political pressure, and managed to stop the reconstruction of the structure as it was before the earthquake. Caltrans worked out a plan with Southern Pacific Railroad (SP) (now Union Pacific) to reroute the freeway at grade level through SP's rail yard. In exchange for the land, Caltrans paid for the design and relocation of SP's operations and facilities. Some operations were consolidated in a much smaller reconfigured Oakland rail yard; others moved to Denver, Colorado.

In 2002, construction began on the Mandela Parkway in the right-of-way of the old Cypress Structure. Completed in 2003, the $1.7 million parkway is lined with trees and plants from various locations throughout the world. The parkway was a critical step in the revitalization and beautification of the neighborhood, which was once blighted and dominated by the double-decker Cypress Freeway Structure.

For decades, the double-decker monstrosity called the Embarcadero Freeway in San Francisco did nothing but end abruptly in mid-air and dump cars out on San Francisco's Broadway Street. Originally, it was supposed to continue on to the Golden Gate Bridge, but soon after it opened in 1959, appalled citizens halted any further construction. Besides being an eyesore, the freeway effectively separated San Francisco from the piers along the Embarcadero. San Franciscans squabbled about what to do with the freeway for decades.

The Loma Prieta Earthquake changed the debate. It shook the Embarcadero Freeway so hard that it was near collapse. After the earthquake, the damaged freeway was closed. Now San Franciscans debated whether to repair it or tear it down. San Francisco mayor Art Agnos argued for tearing it down, claiming that this was "the opportunity of a lifetime," and that San Francisco should not waste it. Eventually, the Board of Supervisors agreed.

In February 1991, demolition of the Embarcadero Freeway began. Few demolition projects have ribbon-cutting ceremonies, but this one did. Senator Diane Feinstein, a former mayor of San Francisco, told those gathered: "I knew one day it would happen. It just needed that push from Mother Nature."[29]

Today, the Embarcadero is a 2.5-mile-long promenade along the Bay and piers. Retro-style trolley cars carry San Franciscans and tourists between Fisherman's Wharf and a new baseball stadium for the Giants. Along the way, piers and buildings are undergoing face-lifts, cruise ships dock along the Embarcadero, and downtown San Francisco is again connected to the piers and the magnificent San Francisco Bay.

THE NORTHRIDGE EARTHQUAKE

It was 4:30 AM on January 17, 1994. Only the early birds were up when the rest of Los Angeles was abruptly awakened when their beds and houses shook. Freeways and buildings collapsed as a 6.7 magnitude earthquake rocked the L.A. basin back and forth for 15 terrifying seconds.

At first, the earthquake was believed to be under the city of Northridge and on the San Andreas Fault—hence the quake's name. However, later calculations revealed the epicenter to be under the city of Reseda, about two miles from Northridge and along a previously unknown blind thrust fault, later named the Northridge Thrust. In a blind thrust fault, an overlying section of the earth's crust moves up at an angle while the underlying section of crust moves down. The rupture does not carry all the way to the surface. Consequently, there is no evidence of the quake at ground level, which is why it is called a blind thrust.

The earthquake caused 51 deaths and over 9,000 injuries. More than 7,000 buildings were severely damaged and made unsafe to occupy. An additional 22,000 suffered minor damage. Over 25,000 dwellings were declared uninhabitable. Nine hospitals suffered damage and had to be closed—the equivalent of 2,500 hospital beds. Portions of 11 major roads in the L.A. area had to be closed, and 9 bridges or highway overpasses collapsed. Twenty-two thousand people were left homeless. In 15 seconds, the Northridge Earthquake became the costliest disaster in U.S. history at the time, with property losses of over $40 billion. (See Figure 5.2.)

The Northridge Earthquake revealed weaknesses in the design standards for the welded joint connections in steel-framed buildings. While no steel-framed buildings collapsed, many suffered damage. The damage came in the form of fractured welded connections, particularly at the connections of beams and girders to columns. The earthquake caused brittle welds to crack. Welded steel-framed structures develop their strength to resist the combination of vertical gravity and horizontal earthquake

FIGURE 5.2 *Northridge Earthquake, 1992. A ruined building on Olympic Boulevard in Los Angeles.* © *Joseph Sohm; ChromoSohm Inc./CORBIS.*

forces by efficiently transferring loads through their extremely rigid welded connections. In structural engineering, rigid steel frames are called "moment resisting" frames because their rigid connections resist the forces trying to rotate or twist the connections apart. In mechanics, "moment" is the tendency to cause rotation around a central point or axis. Cracks in welds seriously compromise a rigid frame structure's ability to properly transfer earthquake loads.

A particularly alarming aspect was that many welded connections failed without damaging adjacent building walls or ceilings. Generally, when structural failures occur, there are telltale signs: walls or ceilings crack and, in severe cases, beams, girders, or columns collapse. Not so with many of the welded connection failures caused by the Northridge Earthquake. Some welded steel-framed buildings that the earthquake damaged were under construction, so the cracked welded connections were visible. This alerted experts to the problem and so they began exploring completed buildings. What they found was a significant number of failed welded connections, leading them to conclude that many welded steel-framed buildings were not sufficiently safe. Structural engineer Stephen A. Mahin, a member of the Northridge Earthquake investigation team, wrote:

> Every earthquake provides new lessons for the earthquake engineering profession. The widespread damage to welded steel moment resisting frame systems was one of the major overall lessons of the Northridge earthquake. The brittle nature of the fractures detected in numerous welded steel beam to column connections, essentially invalidated historic design approaches and code provisions.[30]

Based on findings from the Northridge Earthquake, the 1997 edition of the *Uniform Building Code* incorporated numerous changes in its provisions for earthquake design.

DESIGNING FOR EARTHQUAKES

Over the course of the past century, we have learned much from earthquakes. With each successive generation, we have improved our understanding of them. We have incrementally made improvements in building codes to better resist their devastating affects. Older buildings continually retire; they are torn down and replaced. With each iteration of tear-down and replacement, our buildings and cities become safer.

Designing buildings to resist earthquakes has come a long way since the days of the 1935 UBC. The current earthquake formula used by the 2006 International Building Code is: $V = C_s W$.

Although it may look similar to the 1935 UBC's $F = CW$, the current formula is much more sophisticated and benefits greatly from decades of experience and analyses of buildings after numerous earthquakes worldwide. V is called the "seismic base shear," which roughly means the equivalent lateral shaking force at the base of the building that the building must resist. W is the "effective seismic weight," which is equal to the total dead load, or weight of the building, plus portions of various other building loads such as live loads, snow loads, long-term storage loads, partition wall loads, and stationary equipment loads. C_s is called the "seismic response coefficient," which is determined through a series of formulas and tables and varies depending on proximity to seismic activity, soil conditions, building swaying characteristics, the building's lateral load resisting system, and occupancy importance factors. The code divides buildings into four importance categories, using Roman numerals I through IV. Group IV buildings are called "essential facilities" and include hospitals, power stations, emergency shelters, and fire and police stations. Group IV facilities must resist higher seismic base shear forces than other types of buildings considered less critical.

As we have seen, earthquakes act as wrecking balls, often making planning decisions for us, decisions we did not have the will to make ourselves. We have used earthquakes as pretexts for planning decisions for such things as limiting the heights of buildings and damming rivers. San Francisco's Embarcadero, Chinatown, and Bay Bridge, and the city's water supply from Hetch Hetchy are the way they are because of earthquakes. Earthquakes shape the built environment.

The next big earthquake will test us again. Depending on its severity and epicenter, it may cause terrible destruction, despite all our efforts. If it strikes within a major metropolitan area, it will undoubtedly result in the loss of many lives and considerable destruction of property. It is inevitable. But equally inevitable will be our reaction: We will pick ourselves up, learn new lessons, and rebuild. Again, earthquakes will help shape the buildings and cities in which we live.

6

WIND AND WATER

Thales was the first scientist. Before him, the ancient Greeks explained the world as the work of the gods. Thales, who lived circa 585 BC, explained the world in terms of natural phenomena, that is, the interactions of fire, earth, air and water. According to Thales, water was the most fundamental of the four elements, responsible for everything. The earth floats on a vast ocean. Disturbances of the ocean cause earthquakes and floods.

Anaximenes held another view. He thought air, not water, was the primary element. Everything condenses out of air. The earth rides upon it. Moving air causes the wind, condensing air causes clouds, and clouds splitting make thunder and lightning.

Today, we hold somewhat different views about air and water. In a sense, however, both Thales and Anaximenes were correct. Air and water are essential for life, but under extreme conditions, they can destroy it too. Strong winds can topple trees and blow buildings apart. Winds, in combination with ocean surges, can create destructive and deadly storms. When earthquakes occur under oceans, gigantic waves called tsunamis can form. Racing across the ocean at hundreds of miles per hour, tsunamis create powerful tidal waves that inundate shorelines, destroying everything in their wakes. Wind and water can generate natural disasters of colossal proportions, turning lives and cities upside down.

THE FORMATION OF HURRICANES

Hurricanes are the most powerful weather disturbances on earth. In the western Pacific, they are called typhoons, and in the Indian Ocean, cyclones. Regardless of their name, they wreak havoc. Atlantic hurricanes usually begin as several thunderstorms, called a cluster, in the warm tropical waters off of the western coast of Africa. As the cluster moves west into the Atlantic, it pulls in more moist air from the surface of the ocean, occasionally forming a large storm. Through a process called the Coriolis effect, named after Gaspard Coriolis, who first explained it, the storm spins counterclockwise in the northern hemisphere and clockwise in the southern. As warm air within the storm rises, air pulled in from below rushes toward the center, accelerating the storm's spin. When the wind speed reaches 39 miles per hour (mph), it is called a tropical storm. When it reaches 74 mph, it is called a hurricane. Warm water fuels hurricanes. Consequently, the summer months comprise hurricane season, which extends from June 1 to November 30. Because the Gulf of Mexico is fed by warm ocean currents, it is the perfect pastureland for fattening and strengthening hurricanes.

Categorizing Hurricanes

Atlantic and northern Pacific Ocean hurricanes are categorized by intensity using a scale called the Saffir-Simpson Hurricane Scale. The scale was developed in 1969 by the then-director of the U.S. National Hurricane Center, Bob Simpson, and Herbert Saffir, a civil engineer. Prior to 1969, there was no generally accepted scale for describing the intensity of hurricanes. After Hurricane Camille in August 1969, experts realized that a standard method for predicting storm magnitude and potential devastation was needed in order to better communicate warnings to the general public about the severity of approaching hurricanes.

Influenced by the Richter scale for earthquakes, Saffir and Simpson developed an intensity scale for hurricanes. They established hurricane categories—1 through 5—and measurement criteria for each category, including wind speed, storm surge, air pressure, and potential damage.

Category 1 hurricanes have sustained winds of 74–95 mph, storm surges of 4–5 feet, and a barometric pressure of 28.94 inHg (inches of mercury) measured at the hurricane's eye. The potential damage includes broken tree limbs, upheaval of unanchored mobile homes, minor coastal flooding, and damage to piers, but no permanent damage to building structures.

Category 2 hurricanes have wind speeds of 96–110 mph, storm surges of 6–8 feet, and barometric pressure in the range of 28.50 to 28.91 inHg. Note that the barometric pressure drops as hurricanes become more intense. The potential damage includes loss of roofing materials, breaking of doors and windows, considerable damage to trees and mobile homes, flooding of piers, damage to moored water craft, and some minor damage to building structures.

Category 3 hurricanes have wind speeds of 111–130 mph, storm surges of 9–12 feet, and central pressure in the range of 27.91–28.47 inHg. Potential damage includes possible shearing off of exterior walls of wood-framed buildings, the uprooting of some trees, destruction of mobile homes, considerable flooding along coastal areas, and damage to larger buildings caused by collisions with wind- and/or water-propelled debris.

Category 4 hurricanes have wind speeds of 131–155 mph and storm surges of 13–18 feet. Their central air pressures are very low, in the range of 27.17–27.88 inHg. Potential damage includes the failure of roof structures, extensive exterior wall failures, major damage to buildings caused by flying and water-driven debris, major erosion to beaches, and severe flooding resulting in damage to inland terrain and structures.

Category 5 hurricanes pack wind speeds of 156 mph and greater. Their storm surges are greater than 19 feet, their barometric pressure less than 27.17 inHg. The potential damage from these storms is very great, including the complete structural failures of some buildings and major flood damage to the lower floors of all buildings near the shoreline. The massive evacuation of area residents may be necessary.

Based on the Saffir-Simpson categories and descriptions of wind speeds, storm surges, and potential damage, it became possible to look back at previous storms and classify them using the scale. For example, the Galveston Storm, discussed below, had wind speeds above 131 mph and a storm surge of 15 feet, making it a Category 4 hurricane.

Hurricanes are unlike fires and earthquakes. Fires and earthquakes strike quickly, without warning, and at any time. Hurricanes have a season and, to some degree, they are predictable. Meteorologists can see them forming days before they reach land. Although the science is still not precise, experts can tell a hurricane's general size, strength, direction, and the time and location of landfall. Because there is a period of warning before a hurricane, citizens and authorities generally have time to make preparations and evacuate, if necessary, though, as we'll see, this doesn't always happen.

THE GREAT STORM

The deadliest hurricane in American History occurred in 1900. It has no official name because the National Hurricane Center did not start naming tropical storms until 51 years later. Some call it the Galveston Hurricane, others the Great Galveston Hurricane, the Galveston Flood, or the 1900 Storm. Regardless, when a Galvestonian refers to the Storm, other Galvestonians know which storm is meant.

By the end of the 19th century, the island city of Galveston was the largest city in Texas. Its population of 42,000 lived nestled together on a 30-mile-long island, barely 3 miles wide at its widest point. The island—a long sandbar really—created a natural harbor, Galveston Bay, and the island sheltered the bay from the sea.

The calm, protected waters of Galveston Bay were ideal for the loading and offloading of cargo ships. The cotton business was in full bloom and with it Galveston bankers, merchants, and cotton agents were growing wealthy and complacent. Galveston was the "the New York City of the South." The Strand, the city's most prosperous street, boasted the impressive nickname of "Wall Street of the Southwest." With business brisk, most Galvestonians had hardly a care in the world.

A few had concerns, however. Some worried about what a large hurricane might do. At its highest point, the island was only 8 feet, 7 inches above sea level. Most buildings sat on ground lower than that, some barely above high tide. While many of the mercantile firms along the Strand were well built, constructed of brick and securely anchored to foundations, most houses were not. Houses were generally wood, many hastily constructed with meager foundations or stone footings. Some had little more than wood sill plates setting directly on earth.

Older residents remembered many storms. The storm of September 17, 1877, brought 5-foot flood tides that inundated much of Galveston.

The June 14, 1886, storm brought much worse: Tropical storm winds of 50 mph drove seawater over the island, completely submerging the city. Two months later, on August 19 and 20, another storm struck, packing 50 mph winds and high waves. The year 1888 brought two hurricanes in two months, June 16–17 and July 5. While Galveston continued to withstand the brunt, some residents began to wonder just how long their luck could hold out.

For the city of Indianola, Texas, luck ran out with the hurricane of August 19–20, 1886. Prior to August 1886, Indianola was Texas's leading port city; Galveston its closest rival. Indianola is situated on Matagorda Bay about 150 miles farther southwest from Galveston, down the Texas coastline. Indianola's residents were used to tropical storms. In 1874, Indianola suffered severe damage from strong winds and high tides, but rebuilt. Another hurricane only a year later destroyed approximately three-quarters of the town, killing 176 people. Resilient and stubborn, Indianola's citizens rebuilt again. Additional large tropical storms or hurricanes struck the Texas coastline in 1877 (previously mentioned), and again in 1879, 1880, 1881, 1882, 1885, four times in 1886, 1887, twice in 1888, and in 1891.

Two storms in 1886 were more than most of Indianola's citizens could bear. The first was on August 19–20. It brought winds of over 70 mph to Indianola, collapsing the Signal Office Building and overturning a kerosene lamp that started a fire that burned down a city block even as rain poured from the heavens. The fire went out as Indianola went under water, drowned in a 15-foot storm surge. When the sea retreated, hardly a building stood. The few that did were little more than ruined shells. Many gave up and moved elsewhere. Those who stayed and rebuilt witnessed their efforts washed away in another storm on September 22–23. Waist-deep water driven by 60 mph winds scoured the town. Everyone fled except for one family. The city never recovered from the second storm to regain its past glory. Galveston took the mantle as the largest port city in Texas.

Could a major storm do the same to Galveston? A few of its citizens thought it could, and they began campaigning for the construction of a seawall to protect Galveston from a fate similar to Indianola's. Most Galvestonians, however, believed a seawall was unnecessary. Galveston had weathered many storms. At least ten documented storms had struck Galveston in its 60-year history, and the city suffered little damage from them.

A seawall would be very costly and, they thought, an unwarranted waste of money.

On July 15, 1891, just two days after another tropical storm inundated Galveston, Isaac Cline (1864–1955), the Texas Section Director of the newly formed U.S. Weather Bureau, wrote an article for the *Galveston News*, in which he argued:

> It would be impossible for any cyclone to create a storm wave which could materially injure the city.[1]

Cline believed that only weak storms struck Galveston, and because the city had ridden out many of these in the past, it would do so again. Besides, he argued, if a hurricane hit, the waves it generated would simply wash over the island, continue on into Galveston Bay, and then wash harmlessly onto the sparsely populated Texas prairie beyond.

Galveston did not build a seawall. Instead, it built more buildings and docks. It shaved down sand dunes to fill in low areas of the island so it could build even more.

Galveston's Luck Runs Out

The month of August 1900 brought clear skies and high temperatures along the Texas coastline. Water in the Gulf of Mexico warmed daily, and by the end of the month the Gulf approached the temperature of bathwater. On August 27, a ship about 1,000 miles east of the Windward Islands (the islands of Grenada, St Lucia, St. Vincent, and Barbados) reported unstable weather conditions and rough seas. On September 1, the U.S. Weather Bureau reported a storm had developed southeast of Cuba and was moving west. On September 4, the Weather Bureau in Galveston received the first warning from its headquarters in Washington, D.C., that a tropical storm was passing over Cuba and headed toward the Gulf of Mexico. In the Gulf, the storm grew quickly, fueled by the warm sea water. On September 7, it was closing in on the U.S. coastline. There were reports of heavy damage along the coasts of Mississippi and Louisiana, and large swells in the Gulf. Telegraph lines were downed by high winds. Unsure of the hurricane's eventual landfall location, the Weather Bureau in Washington issued storm warnings for all coastal areas between Pensacola, Florida, and Galveston, and continued tracking the storm the best it could. With few telegraph lines still in operation, communication with the coast was spotty. Somehow, Bureau forecasters concluded that the storm was veering to the east and would probably make landfall somewhere on the Florida peninsula, cross Florida and exit into the Atlantic, and die harmlessly somewhere out at sea. They were wrong.

The next morning, Saturday, September 8, Galvestonians awoke to partly cloudy skies and waves that were only a bit higher and choppier than usual—the infamous calm before the storm. Few of Galveston's citizens evacuated. Most went about their business as they did on any other Saturday morning. In fact, rather than evacuating, people were arriving. A passenger train from Houston arrived in the morning, although late due to track flooding and wind-blown debris on the tracks. The train was carried by ferry from Port Bolivar across the bay to Galveston Island, as was customary.

By mid-morning the wind had picked up considerably and it started to rain. Another train on its way to Galveston was stranded in the advancing storm. The train from Beaumont, Texas, waited on the dock at Port Bolivar for the ferry. Its passengers watched helplessly as the ferry captain tried again and again to dock. Eventually he gave up and left. The train engineer tried to back up, but water had flooded the tracks behind the train. Some of the train's passengers left the train and ran to nearby Point Bolivar lighthouse for refuge. Most of the passengers stayed on the train to wait out the storm.

The rain and wind increased throughout the day. By mid-afternoon, waves washed across the streets of Galveston. As the water advanced, citizens hurried to higher ground. In Galveston, that meant only a difference of a few feet. It staved off their fate for only a short while. By 6 PM, wind speed was 100 mph and still increasing. The wind broke tree limbs and sent them flying like missiles. The hurricane created 15-foot wave surges that cascaded over Galveston, covering it in a deep, watery blanket. Trees were uprooted and buildings floated off their foundations. With terrified occupants still inside, buildings were swept up by the torrent. They careened into one other, breaking into pieces. Debris raced along, smashing into more buildings, docks, and ships.

The eye of the storm passed over Galveston around 8 PM. By 11 PM, the winds had subsided. Sunday morning brought mild breezes of 20 mph. The storm had passed, leaving behind a ruined city. Block after city

FIGURE 6.1 *Galveston Hurricane, 1900.* © *Reuters/CORBIS.*

block were gone. (See Figure 6.1.) In total, three-fourths of the city was washed away. Estimates vary, but somewhere between 2,500 and 3,500 homes were destroyed. Galveston's three bridges were also destroyed.

The death toll was staggering: an estimated 8,000 to 10,000 were killed, at least 6,000 of whom were on Galveston Island. Bodies were scattered everywhere. Many washed up on the Texas shoreline. Some were not recovered for weeks. At first, the bodies were taken out to sea for burial, but many washed back on shore. Funeral pyres were erected and burned for weeks afterwards.

Galveston Learns and Rebuilds

Galveston rebuilt and within three weeks cotton was again being shipped out of its ports. In a sense, Galveston's fate was similar to that of Indianola. The oil business was catching hold. Business and development began shifting north as Houston was beginning its hey-day as an oil town. Galveston competed for a while with Houston, but in 1909, Houston dredged a shipping channel, which dashed any chance Galveston may have had of returning to its former glory.

After the Great Storm, Isaac Cline changed his tune. He wrote another article, this time in support of the seawall. In 1902, Galveston built a seawall, 3 miles long and 17 feet high. Much of the city was raised to the height of the seawall with dredged sand, and over 2,100 buildings were rebuilt at the new height.

In 1915, another hurricane struck Galveston and tested its seawall. The hurricane's 12-foot storm surge did not breach the wall. Over the years, the seawall was extended. Today, it is 10 miles long.

Long ago, cotton disappeared as Galveston's economic mainstay. Today, it is tourism. In 2001, the seawall and the buildings that survived the hurricane were declared National Historic Landmarks and are tourist attractions. Parts of Galveston have expanded beyond the protection of the seawall and, consequently, are not protected. Memories of disasters are short. Only time will tell how wise it was to build beyond the seawall and taunt nature.

THE 1928 OKEECHOBEE HURRICANE

On September 10, 1928, a tropical storm was reported by the ship S.S. *Commack*. Three days later, when the storm struck Puerto Rico, it had grown into what we would now rate a Category 5 hurricane. An anemometer in San Juan, Puerto Rico, measured the wind at 160 mph. Soon afterward, the wind destroyed the anemometer. The hurricane left thousands homeless, 312 dead, and Puerto Rico in tatters.

The hurricane continued on toward the coast of Florida. It made landfall in Palm Beach County near West Palm Beach and headed over Lake Okeechobee. Residents were warned well in advance, and most evacuated ahead of the storm, but the predictions of landfall were incorrect. The storm was late and many residents had returned and were home when the hurricane struck.

The damage and loss of life in Florida were catastrophic. The storm surged over a dike at the south end of Lake Okeechobee and flooded an area of hundreds of square miles, in some places as much as 20 feet deep. The flood wrenched houses off their foundations, and the houses smashed into one another on the way to their final resting place in the Florida everglades. After the eye of the storm passed, the wind direction shifted and blew the floodwaters back across the lake, breaking another dike on the lake's north side.

It took weeks for the floodwaters to recede. For decades, the death toll varied wildly between 1,800 and 3,400. In 2003, it was revised to around 2,500, making it the second deadliest storm in U.S. history.

In the cleanup afterwards, bodies were segregated. The bodies of African Americans and migrant workers were burned or buried in mass graves, while bodies of dead Caucasians were identified, buried in caskets, and honored with memorial services. This racially motivated act has been remembered for generations and created the belief that poor nonwhites are treated differently after hurricanes. In the days immediately following Hurricane Katrina in August 2005, the federal response to aid the people of New Orleans was slow, reminding some of the 1928 Okeechobee Hurricane.

After the hurricane, it became apparent that better-constructed buildings and those with window shutters suffered far less damage than poorly constructed buildings or those without storm shutters. Buildings faced with brick or stone and those with steel frames received very little damage. Some communities throughout Florida began improving their building codes, requiring storm shutters for windows and walls to be made of brick. Unfortunately, most did not. Lessons learned by one community were often learned the hard way by another during a subsequent hurricane.

THE LABOR DAY HURRICANE OF 1935

With wind speeds estimated at 185 mph, the Florida Keys Hurricane of 1935 was one of the most powerful hurricanes to strike the United States. It struck Matecumbe Key on September 2, Labor Day, and completely destroyed the island with its 15-foot storm surge. Not a building or tree was left standing. Roads and railroad tracks were washed away, including the railroad bridge that connected the island to the mainland. An evacuation train was sent from the mainland to rescue island residents and World War I veterans who were living in construction camps while building new roads and buildings. The train never made it. High waves knocked its passenger cars off the tracks. Only the much heavier locomotive remained upright. Those waiting for the train were left stranded, and 423 drowned.

After the hurricane, the financially strapped Florida East Coast Railway was unable to rebuild its destroyed railroad tracks and bridges. The Railway sold its damaged bridges and right-of-way to the state of Florida. Florida built the Overseas Highway, which connects the Florida Keys to the mainland. Opening in March 1938, it reused much of the defunct railroad's bridges and roadbeds. Although much of the Overseas Highway was rebuilt in the 1980s, the highway owes its existence to one of the most powerful hurricanes to ever strike the U.S. coastline.

1965 HURRICANE BETSY

The story of Hurricane Betsy sounds eerily familiar, as if the deadly storm of 40 years ago happened only recently. On September 7, 1965, Category 3 Hurricane Betsy skirted across the southern tip of Florida and entered the Gulf of Mexico. It began feeding on the Gulf's warm waters and grew to near Category 5 strength with winds of 155 mph. Experts predicted landfall somewhere along the ragged boot of Louisiana. Prior to landfall, Betsy's intensity dropped slightly to a Category 3 level, and on the evening of September 9, it marched ashore just west of the mouth of the Mississippi River. As it moved up the Mississippi River, the river's surface raised 10 feet. The hurricane generated giant waves on Lake Pontchartrain and sent them crashing into levees along New Orleans's northern edge. It drove storm surge up the recently completed shipping canal called the Mississippi River-Gulf Outlet. (For more about the Mississippi River-Gulf Outlet, see Chapter 9.) Where the shipping channel intersects New Orleans's Industrial Canal, levees breached, sending floodwaters into the city's Lower Ninth Ward. Floodwaters rose to the height of one-story rooftops. Residents scrambled to their roofs; some drowned in their attics.

Hurricane Betsy killed 76 people and flooded over 160,000 homes. Storm damage was valued at nearly $1.5 billion, making Hurricane Betsy the first noninflation-adjusted hurricane to top $1 billion in damages.

President Lyndon Johnson (LBJ) arrived the next day, promising New Orleanians federal assistance. It took ten days to drain the water from New Orleans. LBJ's promise notwithstanding, emergency response from the federal government was slow. Betsy's victims foraged the best they could until help finally arrived. Weeks passed before emergency trailers were brought in to house the thousands left homeless.

Because of Betsy, the federal government initiated the Hurricane Protection Program, and the U.S. Army Corps of Engineers began rebuilding the levees and building new ones. Damaged levees were replaced, and others were made taller. In areas where land acquisition was either too costly or unavailable, floodwalls were built on top of levees. Funding was sporadic. The work continued on and off for several decades. Forty years later, on August 29, 2005, the day Hurricane Katrina came ashore, the levees in New Orleans were still not complete.

1992 HURRICANE ANDREW

Early in the morning on August 24, 1992, Hurricane Andrew struck the south coast of Florida. Heading in a northwest direction, it plowed a furrow through Homestead, Florida City, and parts of Miami before exiting Florida on the west coast and out into the Gulf of Mexico. With wind speeds in excess of 175 mph, it knocked homes off of foundations, blew out windows and doors, and tore roofs off of houses. Approximately 2 million people had to be evacuated. When it was over, more than 60 people were killed, 82,000 businesses were in shambles, tens of thousands of homes were destroyed, and 250,000 people were left homeless. Property damage was estimated at over $30 billion.

South Dade County (now Miami-Dade County) was particularly hard hit. A poor, working-class area, thousands of people were left homeless and without food or water. Few relief trucks made it into the community, and when they did, they were inundated by hundreds of desperate, homeless, and hungry citizens. The situation worsened over the next three days. Growing angrier and more frustrated with each passing day, Dade County's Emergency Management Director Kate Kole called a press conference and lashed out: "Where in the hell is the cavalry on this one? They keep saying we're going to get supplies. For God's sake, where are they?"[2] Her words shot out over the airways and received an immediate response from then-President George H. W. Bush. The Army, mobile kitchens, and tents were quickly sent to the hurricane victims.

On September 1, 2005, three days after Hurricane Katrina and with 80 percent of New Orleans under water, New Orleans's mayor Ray Nagin, frustrated with the federal government's slow response, lashed out in a similar way:

> This is a national disaster. [Federal government] get every doggone Greyhound bus line in the country and get their asses moving to New Orleans. . . . They are thinking small, man. And this is a major, major, major deal. And I can't emphasize it enough man. This is crazy.[3]

The next day, President George W. Bush visited New Orleans and met with Mayor Nagin.

With government officials so slow to respond after Hurricane Andrew, rumors began to circulate. One claimed that hundreds of migrant farm workers had been killed in the storm, but uncaring government officials had not counted them in the official death tolls. The rumor was untrue, but to those who believed the rumor, it was not so far-fetched. The 1928 Okeechobee Hurricane cast a distrustful and long shadow.

Hurricane Andrew literally exploded houses from the inside out. When its high-speed winds passed over roofs, they created uplift, much like the wing of an airplane. When the wind blew out the doors or windows, wind rushed inside, pressurizing the building, and blowing roofs off and walls out. Flying debris was a major problem. Anything that tore loose became a potentially lethal projectile, pummeling buildings, breaking windows, and smashing into walls and roofs. While most of the destruction caused by Andrew was due to high winds, flooding contributed significantly to the damage in low-lying coastal areas.

Government Response to Past Hurricanes

The 1960s saw many deadly and costly hurricanes with names such as Donna and Ethel in 1960; Carla in 1961; Cleo, Dora, and Hilda in 1964; Betsy in 1965; Alma and Inez in 1966; and Beulah in 1967. Congress was worried about the rising costs of federal assistance in the wake of hurricanes. They saw the costs going up and saw no end in sight. They also saw that a disproportionate amount of assistance went to help residents living in areas that were very susceptible to flooding. In 1968, Congress enacted the National Flood Insurance Act and charged the Federal Insurance Administration (FIA) with overseeing the National Flood Insurance Program (NFIP). The NFIP is designed to reduce the risk of buildings being damaged by flooding. The FIA went to work identifying low-lying areas prone to flooding and developing flood maps. Many of the houses damaged by wind and flood during Andrew were in flood-prone areas as defined by the NFIP.

In 1973, Congress passed the Flood Disaster Act. It required all buildings located in flood hazard areas to have flood insurance as a condition of receiving federal disaster assistance. Federally guaranteed flood insurance was available for buildings in communities that agreed to regulate building construction in accordance with NFIP guidelines and flood maps. In 1979, the newly formed Federal Emergency Management Agency (FEMA) took over the administration of the NFIP.

The NFIP has established what it calls a Base Flood Elevation (BFE). The BFE establishes the elevation at which everything above it has a less than 1 percent chance of flooding in any given year, and everything below it has a greater than 1 percent chance. Put another way, the BFE represents the 100-year floodplain, meaning that it is unlikely that more than one flood a century will exceed the base flood elevation. Consequently, buildings below the BFE are susceptible to flooding on a more frequent basis and are therefore considered to be at unacceptably high risk of flooding. To avoid this unacceptable risk, buildings below the BFE must be raised above it in order to be eligible for federal aid and flood insurance.

In addition to establishing BFEs, the NFIP established what it calls hazard zones, and assigned them letter designations such as V, VE and A, AE. There are many hazard zones, but all start with either the letter "V" or "A." "V" zones are called Coastal High Hazard Areas. These zones are subject to high-velocity wave surges, waterborne debris, scouring, and erosion. "A" zones are not within the Coastal High Hazard Area, although they are below the BFE.

Because V zones are subject to wave action, the NFIP does not permit continuous foundation walls in V zones. Buildings built in V zones must be constructed on open foundations such as piles, elevated posts, or piers. In V zones, houses appear to be raised on stilts. In A zones, houses are permitted to have continuous foundations, because A zones are not subject to severe wave action.

Rebuilding after Hurricane Andrew. Many of the houses in South Dade County were slab-on-grade construction, below the BFE and in A zones. After Hurricane Andrew, many were substantially damaged. The NFIP defines substantially damaged to mean that it would cost more than 50 percent of the house's market value to repair it. To be eligible for federal assistance and low-cost loans, the owners of substantially damaged houses had to agree to raise the lowest floor of their homes above the BFE.

Owners were given a choice: demolish what was left of their homes and build new ones, or repair their homes and elevate the lowest floor as part of the repairs. Most homeowners chose the latter. As a result, many slab-on-grade houses in South Dade County that pre-date Hurricane Andrew are now above the 100-year floodplain and no longer have slab-on-grade foundations. Not all residents rebuilt, however; many chose to leave instead. Approximately 100,000 residents of South Dade County left the county for good.

As Floridians cleaned up after Hurricane Andrew, it became apparent that many buildings were not built in compliance with the standards of the building code at the time they were constructed. As discussed in Chapter 3, the Southern Building Code Congress International was founded in 1940. Headquartered in Birmingham, Alabama, it published the model code called the *Standard Building Code* (SBC). Soon after World War II, cities in Florida began to adopt the SBC, but not all. In the 1970s, Florida mandated that all municipalities and counties adopt and enforce a building code. Most adopted the SBC, with some cities including local amendments. Amendments varied and some communities took code enforcement more seriously than others. Consequently, the quality of construction of buildings and houses varied throughout the state. Hurricane Andrew made it clear that cities and counties were not following the state mandate.

In 1998, the State of Florida passed legislation to develop a single statewide building code that would be enforced by local officials. In 2002, Florida adopted its first statewide building code, the *Florida Building Code*, that superseded all other local buildings codes. The 2004 edition of the *Florida Building Code* is based on the 2003 edition of the *International Building Code*. It includes additional amendments that improve building performance during major hurricanes. The Preface to the 2004 *Florida Building Code* states that studies

> revealed that building code adoption and enforcement was inconsistent throughout the state and those local codes thought to be the strongest proved inadequate when tested by major hurricane events. The consequences of the building codes system failure were devastation to lives and economies and a statewide property insurance crisis.[4]

The 2004 *Florida Building Code* contains the most stringent hurricane-resistant design provisions in the country. It requires all buildings and structures to be designed and constructed to resist very high wind loads. For example, in Miami-Dade County, buildings must be designed to resist winds of 146 mph,[5] which is the equivalent of a Category 4 hurricane.

To prevent awnings and canopies from tearing away from buildings and becoming potentially dangerous projectiles during high winds, Florida's code requires awnings and canopies to be designed to resist sustained winds of 75 mph and 3-second gusts up to 90 mph.[6]

The *Florida Building Code* requires shingles used as roofing materials to be securely fastened. The same is true with roof structures, doors, and windows. Garage doors must be reinforced to resist high winds. The purpose is to reduce the amount of debris flying around during a hurricane.

Hurricane Andrew tore plywood right off of roofs. In an attempt to prevent this from happening again, the *Florida Building Code* requires plywood to be reinforced with additional framing members running perpendicular to roof rafters and roof trusses. The code requires roof rafters and roof trusses to be connected to building walls with metal straps, called hurricane straps. Hurricane Andrew lifted many roofs off of houses. While the code in effect in 1992 required hurricane straps, the law was not well enforced and the number of straps required proved inadequate. The 2004 *Florida Building Code* increased the number of required straps.

In addition to being securely fastened, doors, windows, and exterior wall cladding such as wood siding, brick veneer, and the like, must be designed to resist building pressurization from high winds. Recall from the discussion above that high winds lower the air pressure above roofs of buildings. When windows or doors break, the wind rushes in, pressurizing the house and causing roofs and walls to blow out. To resist pressurization, the building's cladding must not be allowed to tear off, and windows and doors must not break, even if pummeled by flying debris. The *Florida Building Code* states:

> Exterior wall cladding, surfacing and glazing, within the lowest 30 feet of the exterior building walls shall be of sufficient strength to resist large missile impacts.[7]

Wall cladding, surfacing, and glazing located above 30 feet must be able to resist the impact of small flying debris. While it is practical to securely fasten doors and windows to building structures, it is difficult to design doors and windows to resist impact from flying debris traveling at high velocities. Consequently, the *Florida Building Code* provides an alternative. Rather than designing doors and windows to resist impact, the code allows the use of fixed, operable, or portable shutters to protect doors and windows in lieu of impact-resistant doors and windows.

Although the code does not require the front doors of houses to swing out, some homebuilders design front doors to open out. It is much more difficult for high winds to push open doors that open out.

After the 2005 hurricane season, a team of engineers from the University of Florida did a study to determine how houses in Florida held up. They compared the damage to houses built before the enactment of the 2002 *Florida Building Code* to those constructed afterward. The team found that performance increased significantly; however, not all homes built after 2002 survived unscathed. Common failures included damage due to roof and soffit vents, which allowed wind-driven rain to enter roof spaces and soak insulation and damage insulation and ceilings. The research did, however, demonstrate the importance of the *Florida Building Code* in reducing damage caused by hurricanes.

TSUNAMIS

Hurricanes cause high winds and storm surges. As we have seen, it is often the high waves of the storm surge that cause much of the damage. Volcanic eruptions, landslides, and underwater earthquakes can also create waves. Earthquakes can shake laterally and vertically. Under-ocean earthquakes can quickly move large portions of the seabed up and down, displacing millions of tons of water and creating colossal waves called tsunamis, which is a Japanese word meaning "harbor waves." Tsunami waves radiate out from the earthquake in all directions like giant ripples, though these waves are barely discernable in the deep ocean. They can pass under fishing boats virtually undetected, but, as the waves enter shallower waters, the waves' heights are magnified by the rising seabed. Gigantic tidal waves, dozens of feet high, moving at hundreds of miles per hour, strike the shoreline and wash over everything. Depending on the size of the waves and the topography of the shoreline, tsunamis can rush for miles inland, destroying trees, cars, buildings, and entire communities within minutes.

Tsunamis have wreaked havoc throughout history. Generally, there has been little warning. Just prior to landfall, the approaching tidal wave sucks water away from the shoreline, creating an unnaturally low tide. The water retreats so quickly that it often leaves fish floundering on the beach. Historically, this has been the only warning, and it is a short one. Minutes later, the approaching wall of water is visible and crashes ashore. Because a tsunami travels so fast, there is no chance of outrunning it. When tsunami waves retreat, they often cause additional damage. They scour and suck into the sea everything that is not securely anchored: broken trees, cars, destroyed buildings, animals, and people.

When it is over, devastated survivors pick up what is left of their lives. Eventually they rebuild, and generally do so pretty much as they had before. It is only within the past 60 years or so that we have done much in the way of tsunami warning and prevention. As we might expect, it took a tsunami disaster to finally focus our attention on the destructive force of these natural disasters.

TSUNAMI WARNING SYSTEMS

On April Fools Day in 1946, a magnitude 7.8 earthquake occurred in the Pacific Ocean south of the Aleutian Islands in Alaska. The earthquake sent a series of tsunami waves radiating out in all directions. The first land the tsunami hit was the nearby and sparsely populated Unimak Island of the Aleutian chain. The Unimak Island lighthouse, called Scotch Cap Lighthouse, sat upon a rocky cliff about 40 feet above sea level. Built in 1940, the beacon atop the 5-story concrete and steel structure warned passing ships from venturing too close to the rocky shore. With virtually no warning, a 100-foot-high wall of water crashed against the cliff and lighthouse. The wave toppled the lighthouse, killing all five men inside.

In a little less than five hours, the tsunami reached the town of Hilo on the east coast of the island of Hawaii. A succession of a half-dozen 24-foot-high waves washed over Hilo, toppling trees, scouring roads, pushing buildings off their foundations, and killing 159 people.

After the Hilo disaster, it was apparent that most, if not all, of the deaths on Hilo were preventable. It took nearly five hours for the tsunami to reach Hawaii, ample time to have evacuated low-lying areas. What was needed was an early warning system. On August 12, 1948, the

Seismic Sea Wave Warning System (SSWWS) was created, and in 1949, its command center in Ewa Beach on the island of Oahu was put in operation. Today, the SSWWS is called the Pacific Tsunami Warning System. Equipped with seismic detection equipment and tide gauges, it provides tsunami warnings for Hawaii and most Pacific Basin countries.

The SSWWS was fundamentally established to protect Hawaii from tsunamis, hence its location on Oahu, Hawaii. It was Hilo, after all, that was most devastated by the 1946 Aleutian Tsunami. Ironically, the center installed no tide gauges off the Alaska coast when it was created. Tide gauges nearer Alaska would not only give Hawaii more advanced warning, they would have provided warning for coastal areas of Alaska and cities along the west coast of North America as well. But, as we have seen throughout this book, our general approach to disaster planning is to prevent the last disaster from reoccurring, not to prevent new disasters. Today, however, there is a tsunami warning system for Alaska and the west coast of North America. We can all guess why.

WEST COAST AND ALASKA TSUNAMI WARNING SYSTEM

Around 5:30 PM on March 27, 1964, an 8.4 magnitude earthquake occurred off the coast of Alaska, near Prince William Sound, about 55 miles west of Valdez, Alaska. The earth shook for four to five minutes, as the earthquake raised and dropped the seabed. In addition, it caused numerous avalanches inland. At least five separate tsunamis were created as massive landslides plummeted into the sea. The quake also ruptured underwater communication cables.

The earthquake triggered seismic sensors throughout the world. Using triangulation, seismologists at the SSWWS Center in Hilo quickly pinpointed the location of the earthquake. However, with no tide gauges near Alaska and communication lines severed, the Center had no way to know if a tsunami had been created. Approximately 1 hour and 20 minutes after the earthquake, the Center issued its first warning:

> This is a tidal wave (seismic sea wave) advisory. A severe earthquake has occurred at Lat. 61 N., Long. 147.5 W., vicinity of Seward, Alaska, at 0336Z [Zulu time or Greenwich time] 27 March. It is not

known, repeat not known at this time that a sea wave has been generated. You will be kept informed as further information becomes available. If a wave has been generated, its ETA for the Hawaiian Islands (Honolulu) is 0900Z, 27 March.[8]

Note the warning's provincial, Hawaii-biased nature. Note, too, its specificity regarding relatively useless information and its lack of knowledge regarding important information: Was there a tsunami or not?

There was a tsunami, and even if the SSWWS had known it, its warning was too late. The tsunami was already causing death and destruction along coastal areas of Alaska and British Columbia. The tsunami headed down the west coast of the United States. It caused 106 deaths in Alaska and 4 in Newport Beach, Oregon. Most residents had no warning the wave was coming until it hit.

The little fishing and resort town of Crescent City on the north coast of California had some warning. Shortly after 10:30 PM, the SSWWS issued another warning. By this time, contact with Kodiak, Alaska, had been reestablished and Hilo knew a tsunami was on its way. Again, the warning was geared toward Hawaii, but officials on the West Coast interpreted the message and passed the warning along to coastal communities.

Less than an hour and a half later, just a bit before midnight, the tsunami reached Crescent City. Crescent City is so named because the bay it rests on forms a sickle-shaped harbor like a crescent moon. The crescent angles northward, so storm waves coming from the north are funneled into the bay and amplified. Throughout the town's history, it has experienced flooding along Front Street, the town's main street that parallels the bay. To reduce flooding, Crescent City constructed a 2-foot-high seawall between the beach and Front Street.

A total of four waves struck Crescent City. The third was the most destructive. Approximately 20 feet in height, it easily hurdled the seawall and bore inland. The four waves flooded a 12-mile stretch of Crescent City and an area extending as much as 2 miles inland. Eleven people were killed and much of Crescent City was destroyed.

After the 1964 Tsunami, the United States realized that lives could have been saved by an early warning system for Alaska and the rest of the West Coast. In 1967, the United States implemented the West Coast and Alaska Tsunami Warning Center, located in Palmer, Alaska. The SSWWS center was renamed to the Pacific Tsunami Warning Center. Together these two tsunami warning centers serve to warn residents of Hawaii, Alaska, the west coast of North America, and participating Pacific Rim countries of approaching deadly and destructive tsunamis.

2004 INDIAN OCEAN TSUNAMI

On December 26, 2004, the world experienced the worst natural disaster in recorded history. A 9.1 magnitude earthquake occurred in the Indian Ocean, about 100 miles off the west coast of Sumatra, Indonesia. The earthquake raised the seabed along with millions of tons of water, creating a colossal tsunami. With the estimated power of 23,000 atomic bombs, the tsunami radiated outward from the earthquake's epicenter at the phenomenal speed of 600 miles per hour (mph).

Because there was no tsunami warning system for the Indian Ocean, the first warning system to pick up the earthquake was the Pacific Tsunami Warning Center in Hilo, Hawaii. Within minutes after the quake, the Center's scientists were busy analyzing seismic data, trying to pinpoint its location. Meanwhile, the inhabitants and tourists along the coastal communities of the Indian Ocean went about their morning as usual, completely unaware of the danger. The scientists in Hilo determined the earthquake's location in the Indian Ocean. Eighteen minutes after the earthquake, the Pacific Tsunami Warning Center issued its first warning that there had been what they thought was an 8.0 magnitude earthquake in the Indian Ocean.

The Hilo scientists did not know if the earthquake had generated a tsunami, because not all underwater earthquakes do. Earthquakes that move the earth back and forth generally do not, whereas those that move the earth up and down can. This information, however, is not recorded by seismographs. Without tide gauges—and there were none in the Indian Ocean—the scientists in Hilo were unable to determine if a tsunami had been created. Unknown to them, about eight minutes before they issued their first warning, the tsunami had already destroyed most of Sumatra.

It took the tsunami just ten minutes to reach Sumatra. As the tsunami neared Sumatra's coastline, its leading edge sucked water back away from the beach, leaving fish flapping on the wet sand. Dozens of amazed Sumatrans, who had never seen anything like this before, rushed forward to catch the helpless fish. Then the tsunami wave came. It washed completely over the three-mile-wide island, uprooting trees, smashing buildings and cars, and killing nearly 100,000 people. Roughly two-thirds of all those killed by the tsunami were killed in Sumatra. A few minutes later, the wave struck the Anadaman and Nicobar Islands.

About one hour after the earthquake, the wave reached the southern coast of Thailand. Depending on the specific morphology of the coastline, damage in Thailand varied considerably. Deep bays received little damage. Kamata Beach, on the other hand, has a gentle, shallow seabed and it received terrible devastation.

The scientists in Hilo continued to sift through their data. Within an hour they had recalculated the earthquake's magnitude, increasing it first to 8.5 and then 9.0. Eventually they learned that, indeed, the earthquake had caused a tsunami. With no warning systems in any of the countries in the tsunami's path, the Hilo scientists frantically made phone calls. Geologist Barry Hirshorn of Hilo's warning center recalled:

> We started thinking about who we could call. We talked to the State Department Operations Center and to the military. We called embassies. We talked to the navy in Sri Lanka, any local government official we could get hold of. We were fairly careful about who we called because we wanted to call people who could actually help.[9]

Two hours after the earthquake, Sri Lanka was next. Although 1,000 miles from the epicenter, the tidal wave inundated the island, killing over 35,000 people.

Within a few hours, the tsunami decimated hundreds of miles of coastline in 15 countries. It killed an estimated 180,000 people, with over 40,000 still missing. The 9.1 magnitude earthquake was the largest quake in the world during the past 40 years and the fifth largest ever recorded. It was so enormous that the planet now wobbles a bit more than it used to and our days are three-millionths of a second shorter.

LESSONS FROM TSUNAMIS

In January 2005, only weeks after the deadly 2004 Tsunami, the United Nations held an international conference in Kobe, Japan. During the conference, the UN established the Indian Ocean Tsunami

FIGURE 6.2 *Indonesia, Banda Aceh, Tsunami, One Year After, 2005.*
The tsunami damaged Baiturrahim Mosque under renovation in the hard-hit neighbor-hood of Ulee Lheue, Banda Aceh. The mosque was one of the few buildings of the area to survive the tsunami. © *James Robert Fuller/CORBIS.*

Warning and Mitigation System. By mid-2006, it was operational. The system includes seismic detection equipment, tide gauges along mainland and island coastlines, and deep-ocean buoys that measure ocean surface conditions as well as variations in ocean depth. The tide gauges and deep-ocean buoys include satellite transmission equipment to relay data to ground-based advisory centers throughout the region, including the countries of Australia, India, Indonesia, Iran, Malaysia, Pakistan, and Thailand. (See Figure 6.2.) In addition to the monitoring equipment and advisory centers, countries have developed warning and evacuations plans. Thus far, nearly 30 nations have set up functional warning programs or have their development under way.

In addition to the region's tsunami warning system, there were lessons learned regarding the performance of buildings. Tsunamis are very powerful. They are also relatively rare. Designing all buildings to resist the full impact of tidal waves is not practical. However, in the aftermath of the 2004 Tsunami, it is apparent that many mitigation measures are possible to reduce and, perhaps in some cases, eliminate damage.

Damage from tsunamis comes in three ways: (1) damage from the impact of the tidal wave, (2) damage caused by debris picked up and swept along by the wave, and (3) the scouring action caused by the retreating wave. Following is a summary of lessons learned about the performance of man-made structures in tsunamis:

- *Building elevation matters.* Buildings built farther from the beach have a much better chance of survival than those built at or near the coastline. In addition, those built along the beach, but elevated, have a greater chance of survival than those that are built at beach level. Elevated buildings allow waves to pass underneath, greatly increasing their chances of survival. Buildings that suffered the most damage were those built directly along the beach with first floor walls directly facing the ocean.
- *Building orientation matters.* Building walls perpendicular to or facing the ocean sustained considerable damage. Walls oriented with the flow had a much higher survival rate.
- *Strong and deep foundations are important.* Foundations must be strong enough to resist wave impacts and deep enough so that scouring and erosion due to rushing water does not undermine them.
- *Building materials are important.* Buildings constructed of reinforced concrete fared much better than those built of brick and wood. Many two- and three-story concrete buildings survived while their wood-framed neighbors were obliterated.
- *Reducing the flow of debris is important.* Many tsunami victims died because of debris swept along by the waves. Elevated buildings and reinforced concrete structures with strong and deep foundations reduce building damage and, consequently, the amount of debris swept along by the tsunami. Debris can be reduced by locating parking lots and other potential sources of debris away from beaches and on the inland sides of sturdy structures.
- *Improving building codes and construction supervision is necessary.* The area of the 2004 Tsunami is considered a nonearthquake-prone area. Consequently, buildings are not designed to resist earthquakes. This makes them more vulnerable to damage by tsunamis because the buildings are not as strong as earthquake-resistant buildings. Many buildings in the region are constructed without the assistance of architects or engineers during design or construction. This practice should be changed.

- *Waves come in and go out.* Building foundations and retaining walls must be designed to resist erosion caused by incoming and receding waves.
- *Seawalls can reduce damage.* Even if they are overtopped, they can reduce a lot of the surge. They must be continuous and penetrations in them must be protected by floodgates. Walls that slope inland are not as effective as vertical walls or those that slope seaward.

The Netherlands, for example, uses seawalls to defend itself from the sea. With 60 percent of the nation below sea level, flooding was a recurring problem. When the Netherlands flooded in 1953 and killed 1,800 people, the disaster sparked a "never again" attitude. The Dutch built a complex system of dams, dikes, and movable floodwalls. The Netherlands has never flooded since. Like the Netherlands, Taro, Japan, also relies on a seawall for its survival. In 1896, a tsunami killed 1,900 of its 1,940 citizens. Nevertheless, they rebuilt. In 1933, a 25-foot-high tsunami again washed over Taro, killing 900. "Never again," Taro's citizens vowed. In 1934, Taro built a 26-foot-tall seawall with 18 floodgates separating the town from the sea. Taro has not flooded again.

In the United States, the State of Oregon has adopted tsunami design standards. Oregon's 2004 *Structural Specialty Code*, which is the 2003 *International Building Code* with special Oregon amendments, includes requirements for building within the low-lying areas along the Oregon coast, which are susceptible to tsunamis. Oregon's Department of Geology and Mineral Industries (DOGAMI), using a combination of scientific evidence, geological survey data, and tsunami modeling, developed a map defining certain areas of Oregon as Tsunami Inundation Zones. Oregon law prohibits the construction of "essential facilities" and "special occupancy structures" in Tsunami Inundation Zones. In addition, "hazardous facilities" and "major structures" are mandated to seek advice from DOGAMI before constructing within Tsunami Inundation Zones. Oregon defines these categories of structures as follows:

- *Essential facilities:* hospitals, fire and police stations, storage tanks, and warehouses storing emergency response supplies and fire-suppression materials, garages and covered parking areas for emergency response vehicles, standby emergency power generators, government communications centers, and other facilities required for emergency response

- *Special occupancy structures:* public assembly buildings with capacities greater than 300 persons, K-12 school buildings, child care centers with occupancies greater than 250, colleges with more than 500 persons, medical facilities with incapacitated patients, jails and detention facilities, and all structures with occupancies greater than 5,000 people
- *Hazardous facilities:* buildings or structures that contain sufficient quantities of toxic or explosive substances to be safety hazards if accidentally released
- *Major structures:* buildings that are taller than six stories with areas greater than 60,000 square feet, all buildings taller than ten stories, and parking structures over three stories in height with areas greater than 30,000 square feet

Constructing any of the above facilities within Tsunami Inundation Zones requires a public hearing and an exemption. The applicant must demonstrate that "the safety of the building's occupants will be ensured to the maximum reasonable extent."[10] To this end, applicants and their designers shall

- address the relative risks within the zone;
- consider mitigative design and construction strategies;
- consider terrain modifications to mitigate impact of a tsunami;
- balance competing interests and other considerations (the meaning of "other considerations" is not defined); and
- pay for all costs for review of the application and approval process.[11]

Many communities within Oregon, however, lie completely within Tsunami Inundation Zones. If the above rules were strictly enforced, some communities could not build schools or police or fire stations without going through the state's exemption process—a process that does not guarantee that an exemption would be granted. Also, under many circumstances, the cost of mitigation could be considerable and therefore beyond the financial means of many communities. Consequently, the State of Oregon has given communities completely residing within

Tsunami Inundation Zones a major exemption. Oregon Statute ORS 455.447 states that the tsunami inundations requirements do not apply

> to fire or police stations where there is a need for strategic location; and to public schools if there is a need for the school to be within the boundaries of a school district and this cannot otherwise be accomplished. . . . [and the provisions] do not apply to water-dependent and water-related facilities, including but not limited to docks, wharves, piers and marinas.[12]

The exemption undermines the purpose of the law. In effect, communities within Tsunami Inundation Zones can comply or not comply as they see fit.

Nevertheless, the Oregon law is a good first step. It reminds Oregonians of the ever-present threat of tsunamis to low-lying areas along the Oregon coast. In addition, it offers sound advice for placement of various facilities that, if inundated by a tsunami, could cause severe destruction of property, environmental damage, and even loss of life. As we have seen throughout this book, the best way to plan for disaster is planning to avoid it.

Chapter

7

DISASTERS OF ANOTHER KIND

Thus far, we have looked at disasters arising from natural causes: fires, earthquakes, hurricanes, and tsunamis. We have also looked at the man-made phenomena of overcrowding. We have seen how these disasters have shaped the built environment. In addition to overcrowding, there are other types of man-made disasters that affect the built environment. They are:

- Economic disasters
- Social disasters
- Structural disasters

In this chapter, we look at these three man-made disasters. Economic, social, and structural disasters are usually confined to large, complicated, and unique projects. This is because there are more uncertainties associated with these projects. Uncertainties can lead to unintentional mistakes and misjudgments in project management decisions and in the choice of methods and procedures used to direct and monitor the progress of planning, design, and construction. These mistakes and misjudgments adversely affect project execution, and this can cause severe project planning errors, cost overruns, excessive design and construction rework, misspent project funds, slippage in project schedules, and quality control problems. Serious design and quality control problems can lead to injuries and even deaths.

The method of executing the planning, design, and construction of a project is called a project's "delivery system." Misjudgment in choosing a project's delivery system can be the first in a series of mistakes that lead to disaster. For example, the Sydney Opera House in Sydney, Australia, was a colossal economic disaster. Early in the project, a design/build delivery system was selected. In hindsight, this project delivery process proved to be a key factor in the project's seemingly endless escalating costs.

Planning and design assumptions form what is called a project's "design philosophy." Architects and planners base many project-related decisions on design philosophy. A flawed design philosophy can lead to inadequate or defective ways of thinking about, solving, and fleshing out the final design of a project. On occasion, a flawed design philosophy causes unintended disaster. For example, the Pruitt-Igoe Housing Complex in St. Louis, Missouri, a low-income, high-rise housing complex designed and built in the 1950s, is a classic example of a social disaster caused by a fallacious design philosophy.

Mistakes in judgment and failure to follow fundamentally important steps during the design and construction process can result in serious mistakes that can lead to disaster. Particularly important in the design of buildings is the selection and design of a building's structural system. Failure to understand how a building's structural system will behave during severe, yet predictable, conditions can cause structure disaster. The Kemper Basketball Arena in Kansas City, Missouri, is an example. During a heavy rain storm in 1979, its roof suddenly collapsed.

Carelessness in following critical design steps and failure to perform crucial calculations can also cause structural disaster. The 1981 Hyatt Regency Hotel disaster in Kansas City, Missouri, is an example. One hundred and fourteen people died and over 200 were injured when the lobby balcony they were standing on suddenly gave way. Nobody did any calculations during the construction shop drawing review to confirm that the contractor's changes to the balcony support system were structurally sound.

ECONOMIC DISASTERS

Economic disasters are projects characterized by astronomical cost overruns. Frequently, economic disasters are coupled with enormous slippages in project schedules because time equals money in the construction industry. If a project takes longer to design or build, it generally costs more. Economic disasters frequently receive harsh condemnation from experts, the press, government officials, and the public as they are being executed. Often, the reputations of these projects are severely tarnished by the time they are complete. Ironically, some go on to become lasting achievements, outlasting their critics and making important contributions to the very communities that criticized them. Two notable examples are the aforementioned Sydney Opera House in Sydney, Australia, and the Scottish Parliament in Edinburgh, Scotland.

The Sydney Opera House

The Sydney Opera House took 19 years to complete from inception and design to construction, instead of the 6 years originally estimated. Conceived in 1954 and designed and built between 1957 and 1973, the structure cost 15 times more than its original estimate. In 1965, the publicly funded project cost the Labour Party of New South Wales its longstanding control of government, losing to the Liberal-Country Party, who made the Opera House delays and its escalating cost a major—and successful—campaign issue.

The Opera House's distinctive sail-like appearance required a unique structural system. In addition, the size and configuration of the Opera House's main auditorium and stage area were in constant design-flux for a considerable period of time. In an attempt to push the project along as quickly as possible, the New South Wales government committee overseeing the project decided to employ a design/build project delivery method. In design/build, construction begins before the design is completed. While many building projects employ this method with success, it is not a delivery method well suited for unique or complicated projects that require many first-time solutions to unusual design problems. In particular, it is a poor delivery solution when the design team and user group cannot come to a consensus on the building's design.

FIGURE 7.1 *Sydney Opera House as seen from the Sydney Harbor Bridge.* © *Paul A. Souders/CORBIS.*

As the engineering firm ARUP struggled with the building's structural design, and the architect Jørn Utzon continued to design the auditorium and stage, the concrete foundation was poured. Rather than accelerating the project, this instead slowed it down, because once the building's structural system and auditorium design were determined, the foundation was not compatible with the design, and it had to be demolished. Eventually, through a series of trials, tribulations, arguments among team members, and the eventual resignation of the architect, the project was completed, 13 years late and 1,500 percent over budget, a world record for cost overruns on a percentage basis.

Today, the Sydney Opera House has long since weathered the economic disaster and controversy. It has become synonymous with Sydney, Australia. It is a prime tourist attraction and one of very few buildings recognized around the world. (See Figure 7.1.)

The Scottish Parliament

The Scottish Parliament Building in Edinburgh, Scotland, took over four years to design and build instead of the two years originally scheduled. Instead of costing the equivalent of $75 million U.S. dollars as budgeted in 2000, it actually cost $830 million by the time it was completed in 2004, an elevenfold cost increase. The Scottish Parliament was roundly criticized by journalists and experts for the project's mismanagement and cost overruns. In May 2003, before the building was completed, Lord Peter Lovat Fraser was asked to investigate the debacle. He presented his findings to Parliament in early September 2004.

On September 22, 2004, the Scottish Parliament met in the debating chamber of their new Parliament building for a "time of reflection," as they called it, they debated Lord Fraser's findings and discuss the lessons learned from the financial disaster. Lord Fraser's conclusions included:

- *It is necessary to have a well-defined and fixed scope of work.* The original program of spaces, which was a list of all the rooms and functions that were planned to take place within the facility, was poorly formulated and woefully inadequate to meet Parliament's needs. It changed considerably as the design progressed, causing extensive redesign work and doubling the building area from 170,000 square feet to 325,000 square feet. Needless to say, it is impossible to build the same quality building for the same cost if the area of the building nearly doubles.

- *Buildings of complex shapes are expensive to design, detail, and build.* Architect Enric Miralles's postmodern, multifaceted, and nonorthogonal design (the building design had few straight lines and right angles) was very complicated. It required a tremendous number of design hours to work out how the building's organic geometry came together. Miralles's creative vision was so complicated that it was impossible for the designers to anticipate the hundreds of unique and specialized details required to implement the design. The details proved so difficult to visualize in three dimensions that approximately half of them had to be reworked in the field, at considerable cost.

- *Rigorous budget controls are required for complex building projects moving at a rapid pace.* Lord Fraser commented in his report that he was astonished that the government ministers in charge of the project were unaware of the frequent cost increases. In addition, the inquiry revealed that no one told the architect to consider economy while designing the building.[1]

- *Poor communication among design team members leads to coordination problems.* The project was a joint venture between Miralles's Spanish design firm, EMBT, and the Scottish design firm RMJM.

Key design team members had never worked together before. Design ideas generated and loosely sketched by EMBT were fleshed out in detail by RMJM, often with much difficulty, confusion, and reworking.

- *The Construction Management project delivery approach transferred all responsibilities for cost overruns to the Scottish taxpayer.* The Fraser report placed considerable blame on the project delivery process. The project delivery approach did not follow the standard design, bid, and build approach, typical of most publicly funded building projects. In a design/bid/build scenario, the project design is first completed. Next, contractors competitively bid to build the project. The lowest or most responsive contractor is awarded the contract, and then construction begins based on the agreed-to fixed price. In design/bid/build, so long as the construction documents are free of errors and the scope of work does not change, the contractor assumes the risks associated with construction cost overruns. The Scottish Parliament Building was not designed and built this way. Early in the process a decision was made to employ a Construction Management project delivery approach. According to Lord Fraser's report, this is when "the wheels began to fall off the wagon."[2] Near the project's outset, while the design was still quite fluid, a Construction Management firm was selected to oversee the design, construction, cost, schedule, and delivery of the project. The Construction Management firm, however, had no financial responsibility for the project's cost. The costs associated with all changes and technical and managerial misjudgments were paid for by the Scottish Ministry of Finance, which is to say the Scottish taxpayer. In effect, the decision to deliver the project via Construction Management was equivalent to handing out blank checks to all project participants.

In general, the lessons of the Scottish Parliament Building project are characteristic of many unique and complex building projects. Fundamentally, financial disasters are project management failures. Strangely enough, lessons from project management failures are a lot like lessons from natural disasters: They do not travel well. Large and complicated projects worldwide have suffered and probably will continue to suffer from project management mistakes. This may be because

FIGURE 7.2 *Scottish Parliament Building, Edinburgh, Scotland. Photo by Author.*

project management is still not taken seriously as a profession. It is often treated as an adjunct to the design professions or an additional and temporary responsibility for a political body that is often unfamiliar with the intricacies of design and construction. This was true for both the Sydney Opera House and the Scottish Parliament. Neither government entity paid close and thorough attention to the everyday project management and design decisions, which ultimately led to the projects' disastrous cost overruns.

The completed Scottish Parliament is an amazing postmodern architectural achievement. (See Figure 7.2.) In its first six months after opening in 2004, it attracted over a quarter of a million visitors. Within a year, it had become Scotland's number one tourist attraction. With the project complete, the financial bleeding is over. The memory of the disaster will fade, and in its place, generations of Scots will grow to appreciate, enjoy, and be proud of their iconoclastic building. The Scottish Parliament is destined to become a premier example of postmodern architecture.

Boston's Big Dig

The former Central Artery of Boston, Massachusetts, was a six-lane elevated turnpike that cut right through the city. Conceived in a 1948 Master Highway Plan for the Boston Metropolitan Area and built between 1950 and 1959, it was more like a scar than an artery. Raw and ugly, it divided the city in two. Originally designed to accommodate 75,000 vehicles a day, by the 1990s the number of cars using it each day was closer to 200,000. Traffic was bumper to bumper for about 10 hours out of every 24. Accidents were frequent—four times the national average for a road its size. It was the most congested freeway in the United States.

Experts estimated that if nothing was done by 2010, traffic would crawl along bumper to bumper about 16 hours out of every day. Besides the impact on motorists' stress levels, experts estimated that the congestion would cost a staggering $500 million a year in accidents, wasted gasoline, and product delivery delays.

In the late 1940s and 1950s, politicians, highway designers, urban planners, and architects designed and constructed just about anything in the name of progress. After World War II, America had a confident can-do attitude and an overly simplified faith in building and technology. Proponents of Boston's Central Artery claimed that it would unclog city streets and speed cars through the city. More importantly, it would prepare Boston for growth and prosperity during the latter half of the 20th century. So what if the raised highway was unattractive and divisive. So what if people and businesses would have to move or be moved. They were standing in the way of progress. The 1948 master plan stated matter-of-factly that

> the relocation of tenants is an integral part of a highway project. . . . [In] congested areas, particularly those of [a] substandard housing nature, consideration should be given to mass relocation of tenants in new housing projects.[3]

Construction of the Central Artery required the condemnation of acres of property and the relocation of approximately 20,000 Boston residents. Dozens of old buildings in Boston's downtown were demolished and the project displaced approximately 900 businesses. As construction proceeded, it slowly walled off Boston's north end and waterfront neighborhoods from downtown.

When the Central Artery opened in 1959, it carried 75,000 cars a day from the outskirts of Boston to or through downtown. By the early 1960s, Bostonians began to figure out that the Central Artery was an urban planning mistake. It adversely affected the identity and livability of the neighborhoods adjacent to it, and stigmatized neighborhoods and residents who lived on the "wrong side" of the structure. Neighborhood groups began to organize and urban planners began to speak out. In an urban planning report published in 1966, the civil engineer Frederick Salvucci, who later served as Massachusetts State Transportation Secretary during Governor Michael Dukakis's two separate administrations, wrote that the highway destroyed

> something far more difficult to replace: established neighborhoods that enjoy[ed] a deep sense of community. Boston's Central Artery, where it borders on the North end, is a classic example of what highway critics call a "Chinese Wall": a physical and psychological barrier isolating a neighborhood from shopping, jobs, churches, schools and friends.[4]

Throughout the next decade, transportation and highway experts, politicians, and community action and business groups debated about the elevated freeway. All the while, traffic on the Central Artery increased and neighborhoods bordering it continued in decline.

During the mid-1970s, while Salvucci was serving his first stint as State Transportation Secretary, the idea of running the Central Artery underground was proposed to him by highway contractor and engineer Bill Reynolds. Reynolds saw the elevated highway as a "giant billboard that says roads are bad."[5] For Reynolds, roads were bread and butter, and he wanted to improve their perception. Making the Central Artery invisible sounded like a good idea. At first, Salvucci was skeptical that burying the freeway was feasible, but eventually Reynolds convinced him it was possible. Salvucci began to develop a strategy to implement it.

Massachusetts politicians shelved the idea—and the Dukakis administration—for four years. The idea was resurrected when Dukakis regained the governorship in 1982 and he reappointed Salvucci as Transportation Secretary. For the next six years, Salvucci pushed the project forward. Finally, in 1987, with an estimated price tag of $2.5 billion, the project received approval for federal funding, but only after the U.S. Senate overrode President Ronald Reagan's veto. After his veto, Reagan quipped, "I haven't seen this much lard since I handed out blue ribbons at the Iowa State Fair."[6] Regardless, the project was approved and design work began.

The design of the Central Artery/Tunnel Project (CA/T) was colossal in both scope and complexity. The design called for an eight-lane tunnel that would run directly beneath the existing Central Artery. The tunnel would rise up out of the ground, widen, and divide into two bridges crossing the Charles River. CA/T would include connections to other freeways serving the greater Boston area, including an extension of the I-90 freeway to Logan Airport. The old Central Artery would continue to be used during construction. It would not be torn down until after the tunnel was built. The land occupied by the former freeway would then be turned into parks and moderately sized real estate developments. All of this would be done without interruption to Boston's economy. The city would remain open for business during construction of the entire project. While some components of the project would have earlier completion dates, the project's overall completion date would be 1998.

By 1991, the design was well under way and construction was ready to begin. However, the $2.5 billion figure for construction had doubled to $5 billion. The project again went before the U.S. Senate for funding and approval. Because the cost had doubled in four years, some senators wondered if it would increase again. Massachusetts Senator Edward Kennedy reassured them that $5 billion was the budget and said, "There is no intention of repeating or coming back for additional resources."[7] Congress appropriated the money and construction began.

No other project of similar magnitude had ever been attempted in a major metropolitan area. The project required the excavation of 16 million cubic yards of earth. That is enough dirt to cover 2,500 football fields 1-foot deep. Understandably, the project was dubbed the Big Dig.

About one-third of the dirt removed to dig the tunnels was clay. It was hauled to nearby areas to cap off dumps and landfills that were full to capacity. For example, 3.5 million cubic yards of Big Dig dirt was used to cap the dumpsite on Spectacle Island in Boston Harbor. Other statistics that illustrate the colossal size of the project include:

- 3.8 million cubic yards of concrete were poured, enough to cover nearly 600 football fields 1-foot deep.
- 28,000 miles of reinforcing steel was installed, enough to circle the earth.
- The tunnel's ventilation system occupies seven buildings and is one of the largest ventilation systems in the world.
- The Leonard P. Zakim Bunker Hill Bridge that spans the Charles River is the largest cable-stay bridge in the world.

- Crossing the Fort Point Channel required the first use of jacked vehicle tunnels and the greatest use of concrete-immersed tube tunnels in the United States.

The Big Dig was a first in another way too. It has become the most costly and notorious highway project in American history. As of mid-2006, the cost was nearly $15 billion and growing. Although technically completed in January 2006, seven years behind schedule, its total cost is still unknown. Using the $15 billion figure, however, the cost of the project works out to a staggering $93 million dollars per lane mile—the most expensive road in U.S. history.

If the cost overruns weren't bad enough, the Big Dig also leaked. Tunnel inspections conducted in March 2005 discovered more than 2,000 leaks due to cracks, poorly sealed joints, and improperly installed waterproofing. The combination of cost overruns and leaks caused one Bostonian to quip on National Public Radio's Weekend Edition, "$15 billion sure doesn't buy what it used to." Most leaks were considered minor, but a major leak came to the public's attention two months later when contractors were discovered trying to secretly plug a 20-gallon-per-minute leak.

Due to severe cost overruns, auditors began looking into the Big Dig's finances early on in the project. An audit in 2000 concluded that the project was near bankruptcy. Another found it to be "one of the most flagrant breaches of [financial] integrity . . . in the history of the 85-year-old Federal-aid highway program."[8]

In addition to waste and mismanagement, there were also allegations of fraud. In May 2006, employees of one of the major concrete suppliers to the project were indicted by a federal grand jury. The charges alleged that they conspired to deliver and approve approximately 5,000 truckloads of substandard concrete to the project.

On Monday, July 10, 2006, the disaster got worse. Around 11:00 PM, a 200-foot section of tunnel ceiling fell, crushing a motorist to death. State officials immediately shut down portions of the tunnel and adjacent Ted Williams Tunnel to traffic until the cause could be determined. Newspapers throughout the United States carried the tragic story the next morning. In addition to the tragic accident, much of the Big Dig's dirty laundry was again aired. The New York Times article quoted Massachusetts Governor Mitt Romney's reaction to the tragedy.

Romney, a long-time critic of the Massachusetts Turnpike Authority, minced no words:

> People should not have to drive through the turnpike tunnels with their fingers crossed. I don't think anyone can feel safe driving through a tunnel system where just last night someone got killed by a 3-ton piece of concrete falling on their car.[9]

By the week's end, Romney had stepped in to lead an official state investigation of the disaster.

The section of ceiling that fell was composed of four three-ton concrete ceiling panels. Each panel was suspended from bolts that were glued with epoxy into holes in the concrete tunnel structure above. The epoxied connections failed, causing the ceiling to collapse. Within a week or two, other loose epoxied bolts holding up ceiling panels were found. Repairs were made and portions of the tunnel opened again by Labor Day 2006.

The fallout from the Big Dig disaster is not over, but eventually it will die out. The cost overruns will ultimately be forgotten—such is the scenario for most financial disasters. Bostonians will put the cost of the Big Dig in perspective thanks to the world of good destined to grow out of it. When the memories of the disaster wane, Bostonians will see that Boston is a better place to live because of the Big Dig.

Very few cities have the opportunity that the Big Dig has given Boston. Without a fire, an earthquake, hurricane, or tsunami, Boston has the chance to rebuild itself. It can reclaim land that was once lost to the senseless 1950s let's-build-a-freeway mentality that bisected, polluted, and destroyed neighborhoods. The torn-down Central Artery has rid the city of a major disruptive eyesore and cleared the way for the development of parks and redevelopment projects. Boston has plans to build a 40-acre park along the Charles River, giving Bostonians greater access to the harbor. A 30-acre series of parks and landscaped pedestrian paths is planned for much of the land that once lay beneath the elevated freeway. Called the Rose Kennedy Greenway, the parks will extend from Boston's Chinatown through the Wharf District and to the Fleet Center. With plans to make Boston a vibrant, 24-hour-a-day city, modestly scaled, mixed-use development projects are also planned. These projects will combine housing, hotels, offices, and commercial space to create vibrant communities that will be occupied, used, and enjoyed around the clock.

Once used as the depository for Boston's garbage, Spectacle Island was an environmental nightmare, leaking thousands of gallons of eroding and decomposing material into the surrounding harbor. Instead of a dump and eyesore, Spectacle Island is now part of Boston Harbor Islands State Park. The island was capped with 18 inches of clay and diked to prevent future leakage and erosion. The dirt, clay, and gravel used on the island all came from the Big Dig. A 2- to 5-foot layer of topsoil was placed over the clay that will be planted with trees and other landscaping. There are plans to build a dock for public ferries, picnic areas, pedestrian trails, and a visitors' center—all made possible by the Big Dig.

The Leonard P. Zakim Bunker Hill Bridge over the River Charles is another spectacular consequence of the Big Dig. Its 1,432-foot length and 270-foot-tall towers make it the largest cable-stay bridge in the United States. In addition to the eight lanes of traffic that pass between its two towers, two additional lanes are cantilevered along its east side, giving the bridge its unusual yet graceful asymmetrical appearance. It would not be surprising for people to eventually identify the bridge as an icon for Boston much in the way the Golden Gate Bridge is a symbol for San Francisco.

THE SOCIAL DISASTER OF PRUITT-IGOE

Most disasters start when the destruction begins. Not so with the Pruitt-Igoe low-income housing project in St. Louis, Missouri. Its disaster scenario plays in reverse: Its destruction marked the end of the disaster.

Pruitt-Igoe is the most infamous public housing disaster in American history. It is well known because of the spectacular way it ended: It was deliberately blown to pieces in 1972. Since its inglorious end, it has become the poster child for everything that is wrong about low-cost, high-rise housing projects.

Built between 1951 and 1954, the Pruitt-Igoe housing complex was named after Wendell Oliver Pruitt, an African-American World War II fighter pilot, and former Missouri U.S. Congressman William L. Igoe. The complex included 33 11-story buildings on a site of 57 acres. It contained

2,870 tenement units, working out to a ratio of 50 families per acre. Units varied in size from one to five bedrooms. Fully occupied, it housed over 10,000 residents, a staggering 175 people per acre.

Pruitt-Igoe replaced a decaying, crime-infested slum of ramshackle one-, two-, and three-story brick houses filled with the urban working poor and an assorted collection of wrecked cars and filth. The greater St. Louis community was glad to be rid of it. Although St. Louis had some of the most densely populated slums in the United States, the slum that was cleared had far fewer people per acre than the Pruitt-Igoe housing project that replaced it.

Pruitt-Igoe was the well-intentioned pet project of St. Louis Mayor Joe Darst. Quoted in the April 1951 *Architectural Forum* article entitled "Slum Surgery in St. Louis," Darst said:

> We must rebuild, open up and clean up the hearts of our cities. . . . The fact that slums were created with all of their intrinsic evils was everybody's fault. Now it is everybody's responsibility to repair the damage.[10]

Even before it was built, the building's design received praise. *Architectural Forum* claimed that its 11-story buildings would create

> vertical neighborhoods for poor people in a city which up to now has lived 90% in single houses. . . . [T]he new plan saves not only people, but money.[11]

When it opened in 1954, it was hailed as exemplary. It was thought to be a safe, decent, affordable, and efficient way of housing the urban masses. Its glorious image was used in advertisements by materials and systems manufacturers who proudly touted their association with the project. Everyone thought Pruitt-Igoe was a magnificent achievement of urban planning, low-cost housing, and architectural design. Everyone, that is, except those who lived in it.

One by one, Pruit-Igoe's tenants fell victim to its immense size, lack of amenities, poor security, deficient maintenance, and high-rise institutional appearance that branded everyone who lived in it as under-privileged, and therefore different from everyone else. Tenants and their children were inconvenienced by elevators that were deliberately designed to stop only on every third floor. There were no first-floor toilet facilities for children playing outdoors to use. Consequently lobbies, stairwells, and elevators were often used as toilets. Corridors and other public spaces within the project were poorly lit. Concrete block walls in public spaces were left unpainted. Architectural finishes were bleak. Maintenance was virtually nonexistent. By the early 1960s, the buildings were in dire need of repairs. Tenants started moving out. By 1965, conditions had worsened and Pruitt-Igoe was one-third vacant. St. Louis's Public Housing Authority (PHA) began pumping money into the project in an attempt to repair and rehabilitate it. In its December 1965 issue, *Architectural Forum* changed its tune, this time titling an article about the project "The Case History of a Failure," which noted:

> Ten years ago, this St. Louis project was expected to set a new standard of housing design. Now $7 million will be spent in an attempt to save it.[12]

As it turned out, $21 million was spent trying to save Pruitt-Igoe. Nevertheless, the money and efforts were for naught. By the early 1970s, the project was more dismal still and virtually empty.

Shortly after 3:00 PM on the afternoon of March 16, 1972, a rapid series of loud explosions flashed out from the hollows of an empty Pruitt-Igoe high-rise. The building shuddered momentarily, then collapsed in on itself and crashed to the ground. The first of the 33 Pruitt-Igoe high-rises was reduced to nothing more than a bad memory and a smoky pile of debris.

St. Louis's PHA and the Department of Housing and Urban Development (HUD) had planned the demolition for months. In December 1971, they made the decision to demolish 2 of the 33 buildings. It was the first step in their plan—a hope really—to see if by reducing the density of Pruitt-Igoe other buildings within the project could be saved. The plan was to demolish some of the buildings and "top" others, cutting them down to just a few stories in height, thus reducing the project's density. The intent was to save some of the $57 million that had been invested in the complex, which included $36 million spent to construct it and another $21 million spent trying to save it. Beyond calculation was the cost of its contribution to St. Louis crime and its toll on the lives of the thousands who had lived there.

FIGURE 7.3 *On April 21, 1972, the second 11-story building in the Pruitt-Igoe public housing complex was demolished by dynamite.* © *Bettmann/CORBIS.*

On April 22, a second building was dynamited. (See Figure 7.3.) This time local residents gathered to watch. As the decisive moment approached, the crowd grew silent in anticipation. The *St. Louis Post-Dispatch* reported the crowd's reaction in its front-page story the following day:

> The hush, like that of a football crowd awaiting the outcome of a crucial place kick in the last seconds of a bowl game, was ended by sharp explosions. . . . As the reinforced steel and concrete building crumbled into rubble a spontaneous shout arose from the spectators.[13]

PHA and HUD's hopes to salvage Pruitt-Igoe never panned out. On July 15, 1972, there were more explosions. Throughout the following year, wrecking balls and bulldozers finished off the demolition.

How Design Philosophy Contributed to Pruitt-Igoe's Demise

Pruitt-Igoe's purpose had been to provide affordable housing and a safe and livable environment for its residents. It failed miserably. By 1973, it entered the history books as a tragic example of how not to build low-cost housing.

So what happened to transform it from a magnificent planning and design achievement into a colossal failure in just 18 years? Just prior to its demise, many critics claimed that the project was simply too big for PHA or HUD to manage properly. A more complete answer can be summarized this way: Pruitt-Igoe was a victim of its design philosophy. This led to a series of mistakes and miscalculations regarding its scale, planning, and design. It also led to some eventually fatal cost-cutting measures. To better understand how design philosophy played such a vital role in Pruitt-Igoe's design and eventual demise, a brief trip to Paris, France, in the 1920s helps.

In the early 1920s, the Swiss-born architect Charles-Édouard Jeanneret lived and worked in Paris. In 1923, he published a book entitled *Vers une Architecture*, or *Towards a New Architecture*, which was a compilation of articles he had written for his own magazine *L'Esprit Nouveau*. If the name Jeanneret seems unfamiliar, it is because he is known better by his pseud-onym Le Corbusier. In *Towards a New Architecture*, Le Corbusier proposed a revolutionary idea for the design of cities and housing urban workers. In 1926, he published another book, *Five Points of a New Architecture*. In the second book, he advocated an architectural style with large windows, plain exteriors, exposed columns, and interior spaces with few walls and not much furniture. The style was praised as modern, technologically clean looking, devoid of useless ornamentation and unnecessary frivolous furnishings. For Le Corbusier, buildings were "machines for living." Le Corbusier's books were read and praised by architects throughout the world. They began designing Corbu-like buildings.

In 1930, the architectural historian Henry-Russell Hitchcock and the then-recent art history graduate Philip Johnson turned Le Corbusier, along with other architects with a similar design philosophy, into the founding fathers of a new type of architecture. Hitchcock and Johnson dubbed it the International Style. Le Corbusier became world renowned. By the mid-20th century, he was recognized as one of the "Big Three" in architecture, the other two being Frank Lloyd Wright and Mies Van der Rohe.

After World War II, many urban planners, government officials, and architects worldwide struggled with how best to house the ever-increasing number of urban workers. They latched onto Le Corbusier's model from 20 years earlier. In *Towards a New Architecture*, Le Corbusier wrote that building materials of concrete and steel could bring liberation to cities if architects and planners only reject the old way of building—meaning

Beaux Arts Classicism as promoted by the City Beautiful Movement—and instead exploited the potential of the new technologically-advanced building materials:

> [T]he great city is a rising tide. It is time that we should repudiate the existing lay-out of our towns, in which the congestion of buildings grows greater, interlaced by narrow streets full of noise, petrol fumes and dust; and where on each storey the windows open wide on to this foul confusion.[14]

Le Corbusier proposed constructing giant towers made of concrete and steel to house the urban worker. He also proposed locating these towers in parklike settings. Vehicular traffic would be routed around the towers-in-the-parks, thus providing lushly landscaped, safe, clean, and tranquil places for adults to meet and children to play:

> If we take as our basis the vital constructional event which the American sky-scraper has proved to be, it will be sufficient to bring together . . . the great density of our modern populations and to build . . . enormous constructions of 60 storeys high. In these towers, which will shelter the worker . . . all the necessary services . . . will be assembled, bringing efficiency and economy of time and effort, and as a natural result the peace of mind which is so necessary. These towers, rising up at great distances from one another, will give by reason of their height the same accommodation that has up till now been spread out over the superficial area; they will leave open enormous spaces . . . At the foot of the towers would stretch the parks: trees covering the whole town. . . . [T]here indeed is an architecture worthy of our time.[15]

Le Corbusier's first high-rise for housing the urban masses was La Maison Du Fada in Marseilles, an industrialized city located in France. Begun in 1947, it is known today as Unite d' Habitation. Shortly after the construction of Unite d' Habitation began, other high-rise housing projects were on drafting boards throughout Europe and the United States.

In the United States, the Public Housing Authority (PHA) was founded in 1947, replacing earlier organizations that addressed public housing. While these earlier organizations stressed low-rise, walk-up housing projects, the PHA focused on high-rise projects. Beginning with

New York City, high-rise public housing projects soon appeared in American cities.

St. Louis's problem was different than New York's, however. New York was an ever-growing city. More and more people kept coming, particularly rural, poor, African Americans from southern states. Even during the Great Depression, New York City grew, as dissolute people looking for jobs poured in. Not so with St. Louis. During the 1930s, St. Louis lost population, and the trend continued after World War II. In 1947, the St. Louis Planning Commission adopted a plan to encourage working-class families to stay in the city and convince others to move back. Part of the plan included reconstruction of the dilapidated slum known as the DeSoto-Carr district. The neighborhood, home to many poor African-American families, would be demolished and replaced with new two- and three-story row houses and a large public park.

In 1949, the newly elected mayor of St. Louis, Joseph Darst, convinced the Planning Commission to modify their plans. DeSoto-Carr would still be razed, but New York City's high-rise approach to urban housing would be followed. Two high-rise projects for the DeSoto-Carr neighborhood were born: Cochran Gardens and Pruitt-Igoe.

At Darst's request, St. Louis-born architect George Hellmuth and his partner Monoru Yamasaki were chosen as the architects. Their newly formed firm, Hellmuth, Yamasaki & Leinweber, went to work and designed Cochran Gardens first. Their solution: apartment buildings arranged in a parklike setting. Cochran Gardens included five 6-story buildings and four 12-story towers surrounded with lawns, trees, and pedestrian sidewalks. After its phased completion in 1951–1952, the architects received accolades and design awards for their innovative approach to urban housing.

Following the adage that bigger is better, the St. Louis Housing Authority followed Cochran Garden's approach for Pruitt-Igoe. Hellmuth, Yamasaki & Leinweber were again the architects. Pruitt-Igoe included some innovative design features that were praised at the time. Cumulatively, they later proved to bring about its demise.

Skip-stop elevators were one of the innovations. Elevators stopped only at the fourth, seventh, and tenth floors of the 11-story buildings. Tenants who did not live on one of the three floors had to then walk up or down a flight of stairs to their apartments. Considered ingenious, it also reduced costs.

On the floors where the elevators stopped, the architects developed wider, open-air corridors that they called "galleries." Adjacent to the galleries were laundry rooms. The idea was that as moms washed clothes in the laundry room, their children could play safely together in the gallery. Adults could meet in the gallery, sit in soft chairs, and socialize. As residents got off the skip-stop elevators they might meet, greet, and join their friends in conversation. According to the architects, the galleries were "vertical neighborhoods."

No toilet rooms were provided adjacent to the galleries. As part of cost-cutting measures, lighting levels in the galleries were reduced, the concrete-block gallery walls were left unpainted, and no gallery furnishings were provided.

There were no shops or amenities on the ground floor. All were eliminated as cost-cutting measures. Consequently, there was no possibility to make a quick trip down the skip-stop elevator for milk or eggs. There were no coffee shops, drugstores, or hair dressers—nothing but sterile elevator lobbies. There were no first-floor security systems, no surveillance cameras, or security guards. There were no first-floor toilets, either. They, too, were eliminated by cost cuts. When children playing outside did not have the time to take the elevators or stairs up to their apartments, the elevators and stairwells substituted for urinals. Soon the lobbies became unsanitary and unwelcoming.

Another method used to increase the project's financial viability was to increase the number of units. Pruitt-Igoe was originally conceived as only 30 families per acre. The architects developed the design based on that number. Later, PHA increased the density to 50 families per acre. Although the architects protested, their protests were in vain.

The parklike setting that was supposed to surround the high-rise buildings was anything but parklike. To save money, most of the landscaping was omitted. There were only a few trees. Instead of towers-in-a-park, Pruitt-Igoe was towers surrounded by wasteland.

Densely populated, 11-story-tall Pruitt-Igoe was very unlike its residential neighbors. Because most moderate- to low-income housing near it were 2- and 3-story row houses with pitched roofs, tall and flat-topped Pruitt-Igoe stood out like a sore thumb. Consequently, its residents were quickly stigmatized by the project's institutional-looking appearance. They were identified as low–income and, as the situation at Pruitt-Igoe grew worse, branded as petty criminals, gang members, and drug dealers.

The galleries did not function as expected. Cold and poorly lit, parents did not use them as play rooms. Nor did parents let their children play in the grounds that surrounded the buildings. Eventually, the only people out and about were gangs and drug dealers. To stay safe, law-abiding families stayed behind double-locked apartment doors.

Within just a few years, residents began moving out. As the vacancy rate increased, the amount of money coming in decreased. Maintenance and repairs fell woefully behind. As maintenance decreased, still more families moved out and the downward spiral worsened. To keep more families from moving out, rents were lowered. As rents lowered, more welfare families moved in, and so did gangs and drug dealers. More tenants moved out. Soon, welfare families who paid little or no rent were the majority of the tenants. The PHA scrimped on maintenance all the more. Leaking roofs were not fixed. During the winter, water leaking into the stairwells froze on stair treads. Insect screens on windows were not fixed, causing injury to several children who fell out.

Unsupervised children joined street gangs. Vandalism increased. Lobbies and corridors became covered with graffiti. The galleries were used as meeting places for drug deals. In 1968, only 14 years after it first opened, HUD began encouraging residents to move out. HUD called it "depopulation."

Architects and planners learned a great deal from Pruitt-Igoe. Since its destruction, they have paid more attention to how improper design can create unsafe living conditions. Low-rise buildings have become the model for low-cost housing, not high-rise buildings.

Although urban planner and author Jane Jacobs was talking about city streets, her observations about safety apply equally well to public spaces in general. According to Jacobs, public spaces require three things in order to be safe:

1. Clear boundaries between public space and private space
2. Many eyes upon the street
3. Constant activity on the street, not deserted streets

When public space becomes enclosed in spaces like corridors, elevators, and stairwells, the public space loses all three of these ingredients and therefore can become unsafe.

To Jane Jacobs's observations, Oscar Newman, author of *Defensible Space*, added this additional point:

> A family's claim to a territory diminishes proportionally as the number of families who share that claim increases. The larger the number of people who share a territory, the less each individual feels rights to it.[16]

It is tragic that so many lives had to be put through turmoil for architects, planners, and government officials to learn these lessons. Pruitt-Igoe also helped change the role of architects and planners and the importance of technology in solving urban problems. No longer are architects, planners, and technology seen as the saviors of humanity.

STRUCTURAL DISASTERS

Structural disasters are as old as the art of building itself. We have learned to build through trial and error. Over the centuries we have gotten better at it, but there is still much to learn.

Two recent structural examples illustrate this point. After centuries of building, we might conclude that relatively normal weather events such as heavy rain and snow could not possibly cause a modern building to collapse, but we would be wrong. In 1978, the Hartford, Connecticut, Civic Center Arena, completed only four years earlier, collapsed due to excessive roof deflection caused by snow. In 1979, the Kemper Basketball Arena in Kansas City, Missouri, collapsed due to heavy rains and 70 mph winds that caused waves and excessive pounding on the roof. Fortunately, the roofs of both arenas fell on empty seats. Had the collapses occurred one day earlier in the case of the Kemper Arena and only a few hours earlier for the Hartford Arena, possibly thousands would have been injured or killed.

Both buildings were modern steel-framed structures with flexible roof structures—too flexible in hindsight. The Kemper Arena roof structure was concrete poured over a corrugated steel deck supported by open web steel joists. The steel joists were supported by steel trusses that hung from a larger space frame. A space frame is a lot like a three-dimensional truss. It can span long distances in two directions, which

FIGURE 7.4 *Looming over Kemper Arena, a massive space frame supports the building's roof structure and provides the arena with its predominant architectural feature. Photo by Author.*

reduces the number of columns needed to hold up the structure. Figure 7.4 shows the Kemper Arena space frame, which is its predominant architectural feature. The Hartford Arena roof was a series of roof panels, each supported on short steel posts, which were supported by a space frame.

Both failures were "progressive failures," meaning that once one key structural component failed, its failure immediately overloaded adjacent structural components. One by one, they failed in rapid succession, bringing the building crashing to the ground.

Investigations after the disasters revealed the causes of the collapses. Because the roof structures were so flexible, the additional weight of the snow and rain caused their roofs to sag, allowing for the buildup of more snow and rain. Eventually, a single structural component within the roof of each building failed, starting the chain reactions that resulted in their collapses.

Investigations revealed a lack of redundancy in the roof structures of both buildings. Redundancy is an important design factor—it is the reason why a daddy longlegs spider can keep walking after it loses a leg, and it is why buildings can remain standing after localized failures of structural components. Redundancy allows both the daddy longlegs and buildings with redundancy to redistribute their weight and still remain standing. Progressive failures are like a line of dominoes: Once the first domino falls, so do all the others. Understandably, progressive failures are quick, unexpected, catastrophic, and virtually impossible to stop once they start.

During the investigation of the Kemper Arena disaster, calculations revealed that when one key structural component failed—a hanger that supported one of the steel trusses—adjacent hangers were not strong enough to support the additional load. All the hangers failed, one after the other, in a zipperlike affect. The failure brings to mind the old proverb, "For the want of a nail, the shoe was lost; for the want of a shoe, the horse was lost; and for the want of a horse, the rider was lost."

Within three months after the collapse, reconstruction of the arena's roof was under way. Work was completed by mid-1981. Today, the arena looks just the way it did prior to the collapse, except for a few subtle but important differences. The roof trusses and open web steel joists are stouter and can support more load. The hangers that support the roof trusses are welded instead of bolted to the trusses. The center of the roof has been raised 30 inches so that rainwater drains toward the perimeter of the roof. Also, more roof drains were added.

Progressive failures are as old as the pyramids and as recent as the 9/11 World Trade Center disaster, which is discussed in the next chapter. Perhaps the oldest progressive structural failure occurred in ancient Egypt over 4,500 years ago. It literally changed the shape of the pyramids.

The Collapsed Pyramid

The Collapsed Pyramid of Maidum (also spelled Maydum and Meidum) is appropriately named. It was built around 2600 BC during the reign of Pharaoh Sneferu, the first Pharaoh of the Old Kingdom Fourth Dynasty. The Collapsed Pyramid is the second oldest Egyptian pyramid known to have been built. Today, it stands as a stepped-mountain-shaped core of sandstone surrounded by the scattered and broken remains of 250,000 tons of limestone casing blocks that once formed its smooth exterior surface. The pyramid's name tells the story: It collapsed.

Egyptologists do not agree when it collapsed. Some believe that it collapsed just as it neared the end of construction, while others think it collapsed in an earthquake during Roman times. If the latter is true, then why didn't other pyramids in the area collapse during the earthquake? Also, if the Collapsed Pyramid did not crumble until centuries later, how then to explain the shape of another pyramid, built less than a mile away? It is called the Bent Pyramid, and its construction began while the Collapsed Pyramid was still under construction and during Sneferu's reign. Sneferu also built a third pyramid, the Red Pyramid, so called because of the pinkish hue of the sandstone used to construct it. The Bent Pyramid's angle of ascent started out at the steep angle of 52 degrees—the same as the Collapsed Pyramid—and then changed abruptly to the shallower and more stable angle of 43.5 degrees, as if its builders had suddenly learned an important lesson.

The Collapsed Pyramid's core is a stepped pyramid, but its casing stones rise at an angle of 52 degrees. Experts know this from examining the two-ton base casing stones that are still intact. Many experts believe that the idea to increase the pyramid's height, length of the base, and angle of accent came after much of the pyramid was already constructed. The fact that the casing stones do not sit on a hard stone foundation, like other pyramids, supports this view. Instead, the bottom stones are buried in the desert sand. Also, it is important to note that the casing stones are stacked to form horizontal joints or layers of stones.

To understand the significance of 52 degrees, it is worth remembering that the ancient Egyptians discovered π (pi). Pi is equal to the circumference of a circle divided by its diameter (or divided by two times its radius). Pi is a constant—it is always the same, regardless of the size of the circle. Although it is an irrational number, which cannot be expressed as the ratio of two integers, we frequently truncate it to the value of 3.14. The ancient Egyptians' value for it was 3.16, or the square of $\frac{8}{9} \times 2$.

It is not known exactly when the ancient Egyptians discovered pi, but they were fascinated by it and may have thought it had eternal or magical powers. The Collapsed Pyramid's designers decided to work the value of pi into the pyramid's very geometry.

To do so, they likened the perimeter of the pyramid to the circumference of a circle, and the height to the radius of the same circle. This established the angle of rise for the sides, which is 52 degrees. This geometry would eternally embed pi into the basic structure of the pyramid.

Starting at the bottom, limestone blocks with angled exterior surfaces were stacked on top of one another. As the casing work neared the top, the pressure on the limestone blocks near the bottom created a tremendous outward thrust. The sand was unable to resist the force. The blocks slipped along their horizontal joints and the pyramid collapsed suddenly and catastrophically.

Some Egyptologists believe that this is why the designers of the Bent Pyramid changed to the shallower and more stable angle of 43.5 degrees to finish the pyramid. Others believe the Bent Pyramid started to show signs of stress cracks and localized failures of its own, hence forcing the designers to change to the shallower angle.

It is believed that the Red Pyramid's construction started after the failure of the Collapsed Pyramid or after structural problems began to appear on the Bent Pyramid. It was built very quickly—completed in 17 years. Because the Chapel built against the pyramid's eastern face appears hastily finished, it is believed that the pyramid was finished near or just after the Pharaoh's death.

The Red Pyramid is the first true pyramid, with smooth sides rising at a constant angle of 43.22 degrees to a height of 343 feet. All pyramids after the Red Pyramid rise at the steeper angle of 52 degrees. They illustrate lessons learned from Pharaoh Sneferu's three pyramids. They are built on substantial stone bases that slope slightly inward, which makes the stone joints slope inward as well, giving them greater strength to resist horizontal outward thrusting forces. Also, casing stones are more carefully chiseled and fitted into place, providing more uniform load distribution.

The Hyatt Regency Disaster

The 750-room Hyatt Regency Hotel in Kansas City, Missouri, opened in July 1980. One of its main architectural features was its atrium lobby, a 50-foot-high glass-and-steel box. On its north side was the guest room tower, and on the south side was the so-called "function block," which contained conference and dining rooms. The guest tower and function block were connected by three elevated pedestrian walkways that passed through the atrium. The walkways hung from the atrium's steel roof trusses—one on the east side that connected the third floor of the tower with the third-floor function block, and two suspended walkways, one on top of the other, on the west side, connecting the second and fourth floors. Beneath the two suspended walkways on the west side was the atrium's cocktail bar and lounge.

On Friday, July 17, 1981, approximately 1,600 people were in the atrium listening to music and dancing. Many stood, listened, and watched from the walkways above. Suddenly an explosion rang out and the two walkways on the west side fell. Atrium windows shattered and sprinkler pipes broke. The walkways pancaked one atop the other as they crashed to the atrium floor. One hundred and fourteen people died and over 200 were injured.

Immediately, everyone suspected shoddy construction. The building was only one year old. Certainly, the disaster could not have been caused by a design flaw, everyone reasoned, not in this day and age. However, investigations conducted by the National Bureau of Standards showed otherwise. Indeed, it was a design error. The investigation revealed that during construction the contractor proposed a change to the suspension structure of the walkways, which was approved by the engineer (see Figure 7.5). The engineer failed to do the necessary calculations to verify

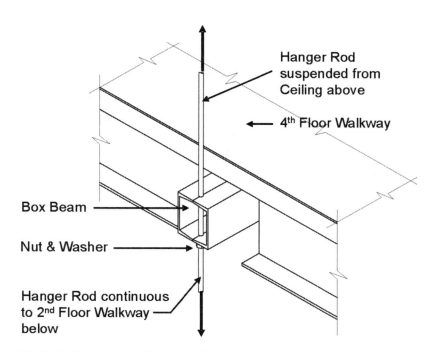

FIGURE 7.5 *Double-Decker Walkway as Designed.*

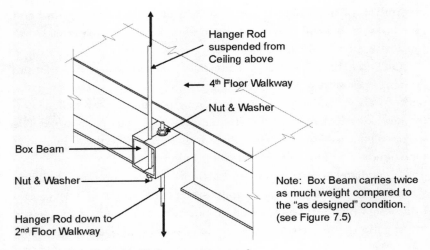

FIGURE 7.6 *Double-Decker Walkway as constructed.*

that the change could handle the design loads. The investigation also revealed that the original design would not have met the requirements of the building code (see Figure 7.6). The result was a design and construction process error that led to a terrible and deadly conclusion—the worst structural disaster in modern U.S. history.

The disaster again exposed the importance of redundancy in building structures. The investigation revealed that the cause of the disaster could be traced to one single connection at the mid-span of the fourth-floor walkway. One of the hanger rods that connected the walkway to the atrium roof trusses above pulled through its opening in the steel box beam that it supported. As soon as this one failure occurred, none of the other hangar-rod/box-beam connections could take the additional load. Those hangers also pulled through their holes in a progressive failure that resulted in the rapid, catastrophic, and fatal collapse of the walkways.

While the Hyatt Regency disaster is considered the worst structural disaster in modern U.S. history, it is not the worst progressive failure. That distinction belongs to the worst building disaster in American history: the 9/11 World Trade Center terrorist attack.

8

WORLD TRADE CENTER

For Americans who are old enough to remember, two events stick in their memories like no others. They remember where they were on December 7, 1941, when they heard about the Japanese attack on Pearl Harbor, and they know what they were doing on November 22, 1963, the day President John F. Kennedy was shot. Now there is a third event that all Americans will remember: the World Trade Center attack on September 11, 2001. Unlike the two earlier events, however, millions watched the horrific tragedy of 9/11 unfold on their television sets.

At 8:48 in the morning, Eastern Standard Time, a commercial jet airliner that had been hijacked by a small group of terrorists slammed into the north face of the 110-story North Tower of the World Trade Center (WTC) in New York City. The plane struck the tower between the 94th and 98th floors, traveling at an estimated speed of 470 miles per hour (mph). Immediately, fire erupted on the affected floors, and within minutes, television networks sent rush-hour traffic helicopters to circle the tower, transmitting live coverage of smoke pouring from the North Tower.

All New York City firefighters were called to the scene. With fire-fighting gear strapped to their backs, they ascended the tower's three stairwells and began to climb to fight the fire and rescue those trapped by the flames.

Fifteen minutes after the first plane struck, a second airplane suddenly appeared on television screens. Viewers watched in disbelief as the craft ploughed into the WTC's South Tower. It struck the east face of the tower between the 78th and 84th floors, traveling at a speed of approximately 590 mph. The plane's impact created a hellish fireball of jet fuel and sent pieces of the plane and the building raining down onto the streets below. Both towers billowed smoke as they burned. Onlookers below screamed as they helplessly watched victim after victim jump to their deaths in panic.

Then, incredibly, at 9:59 AM, only 56 minutes after it was struck, the South Tower fell, disintegrating before the eyes of terrified onlookers. Astonished, millions watched on television. Within seconds, the South Tower was a massive pile of smoke and rubble. Thirty minutes later—1 hour and 43 minutes after the first plane's impact—the North Tower collapsed, taking only a second or two longer than the South Tower to pancake into 500,000 tons of smoldering rubble.

The collapsing towers sent burning shrapnel flying into adjacent buildings. The U.S. Customs Building, the Winter Garden, and the South Plaza Building all suffered severe damage. Neighboring St. Nicholas Greek Orthodox Church was completely destroyed by falling debris. The steel-framed, 40-story Bankers Trust, the World Financial Center 3, and the Verizon Building suffered localized structural damage, but did not collapse. The 47-story WTC7 Building caught fire from falling debris and collapsed after burning out of control for seven hours. Ten buildings, totaling 30 million square feet of office space, were completely destroyed or suffered severe damage. (See Figure 8.1.)

The World Trade Center attack was the largest building disaster in New York City since the Triangle Shirtwaist Factory Fire in 1911. It was the greatest cataclysmic building tragedy ever witnessed by a worldwide audience. In less than two hours, over 2,700 people lost their lives. Incredibly, approximately 1 out of every 8 victims was a firefighter. There were approximately 15,000 office workers in the two towers at the time of the attack, less than half of its normal daytime occupancy. One in 7 of them died. Approximately 1,500 people were trapped in the towers above the crash floors. Only 18 of them managed to escape. Had the attack been an hour or two later, there would have been closer to 40,000 people in the towers and the death toll would have been many times worse.

FIGURE 8.1 *Remaining Section of World Trade Center Twin Tower, 2001. © Bob Krist/ CORBIS.*

Immediately after 9/11, the United States changed. Like the generation of Chicagoans who lived through the Great Fire and thereafter referred to events in their lives as "before the fire" and "after the fire," we as a country now use the terms "pre-9/11" and "post-9/11" to define two very different worlds.

September 11th has also started to affect how we build, though its full impact on the built environment has not yet been fully realized. How we design airports, subway systems, power plants, water treatment plants, and sports facilities are changing because of 9/11. In particular, lessons from the WTC Towers are changing how we design tall buildings.

INVESTIGATION OF THE TRAGEDY

No sooner had the towers hit the ground than laypeople and experts alike began to ask: How could the towers have collapsed so quickly? Once the towers started to fall, it took only about 11 seconds for their 1,360-foot-tall frames to collapse into smoldering heaps.[1] Had a modern-day Galileo dropped a ball from atop one of the towers as it began to collapse, the ball would have beaten the tower—with Galileo in it—to the ground by only a few seconds, assuming the much lighter ball did not buoy in the wind.[2]

Other questions troubling everyone were: Was the collapse of the towers inevitable? Did so many people have to die? In short, what went wrong? Modern steel-framed buildings are not supposed to fail like this. No other steel-framed building in the world had ever collapsed as the WTC Towers did.

The next day, September 12, 2001, the Federal Emergency Management Administration (FEMA) and the American Society of Civil Engineers (ASCE) talked about forming a Building Performance Study (BPS) Team to study the WTC disaster. A team of structural, civil, and fire protection engineers was assembled. After rescue operations were declared complete on October 7th, the BPS Team began its investigation.

The BPS Team sifted through wreckage onsite and in salvage yards. Photographs were taken and studied. Materials were removed and tested. Videos of the collapses were watched over and over for clues. Burned and twisted pieces of steel were examined. All of the towers' major steel components had been marked prior to construction in the 1970s. Identification markings on steel members were compared with construction shop drawings to determine their locations within the towers. Slowly, the puzzle merged into a picture.

As experts investigated and collected data, conspiracy theorists had already jumped to far-reaching conclusions. Bloggers argued that the airplanes alone could not have caused the towers to collapse. They likened the collapses to large-scale building demolition implosions, citing that the towers fell only slightly slower than a free-falling body—just like what happens when professional demolition contractors bring down buildings. They drew attention to the fact that no other steel-framed building hit by an airplane had ever collapsed.

To make their case, conspiracy theorists used as an example another famous skyscraper in New York City, the Empire State Building. The Empire State Building opened for business on May 1, 1931. Fourteen years later, near the end of World War II, it was struck by an airplane, but did not collapse.

On the foggy Saturday morning of July 28, 1945, a disoriented pilot of a ten-ton B-25 bomber drastically miscalculated the distance to New Jersey's Newark Airport. The pilot dropped out of the fog too soon and into downtown Manhattan. He managed to dodge a few tall buildings but then crashed headlong into the north wall of the Empire State Building between the 78th and 79th floors. Traveling at approximately 200 miles per hour, the plane ripped an 18-foot-long and 20-foot-high hole in the side of the building. (Figure 8.2.) The plane disintegrated inside. Airplane fuel and flames spewed out of the building and down the outside. Fuel also spilled forward into the building's interior. The plane's momentum carried one of the engines into the building's core and down an elevator shaft. A portion of the plane's fuselage and landing gear continued completely through the building, drilling through firewalls and stairwells and out the other side. The fiery parts flew across the street and landed on the roof of a building across the street.

Doused with fuel, the combustible office contents on the 78th and 79th floors erupted in flames. The fire burned so intensely that window glass and light fixture lenses melted into the shape of stalactites. Within minutes, firemen arrived. Using elevators to reach the fire, they extinguished it with relative ease. The plane's pilot, 2 crew members, and 11 building occupants died within moments after impact. Dozens of other people were injured.

While all the office contents in the area of the crash were destroyed by fire, structural damage to the building was minor. The Empire State Building was never in any jeopardy. The building opened on Monday morning for business, as usual. Floors involved in the fire were closed for repairs, but they opened again only three months later.

Conspiracy theorists argued that certainly the much newer and technologically advanced World Trade Center Towers would perform better if struck by an airplane than the much older Depression-era Empire State Building. Something even more diabolical than airplanes must have brought the towers to their knees and, for some reason, it was being covered up. While the BPS Team collected data and carefully

FIGURE 8.2 *A view of the hole in the 78th and 79th stories of the Empire State Building made by a U.S. Army Bomber flying in the fog. Part of the wreckage hangs from the 78th story, New York, July 28, 1945.* © *Bettmann/CORBIS.*

considered what their findings meant, the fingers of conspiracy bloggers were busy at their PCs, using the Internet to spread their disinformation: Perhaps additional explosives were used to destroy the towers.

Ockham's Razor, named after the 14th-century monk William of Ockham who first explained it, states that one should not unnecessarily create complexities to explain something. His reasoning has since become a guiding principle of both science and common sense. When faced with two alternatives to explain an outcome, it is better to choose the simpler of the two because it is more likely to be correct. As a general principle, the scientific method works better than the Rube Goldberg mousetrap approach to problem solving.

To begin with, controlled demolition contractors do not simply tie explosives to columns and push a plunger. They study the building carefully beforehand. They determine which structural components to destroy and in what order. Explosions are precisely timed, often milliseconds apart. Demolition experts remove facing materials from structural members, drill holes, and embed explosives. They cut key structural connections and partially saw cut through various structural members to weaken them and shape the way they want a building to collapse. All of this takes numerous calculations and weeks of preparation. In the case of the World Trade Center, thousands of explosives and miles of wiring would be necessary. The selective demolition, explosive devices, and wiring would all be in plain sight. On average, 40,000 people worked in the World Trade Center every day; somebody would have noticed. A cover-up would require the cooperation of tens of thousands of average citizens. The conspiracy theorists' argument stretched credulity and common sense.

On 9/11, Protec, a world-renowned independent demolition and explosives authority, had portable field seismographs in Manhattan monitoring ground vibrations at various construction sites for contractor liability purposes. Columbia University's Lamont-Doherty Earth Observatory in Palisades, New York, had permanent seismographs in operation. The seismographs recorded the ground-shaking collapses of both towers. Hours later they also recorded the collapse of WTC7 after it had burned out of control for seven hours. None of the seismographs recorded any vibrations consistent with explosions prior to recording the collapses of the structures.[3]

The BPS Team published its report in May 2002. Entitled *World Trade Center Building Performance Study: Data Collection, Preliminary Observations and Recommendations,* its Executive Summary explained:

> The purpose of this study was to examine the damage caused by [the 9/11 attack], collect data, develop an understanding of the response of each affected building, identify the causes of observed behavior and identify studies that should be performed. The immediate effects of the aircraft impacts on each tower, the spread of fires following the crashes, the fire-induced reduction of structural strength, and the mechanism that led to the collapse of each tower were studied.[4]

The report offered a more plausible explanation than the conspiracy theorists. The report concluded that it was not structural damage due to the airplane impacts that caused the towers to collapse. Rather, the impacts started fires that grew more intense, setting off chain reactions that eventually led to the failure of many of the towers' structural components. Severe overloading of the towers' structural systems caused progressive collapses of both towers.

By the time the BPS Team published its report, conspiracy theorists had so tainted the discussion that many citizens, particularly many families of the victims, clamored for FEMA to sponsor an additional study. On October 1, 2002, the National Institute of Standards and Technology (NIST) began a new study. Unlike the BPS study, which drew its conclusions mostly from forensic evidence, the NIST study developed a computer model, simulated the tragic event, and drew conclusions from computer simulations. In September 2005, the NIST published its findings and came to conclusions similar to the BPS study, although with a slightly different chain of events leading to the collapses, as explained in a moment. Both studies concluded that the collapses of the towers were caused by the airplane impacts, which started devastating chain reactions.

Everyone who watched the events unfold on television knows that the airplanes themselves did not destroy the towers. Had the first airplane destroyed the North Tower, it would have been a smoking pile of rubble before the television networks ever started transmitting coverage of the tragedy into our homes. Had the second plane caused the collapse, we would have watched the South Tower suddenly and catastrophically fall, just as the Federal Building in Oklahoma City had done six years earlier.

On the morning of April 19, 1995, homegrown terrorist Timothy McVeigh parked a rental truck filled with ammonium nitrate and fuel oil in front of the nine-story Alfred P. Murrah Federal Building in downtown Oklahoma City, Oklahoma. When the truck bomb exploded, it took only four seconds for most of the Federal Building to collapse. What remained of the building was structurally unsafe and later demolished. The incident killed 168 people and injured more than 500. Approximately 80 percent of the deaths and injuries were caused by the building's partial collapse, not the explosion.

The investigation afterward revealed that the truck bomb destroyed three adjacent ground-floor columns on the front of the building. The columns supported a critical girder, which supported the second story and all the other floors above. The girder had no backup support from any other building components. Once the columns supporting the girder were gone, the girder could not carry the additional weight over the greater span, nor could it lighten its load by transferring, or shedding, some of the load to adjacent members because there were none. The girder immediately super-overloaded and failed, bringing most of the building down with it.

How Design Affects Building Stability

Redundancy in structural systems is a bit like backup systems on a spacecraft; should a critical system or component of a system fail, there is another in place to help out in an emergency. There is a marvelous game called Jenga that illustrates the importance of redundancy in the design of tall buildings. The game starts with a tower made of rectangular-shaped wood blocks, three blocks forming each tier or story. The object of the game is to remove as many blocks as possible without collapsing the tower. When a block is removed, the weight of the Jenga tower above quickly redistributes to adjacent blocks, and the tower remains stable. Eventually, the last redundant block is removed. When the block after that is removed, the tower crashes down.

After the Oklahoma City bombing, engineers, architects, and government and code officials debated whether to require certain new buildings that might be attractive targets for terrorists—for example, government buildings with many employees—to have some degree of blast resistance, given the nature of our changing world. In addition, there was discussion about requiring greater redundancy for key structural components. Neither discussion brought forth any changes to the building code.

The World Trade Center did not fail in the manner of the Federal Building in Oklahoma City. Both WTC Towers remained standing after the airplanes' impacts. According to the testimonies of survivors, the towers swayed after impact, but righted themselves again. The airplanes severed several columns, as many as 15 in the North Tower,[5] but building loads quickly shifted to adjacent columns. The BPS report stated:

> Following the aircraft impact into the building [the North Tower], the structure was able to successfully redistribute the building weight to the remaining elements and to maintain a stable

condition. This return to a stable condition is suggested by the pre-liminary analyses and also evidenced by the fact that the structure remained standing.[6]

While the additional load may have exceeded the adjacent columns' design loads, the columns were not overloaded to the point of failure. Redundancy in the towers' structural systems kept them upright after the airplanes' impacts. However, the impacts started domino effects that led to utter catastrophic failures.

For a domino effect to work, components must be arranged in a certain way, or else the chain reaction is broken. To understand how the dominoes were arranged in the 9/11 WTC disaster, it helps to go back 40 years and look briefly at the design of the World Trade Center.

The World Trade Center was designed in the 1960s by Minoru Yamasaki, who also designed Pruitt-Igoe. Construction began in 1968. The North Tower opened in December 1970 and the South Tower in January 1972. At the time, the World Trade Center was the tallest build-ing in the world.

Many architectural critics and laypeople hated the World Trade Center. *Newsweek* called it the "Towers of Mammon," claiming that "the only way to grasp the enormity and ugliness" was from the air.[7] Architectural historian Lewis Mumford called it "purposeless gigantism and technological exhibitionism and megatechnic chaos."[8] The most acidic comment may have come from architectural critic Charles Jencks. Focusing on the towers' plain and monotonous façades, he wrote:

> A musical figure, repeated at length, such as that in Bolero, acts not just as a form of mental torture but as a pacifier. Repetitive architecture can put you to sleep. Both Mussolini and Hitler used it as a form of thought control knowing that before people can be coerced they first have to be hypnotized and then bored.[9]

Yamasaki had a very different view of his work. He called the World Trade Center "a living symbol of man's dedication to world peace."[10] In 1966, while still designing the World Trade Center, he explained his design philosophy to architect and author Paul Heyer:

> There are few very influential architects who sincerely believe that all buildings must be "strong." The word "strong" in this context

seems to connote "powerful"—that is, each building should be a monument to the virility of our society.[11]

For many years after their completion, the World Trade Center Towers suffered from high vacancy rates. Eventually, however, New Yorkers grew to accept them. Because they stood much taller than any of their neighbors, the twin towers became a prominent and recognizable part of the New York City skyline and a symbol of America's economic strength.

September 11th was not the first time the World Trade Center suffered a terrorist attack. On February 26, 1993, terrorists parked a van loaded with 1,300 pounds of explosives in the World Trade Center's underground parking garage. The homemade bomb's ingredients included sodium cyanide to increase its lethalness. At 12:17 PM, the bomb was detonated. The explosion resulted in the deaths of 6 people and injury to more than 1,000. The explosion severed electrical and telephone lines, including electricity to the building's emergency lighting and communication systems. Black smoke laced with cyanide gas filled the stairwells, making it very difficult for the building's thousands of occupants to evacuate. Smoke inhalation and respiratory problems were common injuries.

The 1993 WTC terrorist attack pointed out weaknesses in the building's emergency systems. Improvements were made to the building's emergency communications and lighting systems. Stairwells were retrofitted with ventilation systems to better expel smoke. Fortunately, the building suffered no permanent structural damage.

Perhaps the most telling safety lesson from the 1993 attack had to do with how people exit tall buildings in an emergency. It took more than five hours for all WTC occupants to exit. Had the explosion caused life-threatening structural damage, there would have been a great need to evacuate the towers in far less time. Contrary to what the layperson might think, the exit systems of skyscrapers are not designed to evacuate everyone simultaneously. The assumption is that a building's fire walls, fire doors, and fire sprinkler systems will contain incidents such as fires and keep them from spreading and becoming a buildingwide problem. Skyscrapers are designed with areas of refuge. The idea is that occupants will retreat to these protected areas and wait for rescue. On 9/11, however, the simultaneous and complete evacuation of both towers was required.

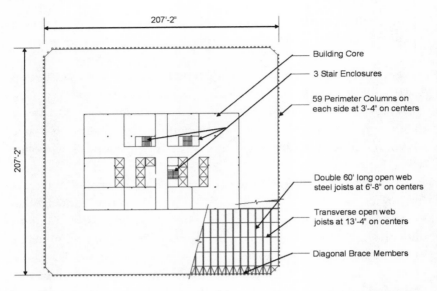

207'-2"

207'-2"

Building Core

3 Stair Enclosures

59 Perimeter Columns on
each side at 3'-4" on centers

Double 60' long open web
steel joists at 6'-8" on centers

Transverse open web
joists at 13'-4" on centers

Diagonal Brace Members

FIGURE 8.3 *Diagrammatic Plan of Typical Floor of the World Trade Center Towers.*

The structural system of the World Trade Center's Twin Towers was innovative and unlike any other. In light of the lessons learned from 9/11, it is unlikely ever to be repeated. The structural system for both towers involved a row of closely spaced exterior columns and a ring of columns around the tower's central core. The core contained elevators, building utilities, three stair towers, and the fire sprinkler systems' main supply pipes, called standpipes or risers. The exterior and interior columns were tied together at every floor with thick steel plates running horizontally, called spandrel plates. The close spacing of the exterior columns gave the towers their strong vertical look. From a distance, the towers' narrow windows between the columns were barely visible.

The exterior columns and core columns were connected by pairs of 60-foot-long open web steel joists—called long-span joists—spaced 6 feet, 6 inches apart. Cross-joists running in the opposite direction braced the long-span joists every 13 feet, 4 inches. (See Figure 8.3.) At the exterior columns, the top horizontal components of the long-span joists—called top chords—sat on angle-shaped support brackets. The angle support brackets were held in place by two $\frac{5}{8}$-inch diameter bolts in slotted holes to allow the connection to move. The bottom chords of the long-span joists were connected to the exterior columns with visco-elastic dampers and held in place with two 1-inch diameter bolts. The stretchable visco-elastic dampers reduced the perception of building motion caused by the wind.

The tower floors, constructed of metal decking covered with 4 inches of lightweight concrete fill, were supported by the long-span joists. At regular intervals, the diagonal web of the long-span joists protruded above the top chord of the joists and then bent back down, forming an inverted "u" that was cast into the lightweight concrete floors, locking the floors and long-span joists together, strengthening the joist/floor assembly by a process called composite action. The columns, spandrel plates, and long-span joists were encapsulated with spray-on fireproofing to protect them from fire. Fireproofing was applied thick enough to give the structural components a three-hour fire rating as required by the building code. A fire rating roughly means how long it takes a fire to burn through.

The original fireproofing contained asbestos. It was soft and could be damaged easily by impact. In the 1980s, the asbestos fireproofing was abated through a combination of encapsulation and removal and replacement with fireproofing material that did not contain asbestos.

The walls that enclosed the core were framed with metal studs and two layers of $\frac{5}{8}$-inch-thick fire-rated gypsum board (or Sheetrock, as many people call it, although Sheetrock is a brand name). The stairwells were also enclosed with metal studs and two layers of gypsum board, giving them a two-hour fire rating, as required by the code. The metal stud and gypsum board system is called drywall. Drywall weighs much less than concrete or masonry, the materials historically and typically used to enclose building cores before the World Trade Center was designed and built.

Weight is a significant factor in the design and construction of tall buildings. Keeping a building's weight down makes it easier to build and less expensive. In addition, reducing the number of interior columns increases the rentable square footage. Fewer columns provide more flexibility in the layout of office spaces. The World Trade Center designers went to significant and pioneering lengths to reduce the building's weight and increase the flexibility and rentable area of its 110 floors. Steel framing, long-span open web joists, spray-on fireproofing, and a drywall building core all contributed greatly toward achieving these goals.

This design also made the World Trade Center Towers different from other tall buildings previously built. Before the World Trade Center, the typical skyscraper was designed with a forest of columns. Columns were typically spaced approximately 30 feet apart in both directions through-out all the floors of the building. The major structural members, such as steel columns, beams, and girders, were encased in hard concrete or cement plaster. Floors were frequently poured-in-place concrete.

The Empire State Building is a typical skyscraper. When the B-26 bomber hit the building in 1945, the airplane never made it to the core, although some pieces of the bomber did, as explained earlier. Interior columns, encased in concrete, were in the way. The office contents on the impact floors burned, but the concrete casing protected the encased steel structure from the heat of the fire. When the fire burned out, the structure was intact, except for a relatively small portion of it where the airplane struck. It was easily repaired.

When originally built, the WTC Towers did not have fire sprinkler systems. Around 1990, the towers were retrofitted with automatic fire sprinkler systems. The fire sprinkler system risers were located in each of the towers' three stairwells.

The World Trade Center was the first nonmilitary/nonnuclear-industry building designed to withstand the impact of an airplane. The airplane chosen for the design standard was the Boeing 707. Although not required by any code requirement, the WTC's owner, the New York Port Authority, took this added precaution, cognizant of the 1945 plane crash into the Empire State Building. The criteria assumed that the 707 would be attempting to land at a nearby airport, traveling at a landing speed of around 180 mph, and that its fuel would be all but spent. Consequently, fuel from the airplane was not taken into consideration in the design. As stated earlier, the planes that struck the North and South Towers were traveling at speeds of 470 and 590 mph, respectively, and each may have been carrying as much as 10,000 gallons of fuel.[12]

Possible Causes of the World Trade Centers' Collapse

The BPS report speculates that when the first airplane struck the North Tower, as many as 15 exterior columns may have been destroyed.[13] It is not known how many open web steel joists were destroyed, but the NIST's computer model suggests that the airplane may have plowed through and destroyed many of them. In addition, the impact knocked off or damaged sprayed-on fireproofing on many of the remaining joists, columns, and other structural components in the immediate vicinity of the impact.

Once past the exterior columns, there was nothing to stop the airplane until it slammed into the columns at the building's core. When the plane struck the core, it caved in the drywall partitions of the three stair towers and broke the fire sprinkler risers, sealing the fate of all the building occupants above the crash floors.

The North Tower swayed from the impact. As it did, the building loads redistributed to adjacent structural members, as explained above. The airplane's fuel started an enormous fire. The BPS report speculates that the fuel was probably consumed in 5 minutes or less.[14] However, the fuel set the building's contents on fire. The fire burned out of control until the tower collapsed 1 hour and 43 minutes later.

Conspiracy theorists claimed that a fire fed by normal building contents could never have achieved a temperature high enough to melt steel. If the temperature was not hot enough to melt steel, then something else must have been responsible for the building's collapse. This is not true.

The hottest an air-fed diffused fire can burn is approximately 1,800°F. However, most normal building fires burn at lower temperatures, in the range of 1,200°F. Steel melts around 2,800°F. But steel does not have to melt in order to fail. Steel begins to yield, that is, elongate and lose strength, at much lower temperatures. At 1,200°F, it loses approximately one-half its strength.[15] In addition, steel twists, bends, and buckles when subjected to high temperatures. Long-span steel joists are considerably susceptible to sagging and buckling when subjected to high heat and high loading conditions. On 9/11, the WTC's long-span joists began to deflect and sag under the severe heat and loading conditions. As they sagged, they pulled with ever-increasing inward force on the exterior columns.

The BPS Team and the NIST Team came to different conclusions about what happened next. The BPS study speculates that one by one the two bolts in the slotted holes that fastened each long-span joist to the exterior columns failed. One by one, the joists fell. This transferred additional load onto the already overstressed, remaining long-span joists, and their bolts gave way. They also fell. All the while, the fire continued to weaken the Towers' columns, with their fireproofing destroyed or partially destroyed. Eventually, enough of the floor system around the area of impact failed and the weight of the floors above the crash became too much. Instantaneously, the sudden impact and great weight super-overloaded the building's structure, and the building pancaked, plummeting to the ground in a process called progressive failure.

The Journal of the Minerals, Metals and Materials Society (JOM), cognizant of the BPS findings, explained the collapse this way:

> As the joists on one or two of the most heavily burned floors gave way and the . . . columns began to bow outward, the floors above them also fell. The floor below (with its 1,300 t[ton] design capacity) could not support the roughly 45,000 t of ten floors (or more) above. . . . This started the domino effect that caused the buildings to collapse.[16]

The NIST study came to a slightly different conclusion. The NIST's computer modeling suggested that the bolted connections did not fail. Instead, the long-span joists sagged more and more, pulling the fire-weakened exterior columns inward, bowing them as much as a few feet. Finally, the columns along the entire exterior face of the tower snapped, exploding into pieces, causing the towers to collapse.

The NIST report answered the conspiracy theorists, stating:

> NIST found no corroborating evidence for alternative hypotheses suggesting that the WTC towers were brought down by controlled demolition using explosives planted prior to September 11, 2001. NIST also did not find any evidence that missiles were fired at or hit the towers. Instead, photographs and videos from several angles clearly showed that the collapse initiated at the fire and impact floors and the collapse progressed from the initiating floors downward, until the dust clouds obscured the view.[17]

The Freedom Tower

Soon after 9/11, the site of the World Trade Center became known as "Ground Zero." There was quite a bit of discussion about what to build in place of the towers. There were those who thought it should be turned into a memorial. Others wanted a park. Still others wanted buildings that were not quite so tall. They argued that the World Trade Center was a mistake to begin with and should not be rebuilt. Others wanted to replace the towers with an even grander tower. Eventually, this view won out.

The plan for Ground Zero is to build four towers varying in size from 58 to 70 stories in height. The crown jewel will be a mammoth tower, the Freedom Tower, the tallest skyscraper in the world. Although only 70 stories, its grand sloping roof will ascend to a height of 1,776 feet. In an attempt to ensure that it will always remain the tallest, an antenna will be placed on top, making it 2,000 feet tall.

At the unveiling of the model in December 2003, New York Governor George Pataki said:

> We will build it in honor of the memories of the heroes we lost. We will build it to show the world that freedom will always triumph over terror and that we will face the 21st century and beyond with tremendous confidence.[18]

At the time of this writing, the architects for the project are Daniel Libeskind and David Childs of the architectural firm Skidmore, Owings, and Merrill. Libeskind is the project's master planner and the New York Port Authority's architect. Childs works for the developer Larry Silverstein. The project will include 2.6 million square feet and cost an estimated $1.5 billion to construct, a staggering $2,000 per square foot!

Childs commented that the Freedom Tower

> must be iconic. . . . Simple and pure in its form, a memorable form, that would proclaim the resiliency and the spirit of our democracy.[19]

The Freedom Tower is not without its critics. Many architects and planners object to it. If the democratic spirit means build big, tall, and out of scale in comparison to the surroundings, then the Freedom Tower certainly delivers. The artist's conception shows the building rising well beyond the height of its neighbors, like the World Trade Center Towers, lording over them as if placed out of scale in a photo montage. Susan S. Fainstein, a professor of urban planning at Columbia University, commented that the "Freedom Tower is a disastrous idea that should be scratched."[20] There is concern among many that downtown New York will experience the same problem it had after the World Trade Center first opened—a glut of office space—because of reluctance to occupy another attractive terrorist target.

LESSONS AND RECOMMENDATIONS

There are a number of lessons about building design and safety from the World Trade Center disaster. The lessons suggest various ways of improving building performance to prevent or delay building collapse and making it possible for more people to safely evacuate buildings in a disaster.

The NIST proposed 30 recommendations as a result of its study of the towers' collapses. Some of the NIST's recommendations addressed improvements in emergency preparedness, response, communication, and training. Many, however, were suggestions for improving the design of buildings 20 stories and taller. The NIST's recommendations fall into the following general groups:

- Increase structural integrity of tall buildings and thereby reduce the likelihood of progressive failure
- Improve the fire resistance of the structural systems of tall buildings and thereby increase the time available for emergency response, firefighting, and building evacuation
- Improve the performance of fireproofing materials, particularly their adhesion capabilities and resistance to impact
- Improve the reliability and redundancy of fire suppression systems (fire sprinkler systems) so that if one part of the fire suppression system is damaged, the system can still function, at least partially
- Improve building exiting systems to reduce the time it takes to evacuate in an emergency and improve the likelihood that everyone can exit during a building-wide emergency

Currently, the International Code Council (ICC), the writers of the *International Building Code* (IBC), is considering a variety of new code provisions for the IBC based on lessons learned from 9/11 and the NIST recommendations. Following is a list of ten significant building design recommendations under consideration for inclusion in future building codes:

1. *Increase the independence of stairwells.* Although the stairwells in both WTC Towers were separated by the required code distances, all stairwells were located in the towers' central cores (see Figure 8.4). When the impacts of the airplanes destroyed the cores, they also

destroyed the stairwells. One of the stairwells in the South Tower was only partially destroyed. This allowed a few of the hundreds trapped above the crash floors to escape by pushing their way past broken drywall partitions and burning debris as they descended the stairs. In the North Tower, all three stairwells were destroyed. Although not yet a code requirement, the designers of the new 57-story 7WTC Building have increased the separation between stairwells. 7WTC is the skyscraper currently under construction to replace WTC7, which collapsed after burning for seven hours. 7WTC is scheduled to open in the spring of 2007.

Stairwells of the new 7WTC are about 110 feet apart, located at opposite ends of the building's circulation core. This reduces the likelihood that both stairwells would be compromised in a disaster, giving building occupants a greater chance to exit safely. In addition, the size of stair landings in the 7WTC stair enclosures are larger than required by current code. This provides more room for those exiting from above to get past those exiting through corridor doors opening onto the stair landings. It also offers a safer place of refuge for those in wheelchairs to wait for rescue.

2. *Increase the strength of building utility cores.* When the airplanes penetrated the towers' cores, they not only destroyed the stairwells, but they also broke the fire sprinkler system risers. They cut off electrical power and rendered all the elevators useless. Drywall is easy to destroy; a hole can easily be made in it with a hammer or sharp object such as a ballpoint pen. Building cores should be hardened to provide better resistance to impact. The core of the Freedom Tower will be concrete. The concrete will be protected by steel cabling to form a strong protective net.

3. *Increase the number and width of exit stairwells.* During the World Trade Center disaster, the building occupants exiting down the stairwells thwarted the firefighters efforts to get up the same stairwells. Firefighters carrying their equipment made it necessary for those evacuating to turn sideways to pass firefighters. This contributed to congestion in the stairwells and resulted in the loss of precious time. Wider stairwells or fewer occupants in the stairwells would make it easier for those descending to pass by those ascending. The ICC's proposed change, *G71—Additional*

Exit Stair, would increase the number of stairwells required in buildings taller than 420 feet (roughly 25 to 30 stories in height) by one additional stairwell. The number of stairwells required in buildings and their overall width is determined by the number of occupants. In general, three stairwells are required when the number of occupants per story exceeds 500 people, and four are required when the occupant load is over 1,000 people. The proposed code change would require four stairwells when the occupant load is greater than 500 and five when the occupant load exceeds 1,000. As the writers of *G71* explained:

> This proposed change is intended to enable rapid full evacuation of very tall buildings by ensuring that ongoing and critical firefighting activity does not reduce the total required exit capacity needed to evacuate the remaining occupants of the building.[21]

The designers of 7WTC employed a similar approach. After determining that the code-required width for their exit stairs needed to be 4 feet, 9 inches minimum, 7WTC designers increased the widths of their exit stairs to 5 feet, 6 inches.[22]

4. *Provide crossover floors.* Current building codes address exiting from floors into stairwells. They establish standards for the widths of stairs and the fire rating of stairwells, but they do not adequately address what happens if a stairwell is blocked below, preventing safe exit. Fire-rated cross-corridor floors located at lower floors could solve this problem by allowing building occupants to safely exit the stairwell at certain designated floors and reenter another stairwell and continue exiting to the street. The design of 7WTC employs a crossover corridor at one of the lower floors, allowing occupants to exit from any side of the building that they choose.

5. *Improve the fire rating and robustness of stair enclosures.* Current building codes require stairwells to have a two-hour fire rating. Future code provisions may increase this to three hours to give building occupants more time to exit in safety. In addition, stair enclosures should be strong enough to resist some degree of external force. Currently, there are no code provisions that require a stair enclosure to have any structural strength other than what is necessary to hold up under normal loading conditions. An ICC member commented that the

stair enclosures of the WTC were destroyed by an aircraft impact. Far lesser events, such as a gas explosion or a vehicle impact (on lower floors) can destroy a stair enclosure, especially when one considers that the Code contains no structural criteria at all. Any structural robustness that existing stair shaft enclosures have is a by-product of the fire rating process; a process that was never intended to provide structural integrity.[23]

The ICC's proposed change *G73—Exit Enclosure Integrity* would establish a two-pound-per-square-inch load resistance standard for exit enclosures.

6. *Improve the integrity of fire sprinkler systems.* The airplanes' impacts severed the WTC's fire sprinkler main risers, rendering the fire sprinkler system useless. 7WTC employs two independent fire risers serving alternating floors. This way, if one is damaged, the other can continue to serve every other floor. The ICC's proposed change to the International Fire Code, *F221—Sprinkler Riser Design,* would increase the redundancy and therefore the reliability of fire sprinkler systems for tall buildings. The proposal would require at least two separate fire sprinkler water supply risers in each vertical zone for buildings over 420 feet in height.

7. *Improved fireproofing of steel structural members.* The fireproofing material that protected the WTC's steel structural system was soft and broke off easily on impact. Because it was lightweight, it was used in lieu of heavier fireproofing materials. Although concrete or cement plaster fireproofing is heavier than the spray-on fireproofing, it is much tougher and more resistant to damage. Consequently, we may see greater use of concrete and cement plaster for fireproofing in the future. In addition, advances will undoubtedly be made in sprayed-on fireproofing, improving both its adhesion and resistance to impact.

8. *Provide greater mass for major structural components.* The use of long-span open web steel joists in the WTC Towers reduced the number of columns and consequently increased the rentable area and its flexibility. Long-span joists are lightweight and difficult to fireproof. The ICC's proposed code change, *S5—Disproportionate Collapse,* would increase the weight and robustness of floor framing members and columns in tall buildings. Structural systems

with greater robustness would enhance their ability to resist impact and fire, and "guard against the possibility of collapse, property loss, and casualties that are disproportionate to the original damaging event."[24]

9. *Pressurized stairwells.* Pressurized stairwells will prevent smoke from entering stairwells when stair doors are opened. When many people are exiting, stair doors are often held open for a long period of time. As smoke enters the stairwell and rises, those exiting from above are often exiting into a smoke filled atmosphere. Pressured stairwells will prevent this.

10. *Initiate a structural frame approach to fire resistance.* Currently, building codes establish different fire-rating requirements for different structural components within a building's overall structural system. The World Trade Center disaster illustrated the interdependency of these various members, calling into question the wisdom of considering them as separate and independent elements. For this reason, the NIST proposed an overall structural system approach for establishing fire-resistance ratings.

Although all of the recommendations listed above will improve the safety of tall buildings, it is doubtful that all will be implemented. For example, the ICC's proposed code—changes as discussed in numbers 3, 5, 6, and 8 above—have already run into resistance. The ICC held its annual Code Development Hearings from September 20 through October 1, 2006. During the hearings, more than 2,000 proposed code changes were debated and acted on. Proposed changes *G71—Additional Exit Stair, G73—Exit Enclosure Integrity, F221—Fire Riser Design,* and *S5—Disproportionate Collapse* were disapproved. Disapproval does not necessarily mean a proposal's permanent demise. All disapproved ICC proposed changes automatically enter a public comment period and may subsequently be reworked, improved, and possibly approved sometime in the future.

If the history of disaster planning is any indication, we will only implement some of the ten recommendations listed above—the easier, more expedient, less costly, and politically palatable ones. The rest we will not, although some future disaster may someday prove that we should have. Such is the course of our centuries-old method of disaster planning.

9

HURRICANE KATRINA

Watching the Hurricane Katrina disaster unfold was a bit like watching an elephant through a picket fence. The nearness and enormity of it made it difficult to fully comprehend. It was the largest natural disaster in American history. More than a year and a half afterwards, we are still picking up the pieces, and we are still emotionally involved. People's lives are still in turmoil. Many are frustrated, disgusted, and incensed that such a tragedy was possible in the United States of America. It will take years, but eventually the disaster will recede far enough away to be put in perspective. So for now, final conclusions about Katrina will have to wait.

This much is known, however: On August 29, 2005, Hurricane Katrina plowed a wide path of destruction, decimating thousands of buildings along a 140-mile-wide stretch of the Gulf of Mexico coastline, extending from Dauphin Island, Alabama, to New Orleans, Louisiana. No one knows what the total cost of recovery will be. Estimates range from $125 to $200 billion. If history is any judge, it will probably cost much more.

Katrina was the third most deadly natural disaster in U.S. history, killing an estimated 1,600 people, placing it behind the 1900 Galveston Storm (8,000–10,000 dead) and the 1928 Ochecheebe Hurricane (2,500 dead). Along the Mississippi, Katrina picked up fishing vessels and barges and tossed them like toy boats into one another and into marshlands. Along the Gulf Coast, it did the same with casino barges, washing them ashore and into other buildings unfortunate enough to be in the wrong place. Katrina flooded 80 percent of New Orleans, a city of approximately 180 square miles with a population of half a million. It destroyed over 300,000 single-family residences, 40,000 apartments, and damaged an additional 300,000 structures. Over one and a half million people were evacuated. Tens of thousands were left living in a state of limbo and turmoil.

This much is also clear: The tragedy of Katrina was not the sole work of a hurricane. The fingerprints of man are all over the disaster. Government failed at all levels. In the immediate aftermath, thousands of New Orleanians were left helplessly stranded on rooftops, bridges, freeway overpasses, and in the New Orleans Superdome as local, state, and federal government officials procrastinated, made excuses, argued, and played political games, illustrating their lack of preparedness and apparent insensitivity to the misery of tens of thousands affected by the disaster.

It took a long time to set up all the dominoes that led to the Katrina disaster. Poor planning, poor judgment, bad decisions, and procrastination over the course of decades set up the tragedy. Generations of unplanned growth combined with an inadequate, poorly designed, poorly managed, and poorly engineered flood prevention system made Katrina much more devastating than it ever would have been without man's missteps. If we are to learn from Katrina, we must take a hard look at ourselves.

NEW ORLEANS

New Orleans was founded in 1718 by Jean-Baptiste Le Moyne, Sieur de Bienville of the French Mississippi Company, a French colonial trading company. He located the original settlement on a narrow, crescent-shaped sliver of high ground along the winding banks of the Mississippi River, hence New Orleans's nickname, the Crescent City. Bienville picked the site because of its proximity to a Native American trading portage—a narrow overland route connecting the Mississippi River with Lake Ponchartrain and Lake Borgne. He also chose the site because he thought it was far enough inland from the Gulf of Mexico to be protected from hurricanes. He was wrong.

One year after Bienville founded the settlement, a hurricane destroyed most it. Undaunted, he had a new city designed by his engineers, Le Blond de la Tour and Adrien de Pauger. Construction of the 7-block by 11-block area known as the French Quarter began in 1721. Bienville named the city La Nouvelle-Orléans in honor of the Prince Regent of France, Louis Phillipe, Duke of Orléans. Streets were named in honor of Catholic saints and royal houses of France. Bourbon Street is not named after the drink; it is named after the Bourbon dynasty that ruled France at the time.

Like all cities built of wood, New Orleans was prone to fires. Between the 1720s and 1760s, New Orleans experienced many. In addition, the hot and humid climate contributed to continual mold and dry-rot problems. In 1763, New Orleans was sold to the Spanish, who instituted tougher building requirements. Roofs had to be clay tile and walls had to be constructed of brick. Today, much of the architecture of the old French Quarter dates from this Spanish period. In 1801, the French regained control. Hence, New Orleans has a French and Spanish history, making it unique among major U.S. cities. In 1803, Napoleon sold New Orleans to the United States as part of the Louisiana Purchase.

By the late 19th century, New Orleans began to outgrow its namesake shape. Portions of Lake Pontchartrain were filled. New Orleanians built levees, drained and cleared Mississippi delta marshland, and constructed buildings in low-lying areas. Throughout the early 20th century, more swampland was drained and built on.

In the 1920s, the area known as the Ninth Ward was bisected by the Industrial Canal. Ever since, the downstream portion, cut off from the rest of New Orleans by the canal, has been called the Lower Ninth Ward. Within the past 50 years, additional portions of the Lower Ninth Ward were drained and occupied.

Levees and Floodwalls

The greater New Orleans area is protected by about 350 miles of levees that follow spaghetti-like routes. They twist and turn as they meander along the banks of the Mississippi River, the shore of Lake

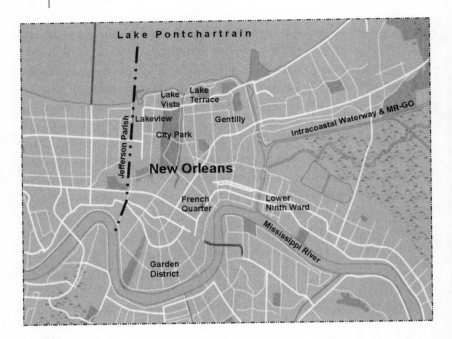

FIGURE 9.1 *Map of New Orleans.*

Ponchartrain, and the sides of narrow drainage canals. In some places, New Orleans's levees are technically floodwalls. Levees are constructed with earth, while floodwalls are made of steel and reinforced concrete. Floodwalls require far less land to construct than levees. Bases of flood-walls are generally about 2-feet wide compared to an earthen levee, which requires 4 feet in width for every 1 foot in height. A 10-foot high earthen levee requires a base 40-feet wide. Where space was tight, floodwalls were constructed. In some areas of New Orleans, floodwalls were built on top of levees to increase the levees' height without having to widen the base.

Most of New Orleans is particularly vulnerable to flooding, because much of it is below sea level and lower than its neighboring bodies of water, the Mississippi River, Lake Ponchartrain, and Lake Borgne. New Orleans is just about surrounded by water. After the original New Orleans settlement was destroyed in 1719 by a hurricane, the engineer Le Blond de la Tour tried to convince Bienville to move the settlement to higher ground, but Bienville did not listen. New Orleanians have been fighting water ever since.

Without protective levees and floodwalls, most of New Orleans would be under water. During Hurricane Katrina, the residential areas along Lake Pontchartrain—Lakeview, Lake Terrace, and Lake Vista—all flooded. These three residential areas were all once marshland or part of Lake Pontchartrain.

Pumps and Polders

Heavy rains would flood New Orleans, too, if it were not for the city's storm water pumping systems. When it rains, rainwater drains to pumping stations located throughout the city (See Figure 9.2). The stations pump rainwater through large-diameter pipes over levees and floodwalls into the drainage canals and Lake Ponchartrain.

The levees and pumping stations divide New Orleans into something akin to a segmented bowl. For centuries, New Orleanians have called their city "the bowl," or, at times, employing their distinctive pallbearer brand of humor, "the damp grave." The Dutch have another name for the segments of the bowl; they call them "polders."

Polders are low-lying areas of land protected by continuous walls around their perimeters. The Dutch are very good at designing, building, and maintaining polder systems. Their system of polders is a marvelous state-of-the-art engineering achievement. The very survival of the Netherlands depends on holding back the sea.

FIGURE 9.2 *View of large diameter storm discharge pipes. These pumps are located along the west side of the Lower Ninth Ward. They convey pumped storm water over an earthen levee and through a concrete floodwall, discharging storm water into the Industrial Canal. Photo by author, 2006.*

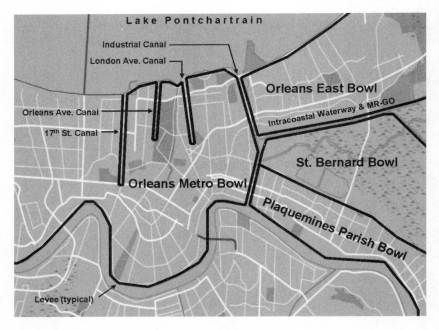

FIGURE 9.3 *Map of New Orleans showing the City's Four Main Polders.*

Not so with the United States. While a few cities and regions in the United States depend on levees to protect them from flooding, our country as a whole does not. Consequently, the design and maintenance of levee systems are, at best, regional problems, not a national priority. Levee funding must compete with everything else for federal attention. In May 1995, after six people in New Orleans tragically died in a massive rainstorm, Congress authorized the Southeast Louisiana Urban Flood Control Project (SELA). SELA was a ten-year, $430 million Corps of Engineers' project to shore-up New Orleans's levees and build new pumping stations. In 2003, with over $250 million of work still to be completed, federal funding was reduced to a trickle due to other competing federal priorities.

New Orleans is divided into four main polders. Within these main polders are smaller polders or sub-basins. In 1965, Hurricane Betsy flooded New Orleans. In its aftermath, the U.S. Army Corps of Engineers began a lengthy process of bolstering New Orleans's four main polders: Orleans Metro Bowl, Orleans East Bowl, St. Bernard Bowl, and Plaquemines Parish Bowl. (See Figure 9.3.)

Downtown New Orleans, including the famous French Quarter and Garden District, are within the Orleans Metro Bowl. The levees and floodwalls that protect the polder hold back Lake Pontchartrain to the north and the Mississippi River along the south edge. In Figure 9.3, notice the long canals that extend well into the Orleans Metro Bowl and along its west side. These canals are drainage canals, lined with floodwalls. From west to east, the canals are named 17th Street Canal, Orleans Avenue Canal, and London Avenue Canal. At the ends of the canals, farthest away from Lake Pontchartrain, pump stations pump rainwater into the canals. The canals are, in effect, fingerlike extensions of Lake Pontchartrain.

After Hurricane Katrina, the American Society of Civil Engineers (ASCE) conducted an investigation of New Orleans's levees and flood-walls. A Dutch member of the investigation team wondered, "Why in the world would you [meaning New Orleans] invite the enemy deep inside your own camp?"[1] The answer is that New Orleans did not intend to. The pump station locations and canals are old, dating from the early 20th century. When the stations and canals were constructed, they were at the edge of the city. The land between the ends of the canals and the current shoreline of Lake Pontchartrain is a combination of drained swamp and fill. The city simply grew beyond the boundaries that pro-vided the original logic for the drainage canals. The outmoded design was never corrected.

New Orleans's system of polders is like a chain. It is only as strong as its weakest link. Any portion of it that is too low or too weak jeopar-dizes the integrity of the entire system. Any overtopping or breaching of levees or floodwalls can cause flooding, in some cases as severe as if there were no polders at all.

MR-GO

New Orleans is a port city. Measured by tonnage, it is the largest port in the United States and the fifth largest in the world. Loaded with oil and other goods, ships navigate the Mississippi River traveling between New Orleans and the Gulf of Mexico and points beyond. Like many industries, time is money in the shipping business. The faster ships can get through the Mississippi River delta and into the Gulf, the better. To that end, Congress approved the River and Harbor Act in 1956, which included provisions for the construction of a shorter route from the Gulf of Mexico to the Port of New Orleans to bypass the Mississippi River. Called the Mississippi River-Gulf Outlet, or MR-GO (New Orleanians pronounce it "Mister Go"), the 76-mile-long canal shortcut was constructed by the Corps of Engineers. Completed in 1965, MR-GO cuts straight through wetlands, connecting the Port of New Orleans directly to the Gulf of Mexico, alleviating the need for ships to navigate the much longer and windier Mississippi River.

The construction of MR-GO required the dredging of a 650-foot-wide by 36-foot-deep channel right through coastal marshland. Wetlands, called nature's "speed bumps," act as natural storm buffers. They reduce the intensity of hurricane winds and storm surges. The carving and dredging of swamps to build MR-GO required moving more dirt than the construction of the Panama Canal.

The 650-foot-wide MR-GO channel narrows to 500 feet wide at the bottom, meaning it has very steep sides, so steep that they are unstable. Every year, portions of the banks slough off, which widens the channel. Every year the Corps of Engineers dredges the channel to keep it clear and deep enough for the passage of ocean-going vessels. Dredgings are loaded on barges and taken out and dumped into the Gulf of Mexico at a cost of approximately $22 million a year to U.S. taxpayers. The erosion and dredging process has continued for decades, increasing the channel's width to the point where parts of MR-GO are now over 2,000 feet wide.

To environmentalists, MR-GO is a disaster. Besides destroying large portions of wetlands to build it, it constantly erodes additional wetlands. Saltwater from the Gulf flows up MR-GO, killing freshwater marsh vegetation growing along its banks, further exacerbating the environmental disaster. In destroying wetlands, MR-GO has also destroyed nature's speed bumps, decreasing the ability of wetlands to slow down hurricane winds and reduce storm surges. Worse than that, MR-GO has formed an expressway for storm surges.

Prior to Hurricane Katrina, researchers at Louisiana State University (LSU) ran computer simulations to study how MR-GO affects hurricane intensities. The analysis concluded that MR-GO could turn a large storm into a catastrophic one. An October 24, 2005, *Washington Post* article reported the following:

> Three months before Katrina, [Hassan] Mashriqui [one of the LSU researchers] told a room full of emergency managers that the [MR-GO] outlet was a "critical and fundamental flaw" in the Corps' hurricane defenses, a "Trojan Horse" that could amplify storm surges 20 to 40 percent.[2]

MR-GO and the Intracoastal Waterway, which connects Lake Borgne to the Industrial Canal, converge and then intersect approximately six miles east of the Industrial Canal forming, in effect, a funnel spout. New Orleanians call it "The Funnel." The water from both waterways squeeze together in The Funnel. The combined water continues on until it ends at the Industrial Canal near the Lower Ninth Ward.

During Hurricane Katrina, storm surge generated in the Gulf traveled unimpeded up MR-GO. Storm surge and strong winds on Lake Borgne drove water up the Intracoastal Waterway. The surges traveled down The Funnel and combined where MR-GO and the Intracoastal Waterway intersect, amplifying the storm surge. Levees overtopped and broke where the two combined (see Figure 9.4), flooding St. Bernard Parish. The amplified storm surge continued down the Intracoastal Waterway/MR-GO canal. When it reached the dead end, it slammed into the floodwalls along the Industrial Canal. The floodwalls breached, flooding the Lower Ninth Ward with a deadly avalanche of water.

During the 1980s, the Corps of Engineers started extending the heights of levees. Some had settled, others had deteriorated, and some just weren't tall enough to provide adequate protection.

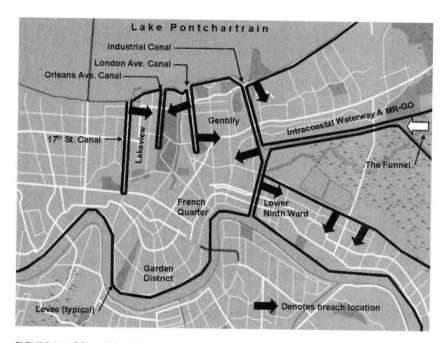

FIGURE 9.4 *Map of New Orleans showing locations of major breaches in levees and floodwalls.*

Rather than extending the levees' height using earth, which would require increasing the widths of the levee bases, the Corps constructed floodwalls on top of the levees. To determine the depths needed for the floodwall footings, the Corps performed soil tests and determined that many levees were setting on a thick organic layer of mud called peat. Peat is soft, spongy, and very compressible. It is a poor substrate material for supporting structures, particularly heavy structures like levees. Heavy levees can sink, and many levees protecting New Orleans had done just that, in some cases as much as two feet.

The Corps designed the floodwall foundations to extend through the peat. Steel pilings were driven down through the levees to a depth of 20 feet and the floodwalls anchored to the pilings. Unfortunately, 20 feet may not have been deep enough in some places to get down below the peat. Also, some of the pilings did not extend that deep. During construction there was difficulty lining up some of the steel piles with the concrete floodwalls because the piles had moved. The *Washington Post* article stated that

> problems with the soft underlayer began to surface even before the floodwalls were finished. In 1994, the now-defunct Pittman Construction Co., a New Orleans firm involved in levee construction, claimed in court documents that floodwall sections were failing to line up properly because of unstable soils.[3]

Storm surge can get past levees and floodwalls in several ways. It can overtop them or it can breach them, meaning it can break them or push them over. It can go underneath them and undermine them from below. Water can also get past a levee or floodwall by overtopping it and then scouring or eroding away the dirt on the dry side, undermining the structure and causing a breach.

A breach is considered a structural failure; overtopping is not. Depending on the circumstances, overtopping can be caused by a design error or by no error at all. Design errors are caused by errors in judgment, assumptions, or miscalculations of the height of a levee or floodwall. Storm surges that exceed reasonable expectations and overtop levees because they are greater than anyone could have imagined are not considered design errors.

New Orleans is a city shaped by water. It is also shaped by the flood control system designed to keep water out. Its system of levees, floodwalls, and canals is an ever-present reminder to New Orleanians that they live on borrowed land, and that they are in a never-ending battle with the water that surrounds them. If mistakes or miscalculations are made, the water wins. In his poem *Nasty Water,* New Orleanian poet James Nolan summed it up:

> New Orleans is a shimmering
> mirage floating on nasty water . . .
> nasty, water,
> nasty, water,
> proud to call it home.[4]

On the morning of August 29, 2005, Katrina and the nasty waters that surround New Orleans ganged up on the city. The hurricane, The Funnel, MR-GO, and the eroded wetlands put New Orleans's all-too-human defense system of serpentine-like, unfinished, and poorly maintained levees and floodwalls to the ultimate test.

BILOXI, MISSISSIPPI

New Orleans was not the only city devastated by Hurricane Katrina. Many cities along the Mississippi Gulf Coast were also hit hard. Biloxi, Mississippi, was one of them. Like New Orleans, Biloxi unknowingly began planning the magnitude of its Katrina disaster many years earlier.

The Choctaw and Chickasaw Native American tribes, who lived along the Mississippi Gulf Coast before the Europeans arrived, were gamblers. A popular pastime was for players to bet on the outcome of *ishtaboli,* a stick-ball game played with two teams of players. Players often bet all of their possessions on the game's outcome. The early French settlers were gamblers, too, although they preferred wagering on card games, checkers, and billiards. The Spanish introduced horse racing and built a race track in Natchez in 1795. Mississippi became a state in 1817. During the 1830s, Mississippians vacationed along the Gulf Coast, frequenting the many hotels that offered gambling. Biloxi was one such destination, with gambling hotels sporting colorful names such as Magnolia Hotel,

Madame Pradat's, and the Shady Grove Hotel. Gambling prospered along the Mississippi coast until 1942. During World War II, the state passed a law prohibiting gambling, but nevertheless, gambling continued along the Mississippi coast. It took a hurricane to stop it.

Hurricane Camille struck the Mississippi coastline on August 19, 1969. It destroyed homes, businesses, and the gambling hotels. For more than two decades afterwards, Mississippi's coastal economy floundered. In 1988, the U.S. Congress passed the National Indian Gaming Act. Mississippians along the Gulf Coast saw the Gaming Act as a way to bring gambling back to Mississippi and to pull the state out of its economic doldrums. In 1990, Mississippi's legislature passed the Mississippi Gaming Control Act, which permitted dockside casino gambling along the Mississippi River and Gulf Coast. Dockside gambling meant the casinos had to float. Technically, they were not on Mississippi soil.

Biloxi built its first casino barge in 1992, and more followed soon after. Mississippi's Gulf Coast was booming again. Tourists—meaning mostly gamblers—were back, with over 42 million of them visiting the area in 2004. There were more than 30 casinos along the Gulf Coast, including 7 in Biloxi.

Casino barges are not very seaworthy. A typical casino featured a gaming floor built on top of a watertight hull that was surrounded by water on three sides. Beneath it was just enough water to support the rationalization that the casino floated. The fourth side of the barge was connected to the rest of the casino complex—the entrance lobby, hotel, shops, and dining establishments. Because the gaming floors were tethered like boats to a dock, they moved up and down with the tide. There is a limit, however, to how much up-and-down movement a floating casino can take before it breaks loose from its moorings.

One of Biloxi's gaming barges was the Grand Casino, which boasted a 106,000-square-foot floating casino and a 975-room hotel. Owned by Caesars Entertainment, it was sold in early 2005 to Harrah's Entertainment. Harrah's planned to make improvements and change the casino's name. Katrina considerably changed those plans.

The late-19th-century philosopher Frederick Nietzsche suggested that to live life to the fullest, one must experience the full range of human emotions, including the exhilaration of fear. "Build your temples on the banks of Vesuvius," he encouraged. The casino owners along the Mississippi Gulf did Nietzsche one better: They built right in it.

HURRICANE KATRINA

Hurricane Katrina was relentless. It struck the U.S. coast a total of three times. Around 6:30 PM on August 25, 2005, it made landfall between Hallandale Beach and North Miami Beach on the east coast of the Florida peninsula. A Category 1 hurricane with winds of 80 miles per hour (mph), it tore southwest through the Florida peninsula, breaking trees and power lines and dropping as much as 15 inches of rain.

Although Katrina caused considerable damage, Floridians were much better prepared than they had been for Hurricane Andrew in 1992. The State of Florida learned many lessons from Andrew. As discussed in Chapter 6, Florida adopted a statewide building code after Andrew, with strict high-wind and flood design standards. The step was instrumental in reducing the number of torn-off roofs, broken windows, collapsed houses, and associated flying debris during Katrina. Millions of Floridians lost electricity, but only seven were killed. They died from falling trees, not from crumbling buildings or flying debris.

Although the states of Alabama, Mississippi, and Louisiana could have bolstered their building codes in the wake of Hurricane Andrew, they did not. The three states had adopted the International Building Code (IBC) for state-funded projects only. For all other buildings, local jurisdictions had the freedom to adopt a building code of their own. Most enforced various editions of the Standard Building Code (SBC). Some had no building code at all.[5]

Katrina passed through Florida and entered the Gulf of Mexico. It began feeding on the warm Gulf water, growing in both size and intensity, until reaching Category 3 status on August 27. By noon on August 28, Katrina had reached Category 5 status with sustained wind speeds of 175 mph, creating colossal storm surges. Meteorologists and local, state, and federal officials watched closely, trying to determine where and when Katrina would strike land next.

Hurricanes in the Gulf of Mexico are trapped, because the Gulf is surrounded on three sides by land. At some point, Gulf hurricanes must strike land. Eventually, meteorologists predicted Katrina would come ashore near New Orleans. On Sunday morning, August 28, 2005, the National Weather Service issued an unprecedented and dire warning:

> Devastating damage expected. . . . Most of the area will be unin-
> habitable for weeks. . . . At least one-half of well-constructed homes
> will have roof and wall failure. All gabled roofs will fail. . . . Majority of
> industrial buildings will become nonfunctional. . . . All wood-framed
> low-rising apartment buildings will be destroyed. High-rise office and
> apartment buildings will sway dangerously. . . . All windows will be blown
> out. . . . Persons...pets...and livestock exposed to the winds will face
> certain death if struck [by blown debris]. . . . Do not venture outside.[6]

Hurricane Katrina and New Orleans

Although the winds died down before Katrina made landfall, its Category 5 storm surge was already moving ominously with the hurricane toward the Gulf Coast. At 6:10 AM on August 29, Katrina made landfall near Buras-Triumph in Plaquemines Parish, Louisiana. It struck as a Category 3 hurricane with sustained winds of 125 mph. At first, this was considered by many to be good news—a Category 3 storm is much less intense than a Category 5.

The hurricane reentered the Gulf for a short period of time and then came ashore again near the Louisiana/Mississippi border. Katrina knocked out power and telephone lines and mobile phone stations, cutting off virtually all forms of communications in and out of the area.

There is an adage that says, "No news is good news." There is a Zen koan—a paradoxical riddle—that poses the question, "Does a tree falling in the forest make a sound?" August 29 put both of these sayings to the test. For the few hours that Katrina poured rain, pounded against levees, and tossed buildings, neither officials nor reporters knew exactly what was going on in New Orleans. Everything in Katrina's grip was out of touch and silenced by the deafening roar of the storm. Electricity, phone lines, and cell phone systems were dead. Once Katrina moved far enough inland and its winds dropped, many outside the area believed the worst was over and, with no news forthcoming to the contrary, assumed that New Orleans had dodged a bullet. In the early afternoon of August 29, the view was somewhat reinforced when CNN showed New Orleanians walking around on Bourbon Street. Those outside the area and unaffected by the storm breathed a sigh of relief.

Unfortunately, the worst was not over. Unknown to everyone except to those who were living it, the disaster had just started. No news was not good news. Trees falling do make a noise—so do 100 mph winds and breached levees. On that Monday morning, however, those New Orleanians who knew about the breaches and the sounds of howling wind, uprooted trees, and houses being plowed off their foundations by floodwater had neither the time nor means to report their hellish experiences. They were struggling for their lives.

After the hurricane, some residents of the Lower Ninth Ward claimed they heard what sounded like an explosion when the levee broke and their homes were suddenly swept up in violent and deadly floodwater. Government officials must have blown up the levee, they thought, to save Orleans Metro at the expense of the Lower Ninth, just as officials had done generations before.

In 1927, heavy rains upriver from New Orleans caused the Mississippi River to overtop and break portions of the many levees designed to permanently steer and channel the mighty river's course. To prevent New Orleans from flooding, government officials dynamited portions of levees, resulting in the deliberate flooding of the Lower Ninth Ward and St. Barnard Parish. In 1965, when Hurricane Betsy broke levees and flooded the Lower Ninth, residents also thought they heard an explosion. Eighty years after the deliberate 1927 flooding and 40 years after the alleged deliberate flooding, some residents of the Lower Ninth still remembered and jumped to the conclusion that officials had done it again. Rather than dynamite, however, the explosion the victims of Katrina heard was much more likely the sound of a giant steel barge slamming into the levee and floodwall along the Industrial Canal. Eventually, that barge came to rest against flooded and destroyed houses in the Lower Ninth Ward.

Before Katrina made landfall, MR-GO was already magnifying the storm's surge. Storm surge traveled up MR-GO, eroding away portions of the levees that protected St. Bernard's Parish. Waves traveling down the six-mile-long funnel spout pounded against the levees lining the Industrial Canal, eventually causing portions of them to breach, spilling water into Orleans Metro and Orleans East. Then, after hours of pounding, the southeast portion of the Industrial Canal broke, catastrophically flooding the Lower Ninth Ward and St. Bernard Parish.

The levee at the foot of Orleans Canal and a one-mile-long section of levee along Lake Pontchartrain overtopped. Sections of the flood-walls along both sides of the London Avenue Canal and one side of the 17th Street Canal breached, flooding Orleans Metro. (See Figure 9.4.) New Orleans, shaped by water, was now going underwater.

Hurricane Katrina and Biloxi

U.S. Highway 90 runs along the Mississippi coastline. Between Gulfport and Biloxi, Mississippi, nothing but beach and a few mea-ger feet of elevation separates the highway from the Gulf. Along the north side of the highway—the inland side—were mile after mile of motels, houses, and historic mansions, some dating from before the Civil War.

Jefferson Davis built his home and library in Biloxi in 1853. The Greek-Revival-styled Tullis-Toledano manor was constructed in 1856. Local historians claim that the $2\frac{1}{2}$-story Tullis-Toledano was built adja-cent to a much older hotel that was the first gambling site in Mississippi. Across the highway several hundred yards to the southeast, was the Grand Casino, tethered in the Gulf, floating in a few inches of water.

On the morning of August 29, Katrina tore along the Mississippi coastline with winds of 120 mph and a storm surge as high as 30 feet in some locations. It flooded over Highway 90, destroying just about everything in its path—portions of the highway, trees, houses, hotels, commercial buildings, churches, gas stations, parking garages, restau-rants, and casinos. Most of Biloxi was submerged under 10 feet of water. The Biloxi-Ocean Springs Bridge washed away. The flooding and dam-age extended as far as 6 miles inland. The surge wrenched casino barges off their moorings, pushing some of them ashore. It shoved the Grand Casino barge into Tullis-Toledano, where it came to rest, crushing the manor beneath its massive 35,000-square-foot hull. Although hurricane winds and the surge did considerable damage to Jefferson Davis's house, it managed to survive, protected somewhat by the higher ground and stone fence between it and the Gulf. By the time Katrina moved on, the Mississippi coastline looked like a battlefield. One hundred and twenty-six people were dead, and nearly 70,000 houses were destroyed and another 150,000 damaged.

In Biloxi, most of the hotels, restaurants, and houses along Highway 90 were washed away. In many cases, only concrete driveways and front steps leading to nowhere were left. Biloxi's restaurants, hotels, and all seven of its casinos were gone. Gone with them was Biloxi's economic mainstay, tourism. The casinos had employed 14,000 workers. Within days, Biloxi's unemployment rate was near 25 percent.

NEW ORLEANS IN THE AFTERMATH

For nearly a month after Hurricane Katrina, most of New Orleans remained underwater. For much of this time, New Orleanians were forbidden to return to their houses. Floodwaters contained toxic chemicals, oils, gasoline, human and animal waste, and dead bodies. National Guard members from throughout the United States were summoned to New Orleans. They went from house to house looking for survivors, victims, and abandoned pets. Every house they visited was marked with spray paint, using a cryptic system to convey basic information. An "X" was made on the wall or door and information painted into each quadrant. The top quadrant told the date of the visit. As Figure 9.5 shows, this house was visited on 9/11. The left quadrant designated the National Guard recovery team that had made the visit. The right quadrant stated whether the house was entered or not. The bottom quadrant told the number of victims found.

It took nearly a month to drain New Orleans. The breaches were temporarily plugged. Dozens of portable pumps, running day and night, pumped the water out, into Lake Pontchartrain and the Mississippi River. After the floodwaters subsided, it was possible to better assess the

FIGURE 9.5 *View of typical "X" symbol used by Guard Troops to designate that the house was visited. This house was visited on 9/11/05, by the California 3rd Search and Recovery Team. Viewing through windows, they determined no bodies were inside. Photo by author August, 2006.*

FIGURE 9.6 *View of a destroyed house in the Lower Ninth Ward one year after Katrina, August 2006. Photo by author.*

extent of the damage. It was astounding. House after house and block after block looked like a war zone. Roofs were torn off, windows and doors were broken, houses were off their foundations. Some houses came to rest in the streets. Others slammed into neighboring houses. Others collapsed outright. (See Figure 9.6.)

Soon after the water was gone, city building inspectors went door to door, assessing the damage to every house. Based on inspections, houses were tagged green, yellow, or red. A green tag meant that the house suffered little damage and was safe to reenter and occupy. Houses that were yellow-tagged had nonstructural damage such as broken windows or doors, destroyed roofs, water damage, and minor, repairable structural damage. Partial occupancy was granted for yellow-tagged houses, and homeowners were given a list of repairs that had to be made. A red tag meant that the house was structurally unstable and unsafe to enter. Occupying it was unlawful. Thousands of houses were red-tagged.

Within four months of Katrina, the 11 Louisiana parishes (counties) hit hardest by Katrina had new building codes. In a special legislative session in December 2005, the State of Louisiana passed a bill requiring all parishes in the state to begin enforcing the 2003 International Building Code. Prior to Katrina, only state-funded buildings had to comply with the safer wind and flood design requirements of the IBC. In addition, the law also established a 19-member state commission to oversee building code enforcement by local officials.

Most of the badly damaged houses were in areas that were severely flooded. In 1984, FEMA had established Base Flood Elevations (BFEs) for New Orleans. To participate in the National Flood Insurance Program (NFIP), communities must require houses and buildings that are more than 50 percent damaged to be raised above the BFE. Thousands of New Orleans houses fell into this category.

After Hurricane Katrina, FEMA decided that the BFEs for New Orleans were outdated. The BFEs varied between elevations of –1.5 to 4.5 feet, and were predicated on the assumption that New Orleans's levee system would hold. Consequently, the BFEs only took into account water associated with heavy rains, not flooding associated with over-topped or breached levees. Post-Katrina, FEMA concluded that the BFEs were too low for most of New Orleans and that new maps with higher BFEs were needed. It would take time to collect and analyze the data and prepare the new maps—time that New Orleanians living in trailers or staying with family or friends did not have.

Over one-half of the houses in New Orleans are below the 1984 BFEs. Raising the BFEs would only make it more difficult and costly to rebuild. Not knowing the eventual elevations made it difficult, if not impossible, to begin reconstruction. Some homeowners and community action groups complained. Months went by as city residents waited. A *USA Today* census of the New Orleans population revealed that by the end of May 2006, 40 percent of New Orleans's population had still not returned.[7] Many others lived in FEMA trailers parked in front of their storm-damaged houses.

By April 2006, FEMA had worked out a solution for the BFEs. It established what it called an "Advisory Base Flood Elevation." It required houses and buildings located in FEMA-designated floodplains to be raised to the 1984 BFE levels or three feet above the highest existing adjacent grade (level of the ground), whichever was higher. In addition, it required all houses and buildings with 50 percent or greater damage, but not in the floodplain, to be raised three feet as well. In effect, this meant that every existing house and building in the city of New Orleans that was significantly damaged by the hurricane or flood had to be raised at least three feet.

FIGURE 9.7 *FEMA Trailer parked in front yard of house that is still unlivable, August 2006. Note the stacked cinder blocks used for the trailer's foundation and to support the trailer's sewer line. Photo by author.*

Now New Orleanians knew the rules and construction could get under way. Still, most New Orleanians took a wait-and-see attitude. They waited to see how the Corps of Engineers did in rebuilding the levees. They waited to see what the City of New Orleans so-called "rebuilding plan" would involve. They waited to see how much insurance money they would get, waited to see what their neighbors did, and waited to see what another hurricane season would bring. A year after Katrina, most of the houses were still as Katrina had left them, damaged and empty. Instead of floodwater around the damaged and empty houses, there were weeds and FEMA trailers. (See Figure 9.7.)

THE MISSISSIPPI GULF COAST

Recovery moved more quickly for the casino owners in Mississippi. There was never a question about whether the casinos would be rebuilt; it was just a matter of where and how quickly. There is a lot of money in gambling. One-third of Biloxi's tax revenue came from its seven pre-Katrina casinos, causing Vincent Creel, the city's spokesperson, to quip, "Some people say casino gambling is the engine driving the [Biloxi] economy. It's really the whole train."[8] Gambling also supported the state of Mississippi to the tune of $200 million in annual tax revenue.

Never reticent and aware of the importance of their industry to the Gulf Coast economy, casino owners spoke up quickly. They advocated rebuilding onshore. Phil Satre, Chairman and Chief Executive of Harrah's, which had purchased the destroyed Grand Casino only a month before Katrina, complained about having to rebuild offshore: "It's not simply an inconvenience, it's a public problem."[9] The president of Treasure Bay Casino in Biloxi threatened, "If we don't get this [permission to build onshore], I will be one that will not be back."[10]

On September 27, 2005, less than a month after Katrina, the Mississippi legislature held a special session. Governor Haley Barbour addressed the legislature:

> You've seen the catastrophic destruction of the casinos and the destruction wrought by those behemoths when they crashed into buildings and vehicles. . . . We can't return the casinos to the way they were. It would be irresponsible.[11]

The legislature approved a bill that allowed casinos to be built on dry land within 800 feet of the Gulf shoreline. On October 17, 2006, the governor signed it into law.

Casinos immediately began to plan their reconstructions, reopenings, and expansions. In December 2005, two casinos in Biloxi reopened with temporary gaming rooms: the Isle of Capri Casino and the Palace Casino Resort.

On April 14, 2006, the Mississippi legislature passed a bill requiring the counties along the Gulf Coast to "enforce, on an emergency basis, all the wind and flood mitigation requirements prescribed by the . . . 2003 *International Building Code*,"[12] until the local counties' and cities' supervisors amend their local regulations to adopt the latest edition of the IBC. A 26-member state board was formed to ensure enforcement.

On August 17, 2006, the Biloxi Grand Casino opened in the BayView Hotel located across Highway 90 from its pre-Katrina location. On August 29, one year after Katrina, the Beau Rivage reopened.

Harrah's purchased the Casino Magic property adjacent to its former casino and plans to build a $1 billion destination resort. In addition, design or construction of many other casinos along the Gulf Coast is under way. Combined, the Mississippi casino projects total billions of dollars.

Hurricane Katrina is in the process of transforming the Gulf Coast. For better or worse, if local communities do nothing to curb it, by 2010 it is possible that Katrina will have turned the Mississippi Gulf Coast into a 75-mile-long version of the Las Vegas strip.

NEW ORLEANS'S LEVEES

At first, the Corps of Engineers claimed that New Orleans's levees did not fail; rather, they were overtopped by a Category 5 storm surge, and because the levees were designed to only withstand a Category 3 storm surge, overtopping was not technically a failure. The Corps argued that the levees that failed were first overtopped. The overtopping caused scouring on the back side of the levees, which eroded away the earth and weakened them, causing breaches.

As soon as the floodwaters were drained, the Corps began rebuilding levees, working 24 hours a day, 7 days a week. The Corps had two goals: (1) to rebuild to pre-Katrina conditions, and (2) to finish before June 1, 2006, which marked the beginning of the next hurricane season. The task was daunting. The levees had broken in at least 50 different locations, and damage to the levees that had not failed was considerable. Katrina damaged almost half of the 350-mile-long levee system and over 30 of New Orleans's 71 storm water pumping stations.

The Corps had taken 40 years since Hurricane Betsy to build the levee system. Some portions were still incomplete when Katrina slammed into them. Now the Corps vowed to fix the entire system in 10 months. Understandably, many observers were skeptical.

As the Corps worked to rebuild the levees, other engineers tried to figure out what happened. On September 28, 2005, a group of engineers from the University of California–Berkeley (UCB), the American Society of Civil Engineers (ASCE), and other engineers and scientists began an extensive investigation of New Orleans's flood prevention system.

The Corps began its own investigation as well, forming a 150-member team called the Interagency Performance Evaluation Task Force (IPET).

On March 6, 2006, Lieutenant General Carl Strock, commander in chief of the U.S. Army Corps of Engineers (USACE), gave a White House press briefing. In it he summarized the progress of the Corps's work:

> [I]n the [Katrina] event, 169 miles were damaged or destroyed; 34 of the 71 pump stations in the city of New Orleans were also damaged. . . . [T]o date, we have restored about 100 of those 169 miles of levee, or about 45 percent of the levees have been restored to their pre-Katrina and authorized levels. About 85 percent of the pumping capacity has been restored to pre-Katrina. . . . In terms of objectives, we're well on track to meet our 1 June commitment to have the flood protection system around New Orleans equal to or better than it was prior to Katrina.[13]

By "equal," Strock meant that the Corps was restoring the levees to their presumably Category 3 conditions and completing the sections that were not completed prior to Katrina. By "better than" he explained:

> [W]e will have it enhanced in the sense that we will put three temporary closures on the canals that presented problems during Katrina . . . the Canal at 17th Street, the Canal at Orleans, and the London Avenue Canal. . . . [A]ll of those will have closures so it will prevent the storm surge of a future event from getting into those that we think are vulnerable areas.[14]

On May 22, 2006, the UCB/ASCE engineering group issued its draft final report entitled *Investigation of the Performance of the New Orleans Flood Protection Systems in Hurricane Katrina on August 29, 2005*. By then, the Corps had rebuilt over 90 percent of the levees and the beginning of yet another hurricane season was less than two weeks away. The report concluded:

> Hurricane Katrina was . . . the root cause of the natural disaster. This disaster grew to a full blown catastrophe, however, principally due to the massive and repeated failure of the regional flood protection system.[15]

The investigations revealed that some levees failed without being overtopped, including the floodwalls on both sides of the London Avenue Canal and one side of the 17th Street Canal. The investigations revealed that the levees's sheetpile foundations did not extend deeply enough. Water seeped beneath them and weakened the soil, allowing the water in the canal to push them over. These three breaches were responsible for 80 percent of the floodwater that inundated the Orleans Metro Bowl.

Another failure occurred at The Funnel. The storm surge coming down the GIWW/MR-GO slammed into the composite earthen levee and concrete floodwalls on the west side of the Industrial Canal. Water overtopped the composite levee/floodwall. This eroded away the earthen back side, weakening it to the point where the floodwall breached, inundating the Orleans East Bowl with floodwater. The report concluded that this breach

> could have been prevented at little incremental cost if erosion protection (e.g., a concrete splash pad, or similar) had been emplaced along the back side of the concrete floodwall at the levee crest, but the USACE felt that this was precluded by Federal rules and regulations regarding authorized levels of protection.[16]

On the east side of the Industrial Canal and just south of the GIWW/MR-GO intersection, water in the canal seeped under the sheetpile foundations of the floodwalls sitting atop the earthen levee:

> Like many sections of the flood protection system, these sheetpiles were too shallow to adequately cut off . . . these underseepage flows. The result was two massive breaches that devastated the adjacent Ninth Ward neighborhood.[17]

The report concluded that the major flooding of New Orleans was due to engineering failures, not just overtopping from storm surges that exceeded the heights of the levees and floodwalls.

On June 1, 2006, IPET released its draft report. The 6,615-page document came to conclusions similar to that of the UCB/ASCE engineers. IPET concluded that various design shortcomings combined with extremely severe and unprecedented storm conditions caused the levees' failures. In a press conference held on June 1, Strock said that the Corps accepted full responsibility for its first project failure in its 230-year history. He went on to say:

> This has been sobering for us, because it is the first time the Corps has had to stand up and say we had a catastrophic failure at one of our projects. . . . [It] weighed heavily on our minds.[18]

The Corps did not make its June 1, 2006, deadline, although it came close. By June 1, work was not yet complete at the Lake Pontchartrain end of the 17th Street Canal. Also, a 400-foot-long section of levee in Plaquemines Parish still needed repair.

The ASCE performed an independent review of the Corps' IPET report. In August 2006, the ASCE's Hurricane Katrina External Review Panel issued a series of recommendations in the form of "call-to-action" items based on its review of the IPET report. Prior to listing its recommendations, the Panel said:

> [The Panel] believes that the failures in New Orleans' hurricane protection system constitute one of the worst catastrophes ever to befall this country. The flaws uncovered as a result of Hurricane Katrina must serve as a sobering reminder to engineers everywhere that their work has life or death implications. Whatever the constraints . . . engineers must continue to uphold the highest standards of their profession, knowing that people's lives are at stake.[19]

The ASCE's Panel made a number of recommendations, which are summarized below:

- *Public safety should be the highest priority.* This seems so obvious that it should not need to be stated. However, in the past, New Orleans's levee design was debated among the Corps, the State of Louisiana, and New Orleans stakeholders. Compromises were made to reconcile preferences and political differences; the result was that safety sometimes took a back seat.
- *The public should know the true degree of safety that New Orleans's flood prevention system provides.* New Orleanians assumed that the levee system was designed to withstand a Category 3 storm. Based on this assumption, the State of Louisiana, the City of New Orleans, and its citizens made assumptions about their city, their lives, and where

to live. So did FEMA when it established its Base Flood Elevations in 1984. The true risks to the levee system should be determined and conveyed to the public. Only then can New Orleanians make intelligent and informed decisions about their future.

- *The redundancy of the flood prevention system should be increased.* The current system has few, if any, backup components. If the first line of defense is breached, there is no second line of defense.
- *One person should be put in charge of the entire system.* This person should be a licensed engineer, not a political appointee.
- *The whole system needs to be rethought.* Reassess its effectiveness due to age and settling. Make the levees survivable if overtopped and strengthen the system. Upgrade the city's floodwater pumping system.
- *The City of New Orleans should make prudent land-use decisions.* It should consider limiting development in flood-prone areas or, at least, establish minimum first-floor elevations in flood prone areas.

The ASCE's land-use recommendation cited above has profound social consequences for New Orleans. In the months following Katrina, New Orleans began cobbling together its recovery plan. Appropriate land use and land-use alternatives were heatedly debated. The outcome of the debate resulted in something no one expected. By the end of July 2006, New Orleans had embarked on a new course, unprecedented in the history of city planning.

REBUILDING NEW ORLEANS

Hurricane Katrina presented New Orleans with an opportunity that few cities ever have: the chance to plan and rebuild on a more comprehensive and sustainable basis. With 80 percent of its neighborhoods and housing destroyed, New Orleans now had the possibility to address and perhaps resolve its entrenched generational poverty. It had the chance to address its communities segregated along economic and racial lines. It had a chance to fix its blighted neighborhoods. The Lower Ninth, for example: one of the poorest and most segregated areas of New Orleans, with an average personal income of $27,522 and a 99.5 percent black population.[20] Katrina gave the city the opportunity to assess improvements for its pumping stations, neighborhoods, roads, canals, and freeway system, some of which bisected and cut off neighborhoods that once thrived. It gave New Orleans the opportunity to decide which areas were more vulnerable than others, change the use of those areas, improve city land use, consider rezoning in order to develop multi-use commercial and residential zones, build parks, and restore marshlands. New Orleanians had a chance to take what was great about their city and build on it, and take what was wrong and fix it.

A comprehensive rebuilding master plan would be the first step in the rebuilding process. Items in the master plan would be prioritized. The best experts from around the country—indeed the world—would jump at the chance to help. It would take a little time to develop, but it would be well worth the wait in the long run.

At first, New Orleans thought along these lines—develop a comprehensive plan for the rebuilding of the city. A committee was formed by Mayor Nagin in October 2005 that included dozens of experts in both urban and post-disaster planning. Called the "Bring New Orleans Back Commission" (BNOB), it set to work planning the rebuilding of New Orleans. With advice from the Washington, D.C.-based Urban Land Institute (ULI), the BNOB hired the Philadelphia-based planning firm of Wallace Roberts & Todd, LLC, to develop a master plan for rebuilding New Orleans. In addition to addressing New Orleans's needs, the plan also had to address specific federal requirements. One was of paramount importance. In order to secure federal funding, all buildings damaged by more than 50 percent of their market value had to be raised or torn down and rebuilt above the BFE. In the months immediately following Katrina, FEMA was still trying to determine just what the base flood elevations should be.

On January 11, 2006, Wallace Roberts & Todd and the ULI team presented a proposed master plan to a capacity crowd of BNOB commission members, New Orleanians, and reporters. The presentation was an overview of a comprehensive rebuilding plan, details of which had not yet been worked out. Called a "citywide framework for reconstruction," the proposed master plan divided the rebuilding effort into four main categories: (1) flood and storm water protection, (2) transit and transportation, (3) parks and open space, and (4) neighborhood rebuilding.

The master plan proposed that the New Orleans flood protection system be upgraded to resist Category 5 hurricanes. It proposed restoring wetlands and closing MR-GO. It proposed moving the large canal flood pumps to the edge of Lake Pontchartrain next to permanent floodgates that would prevent floodwaters from flooding the canals. It proposed lining the canals with fingerlike parks. It proposed consolidating the levee and flood pumps into a single district and putting just one entity in charge of it all.

Construction of a citywide, high-speed, light rail transit system was proposed. The transit system would connect neighborhoods to downtown, other centers of employment, and the airport. It proposed the construction of new roads with wide medians for landscaped open space and pathways for pedestrians and bicyclists. It proposed new parks, with likely locations including properties in flood-vulnerable areas. These properties would be acquired through the eminent domain process—owners would be paid fair values for their properties.

The developers of the master plan assumed that the city would not be as large as it was prior to Katrina for many years to come. Immediately after Katrina, New Orleans's population plummeted from half a million to around 150,000. The planners assumed that by September 2008, three years after Katrina, the population of New Orleans would be only 250,000, approximately half of what it was pre-Katrina.

Another assumption of the master planners was that the creation of mixed-income communities was desirable. Many neighborhoods of New Orleans were stratified by income and race. This was readily apparent to all television viewers during the days of the flood.

These two assumptions drove much of the proposals for rebuilding New Orleans's neighborhoods. The planners suggested the creation of economic and racially diverse neighborhoods by providing housing in neighborhoods that would meet the needs of people with different income levels. It proposed relocating housing from low-lying areas, prone to flooding, to higher-ground areas and increasing the housing density in these higher-ground areas. It proposed rezoning some single-family residential areas to mixed-use areas, allowing multifamily housing, commercial-retail, and services such as beauticians, barbers, and medical facilities. These areas would become new mixed-use communities, incorporating housing and commercial uses with schools, libraries, and cultural and community centers. These communities would be connected by a new light rail transit system to downtown and major areas of employment.

Areas such as the Ninth Ward were identified as "Infill Development Areas." The most severely destroyed, blighted, or underutilized properties in these Infill Development Areas would be consolidated and turned over to private or publicly owned developers for redevelopment. The city would acquire these properties through eminent domain, solicit proposals from developers, and select developers and projects that the city believed most desirable.

The master plan was not well received and quickly fell apart. The plan's attempt to consolidate and relocate housing from low-lying areas to less flood-prone areas was considered by many New Orleanians to be a racist attempt to drive some people out of their homes and away from New Orleans. As far as many irate New Orleanians were concerned, the master planners made two fundamentally flawed assumptions. The first was that city residents would not come back in full force. Many New Orleanians felt that there was no need to consolidate into a smaller footprint on higher ground. The city would fill up again, low-lying and high-ground areas alike. The second was that New Orleanians wanted something other than their own homes and neighborhoods back. New Orleanian homeowners liked their neighborhoods the way they were. Most New Orleanians wanted their homes to be the way they were before Katrina and the botched levee system took them away. Now running for reelection, Nagin sided with the irate New Orleanians. The BNOB committee soon disbanded.

By the time Mayor Nagin was reelected on May 20, 2006, another approach to rebuilding New Orleans was taking shape. Instead of the planning process being led by a small group of experts, it would be led by the people themselves. The planning process was turned over to a local charity called the Greater New Orleans Foundation (GNOF). In April 2006, the GNOF created the New Orleans Community Support Foundation (NOCSF) and a nine-person oversight subcommittee called the Community Support Organization (CSO). Nagin embraced the new process.

The process would work this way: New Orleans's 73 neighborhood groups would consolidate into 12 districts. Each district would interview and select a planner from NOCSF's list of preselected, qualified planning firms. Working with the planning firm that they selected, each district would come up with its own plan, addressing the needs and desires of its various neighborhood groups. The City of New Orleans would come up with its own infrastructure plan. The 12 district plans and the city's infrastructure plan—13 plans in all—would then be stitched together into a comprehensive, single plan for the rebuilding of New Orleans.

The process would be funded by a $3.5 million grant from the Rockefeller Foundation and an additional $1 million that the GNOB had raised on its own. The process was named the Unified New Orleans Neighborhood Plan, but within a few months the name was shortened to the Unified New Orleans Plan (UNOP). In addition, its funding was increased to $5.5 million by contributions from the Bush-Clinton Fund.

In May 2006, the NOCSF solicited qualifications from planning firms throughout the United States. By the end of June, it had received responses from over 60 interested firms and selected 15 (Wallace Roberts & Todd, LLC, was not one of them).

In his July 5, 2006, press release, Mayor Nagin told New Orleanians that the Unified New Orleans Plan

> is an opportunity for all of us to work together toward our common goal of rebuilding the city that we love. So many people have taken initiative to get started already. It is democracy in action, just as it should be. . . . The final plan for New Orleans will be one that we will all be proud of, partly because we will all play an important role in making it happen.[21]

On July 30, 2006, 73 neighborhood groups interviewed the 15 preselected planning teams and discussed their neighborhoods' problems and concerns in order to determine with which team they would like to work. By August, the planning process was under way. New Orleans had embarked on a great experiment, an untried and untested grassroots planning process, its outcome uncertain.

By law, the Louisiana Recovery Authority (LRA) can only release federal funding to communities that submit a plan explaining how they propose to rebuild and meet various federal requirements. In September 2006, while New Orleans was still in the throes of its UNOP process, the LRA began releasing $7 billion in federal money to individual homeowners in various Katrina-affected areas. Another $7 billion was earmarked for New Orleans, but without a recovery plan, the money sat idle.

By November 2006, over one-half of New Orleans's residents still had not returned home. To ensure that as many displaced New Orleanians as possible could participate in the UNOP planning process, a five-city town hall meeting was held in December 2006. Displaced New Orleanians living in Atlanta, Baton Rouge, Dallas, and Houston participated via interactive television.

One concern that some critics of the UNOP planning process have is that the city will only repair itself, not rebuild with a vision for a better New Orleans. With the planning process entrusted to hundreds of individuals who are not planners by profession, critics fear that New Orleanians will think of planning solutions in terms of the way things were before Katrina. Such thinking greatly limits opportunities and carries with it the risk that New Orleans will fall back on failed solutions. Lawrence West, an expert in urban planning from the Massachusetts Institute of Technology, commented:

> Cities do come back from tremendous devastation. But resilience means bouncing back, and that's not the same as bouncing forward. The forces of pre-disaster inertia are very powerful, for the good and for the ill.[22]

How can a truly grassroots and organizationally flat decision structure resolve the tough decisions that must eventually be made? This remains to be seen. At the time of this writing, February 2007, the UNOP process is incomplete. The process is generating multiple plans that must somehow be wover together. To do so will, require hard compromises, and strong city leadership. John McIllwain of the Urban Land Institute and a member of the BNOB commission commented in July 2006 that New Orleans is

> virtually a city without a city administration and it's worse than ever. . . . You need a politician, a leader that is willing to make tough decisions and articulate to the people why these decisions are made, which means everyone is not going to be happy.[23]

Meanwhile, New Orleans is rebuilding—one pioneering homeowner at a time. It is doing so without a plan, although some critics suggest that this is, in fact, the real plan, a "laissez faire" approach to city planning that lets New Orleanians rebuild as they see fit.[24] By August 2006, one year after Katrina, the New Orleans building department had already issued 40,000 building permits. Tens of thousands have been issued since. Federal guidelines allow buildings that were not damaged more than 50 percent to be rebuilt without being raised to a higher elevation. Consequently, houses with crawlspaces barely above the city mud and even slab-on-grade houses are being rebuilt throughout the city. Neighborhood plans developed through the UNOP planning process will undoubtedly be affected and restricted by New Orleanians who have already rebuilt.

10

LEARNING FROM DISASTERS

In 1086, William the Conqueror sent census takers throughout England to determine how much land and livestock his subjects held. When the census takers returned, they recorded their findings in the Book of Winchester. King William used the book to determine how much tax his subjects could afford to pay. Once the amount was determined, it was the Crown's final judgment and nonnegotiable. Because everyone's fate was sealed within its pages, Englanders called it the "Doomsday Book."

Ever since, there have been many doomsdays. Every large natural and man-made disaster brings with it somebody's doomsday. This is how the world ends: incrementally, one doomsday at a time. This is also how we improve the safety of the built environment: one disaster at a time. This has been our approach to disaster planning for centuries. In recognition of this approach, the American Society of Civil Engineers (ASCE) Hurricane Katrina External Review Panel commented:

> The nation learns lessons after every major disaster: lessons in decision making, structural integrity, disaster response, and communications.[1]

As we have seen throughout this book, we improve the way we plan and design based on what disasters have taught us. We have also seen how procrastination, poor planning, and failure to heed warnings helped to create conditions that led to disasters or made them worse. We constructed the stage and arranged the scenery; natural processes played their roles and catastrophes were the result.

We are not fast learners. Often, it takes a few disasters before we "get it." A snippet of the philosopher George Santayana's insight regarding the importance of learning from past events was quoted in Chapter 1. A more complete quotation follows:

> Progress . . . depends on retentiveness. . . . [W]hen experience is not retained, as among savages, infancy is perpetual. Those who cannot remember the past are condemned to repeat it.[2]

It has taken centuries' worth of disasters and trial-and-error learning to make the built environment as safe as it is today. As recent disasters demonstrate we have not learned nor retained all our lessons. Consequently, we still are not completely safe. We have a long way to go.

We have seen that our approach to improving building safety is pragmatic. We develop better ideas about planning and design based on lessons learned from disasters. We then test our ideas in real-world situations and judge their merits by the results. In the world of pragmatic decision making, the horse does not come before the cart. The cause-and-effect relationship works the other way around: Outcomes determine the values of the ideas that brought them to fruition. As Santayana put it: "For things are called great because they are memorable, they are not remembered because they were great."[3] In the Book of Genesis, God created the heavens and earth. Only afterwards did He judge it "good."

Pragmatic solutions to planning and design employ three tools of inference: deduction, induction, and abduction. Deduction is the method of reasoning by which a specific conclusion logically follows from a set of premises. Induction is inferring a general conclusion from a small set of observations. While the first two are commonly regarded as tools of logic, the third tool is most commonly employed by architects, engineers, planners, and government officials. There are few things about the built environment that are certain enough to be resolved only by deduction and induction. The real world is much too complicated, uncertain, political, and filled with too many unknowns to be so simple. Abduction is educated guessing based on past experiences, coupled with practical considerations and artful compromises. This is how most decisions regarding building planning and design are made. Generally, decisions cannot wait until all information is available. Instead, choices are based on educated guesses, and weighing the available and sometimes conflicting data. This is how we plan and design the built environment. Once a decision is implemented—for example, constructed in stone, concrete, and steel—it is tested in real-world situations. This is how we judge how well we plan and design.

Having now looked at many disasters and having seen how they affected the way we planned and built afterward, we can list the basic steps of our centuries-old approach to disaster planning:

1. We build. If it creates or contributes to unsafe conditions, experts warn us of impending disaster.
2. We do not heed their advice. We continue on our course.
3. The disaster strikes, and destroys lives and property.
4. Horrified and grief stricken, we pick up the pieces (on occasion, we instead move on).
5. Government officials vow to never let the disaster happen again.
6. Experts, usually in the form of committees, study the disaster, collect data, learn valuable lessons, and make recommendations about how to better plan and design to avoid a repeat of the same disaster.
7. After debate and sometimes protest, officials implement only the most practical and politically palatable of the recommendations.
8. We rebuild following the new, improved requirements, with the goal of preventing another disaster like the one that has already occurred.
9. Buildings, cities, and/or structures are better built, and are safer as a result.
10. The next disaster tests the merits of our improvements.

First, we build. Perhaps we have a plan or no plan at all. What we build is either safe or it increases the likelihood or potential magnitude of a disaster. If it is the latter, experts frequently warn us of impending disaster if we continue our current path. We do not heed their warnings. At the end of the 19th century, Galvestonians were advised about the necessity of a seawall. They had witnessed—albeit from a distance—the destruction of Indianola farther south along the Texas Gulf coastline.

Some Galvestonians were convinced that to keep their city from a similar fate, a seawall was needed to protect it from the storm surges of strong hurricanes. Yet, no wall was constructed. Prior to Hurricane Katrina, there were warnings about what a large hurricane might do to New Orleans. In July 2004, the Center for the Study of Public Health Impacts of Hurricanes at Louisiana State University ran a computer simulation of a hypothetical storm hitting the boot heel of Louisiana. Realistic storm data for an imaginary Category 3 hurricane, dubbed "Pam," was provided by the National Weather Service. Computer animation showed Pam flooding New Orleans. Particularly devastated were the areas around the intersection of the MR-GO/Intracoastal Waterway and the Industrial Canal. The computer simulation illustrated how the loss of Louisiana wetlands contributed to the flooding. The Federal Emergency Management Agency (FEMA) was aware of the Pam results months before Katrina.

Disaster strikes and destroys lives and property. Throughout history, tens of thousands of people have died due to lack of planning, planning mistakes, misjudgments, procrastination, and lack of enforcement of building codes. The Great Fire of London in 1666 consumed virtually the entire medieval city. London had laws prohibiting thatched roofs for hundreds of years prior to the Great Fire and prohibitions against the use of jetties for generations. Yet Londoners and city officials ignored the laws.

After a disaster, we pick up the pieces. Government officials take action, vowing to never let the disaster happen again. After the Iroquois Theater Fire in 1903, the Mayor of Chicago closed all public assembly buildings in Chicago until officials could determine the reason why so many theater patrons had died in the fire. Soon after the fire, Chicago made many improvements to its building ordinances. After Hurricane Betsy in 1965, the federal government began to repair and improve New Orleans's levee system. Forty years later, it was still incomplete. Katrina's storm surge overtopped levees and floodwalls that had not yet been raised, and water seeped under and plowed through others. As soon as New Orleans was drained, the Corps of Engineers went to work reconstructing levees and floodwalls.

Experts study disasters to determine what went wrong. They collect and analyze data and draw conclusions about how to improve building safety. For example, after the 1904 Great Baltimore Fire, cities and firefighters understood the need to standardize firefighting equipment. Baltimore was not the first city in the United States to be decimated by fire. Insurance underwriters saw the need to develop a model building code. Cities saw the need to adopt and enforce a building code. After 9/11, engineers and code officials studied the collapse of the World Trade Center. From their studies, experts drew conclusions about ways to improve stair enclosures and other elements of building evacuation systems. They learned valuable lessons about the locations of exit stairwells, fire sprinkler systems, drywall used as firewalls, and the performance of steel structural systems when portions of their protective fireproofing is compromised. As discussed in Chapter 7, code officials are considering a number of improvements regarding the design of tall buildings. If they are implemented, they will benefit all of us, making tall buildings safer. After Hurricane Katrina, the American Society of Civil Engineers and the University of California–Berkeley undertook a study to determine why the New Orleans levee system failed. Also, the Corps of Engineers began its own internal study to determine what went wrong. What they learned from the levee failures will make New Orleans's levees safer.

After a disaster we only implement the most practical and politically palatable recommendations. After the Great London Fire, Christopher Wren developed a wonderful, although impractical, plan for building a new London. It was not implemented. After the 1906 San Francisco Earthquake and Fire, officials briefly entertained implementing Daniel Burnham's master plan for a new San Francisco. It was eventually abandoned because its implementation would have threatened the property rights of too many San Franciscans. After Hurricane Katrina, New Orleans briefly explored a comprehensive rebuilding plan that would have changed New Orleans's neighborhood districts. Shortly after the first public airing of the plan, it was abandoned. New Orleans started its rebuilding plan all over, albeit on a much smaller, less ambitious, and more politically palatable scale.

We rebuild with new and improved regulations established to prevent another disaster like the one that just occurred. Buildings, cities, or structures are better built and are safer as a result. The Great Chicago Fire spread quickly through the Windy City's downtown, from wood building to wood building. After the fire, Chicago required buildings constructed within downtown to be noncombustible to prevent another great fire. After the Iroquois Theater Fire, Chicago required all exit doors to swing outward and prohibited the use of locking devices that required special knowledge to operate. After the Coconut Grove Fire in Boston, exit doors were required adjacent to revolving doors. After the Triangle Shirtwaist Factory Fire, laws for the safety of workplaces were established. After the 1906 Earthquake, San Francisco added a requirement for steel-framed buildings to resist lateral loads. After the 1933 Long Beach Earthquake destroyed dozens of elementary schools, the State of California enacted the Field Act requiring the State's review of all school building designs prior to construction. After the Great Storm of 1900, Galveston built a seawall. The list could go on and on.

A disaster must be bad enough and close to home or else lessons are not learned. Dozens of hurricanes had struck Florida prior to Hurricane Andrew in 1992. The damage from Andrew was enormous. This prompted the State of Florida to finally adopt a statewide building code with hurricane design requirements. In 2004, Florida improved its state code, basing it on the 2003 *International Building Code* (IBC) and bolstering the IBC with additional hurricane and flood design requirements. The states of Mississippi and Louisiana are not immune from hurricanes. Yet, prior to Hurricane Katrina, neither state had a statewide building code. It was only after the devastation of Hurricane Katrina that Mississippi and Louisiana adopted statewide building codes based on the IBC. The Great London Fire burned medieval wooden London to the ground. Afterwards, the London Rebuilding Act required its four types of houses to be faced with noncombustible brick. Over two centuries later, wooden downtown Chicago burned before Chicago required noncombustible buildings in its downtown fire district. New York City and Boston burned several times before these two cities did likewise. San Francisco burned many times before it established a downtown fire district.

The types of building materials we use; the heights of buildings; buildings' distances (setbacks) from property lines; the number of stairwells in buildings, their locations, and their distance from each other have all been determined by disasters and our trial-and-error approach to disaster planning. The fire-resistance ratings of various building structural components and the fire ratings of walls, doors, windows, and corridors are all the result of lessons learned from disasters over the course of generations.

Eventually, another disaster comes along and tests the merits of our improved requirements and regulations. When it does, the building materials, systems, or arrangements that factored into the loss of property or life are reevaluated. If necessary, changes are implemented to make the built environment safer.

We are rarely ahead of disasters. Only after the Great Chicago Fire did the city enact comprehensive building requirements. Although the code addressed many other building safety issues, fire prevention was the primary impetus for the building code. After the Great Fire of London, officials were able to write the London Rebuilding Act quickly because most of its requirements were based on laws that were already in effect, but not enforced. After the fire, London enforced its building laws with much greater vigor than it had in the past. After the Draft Riots in 1863, New York began to take the unsanitary and deplorable living conditions within tenement buildings more seriously. Only after the riot were laws regarding tenement hygiene and safety enacted.

This is our method of disaster planning. We have employed it consistently throughout history. Incrementally, we work toward "getting it right." But, because we are human, we can only work toward perfection; we can never achieve it. The trial-and-error process of disaster planning is never ending.

Doomsdays are incremental endings, but they are also beginnings. They begin the next part of the cycle. We mourn our losses, learn from our mistakes, improve how we plan and design, and we move on. No matter how great the tragedy, we move on. Such is the human condition: mourn, pick up, and continue. There are potential disasters looming on the horizon. We cannot quite make out their details, but they are there. Yet, because they are not eminent, we do not act. Like New Orleans, many areas of California are protected by levees. There are more than 2,300 miles of levees in California, approximately 1,600 miles along just two rivers, the Sacramento and San Joaquin Rivers in northern California. The levees are poorly maintained and have suffered from neglect for generations. Some levees were constructed over a hundred years ago. Experts predict that heavy spring rains, accompanied by a large and sudden snow melt, could overtop or breach these poorly maintained levees, flooding heavily populated adjacent low-lying areas. California is also prone to earthquakes, and a major earthquake could easily break deteriorated levees. If the levees fail, hundreds of thousands of residents could be flooded out of their homes. In addition, the drinking water of tens of millions of Californians could become contaminated.

Past estimates have placed the cost of repairs at $3 billion. These levees must be fixed.

Flooding and minor levee breaks occur now and again, often costing tens of millions of dollars in damage. A few have cost much more. In March 2006, California Governor Arnold Schwarzenegger declared a state of emergency after heavy spring runoffs caused flooding. The Governor and U.S. Secretary of Homeland Security Michael Chertoff toured the flooded area by helicopter. The Governor requested $3 billion from the federal government for levee repairs. The request was denied.

After the federal government denied funding, the California legislature worked on a levee repair bill. The first draft of the bill did not please real estate developers because it restricted development in areas below the 100-year floodplain. California's strong real estate lobby pressured the Governor to insert compromise language that permitted the building of small housing projects below the 100-year floodplain with the promise that developers would somehow mitigate the flood risk within 10 years. The Governor and the legislature could not come to an agreement, and by mid-August 2006, the bill was dead. Without an immediate threat, politicians chose the easier and less-responsible course of action: They did nothing.

Because the politicians could not or would not make the difficult decisions, the subject of levee construction instead went before the California voters. On November 7, 2006, Californians passed Ballot Measure 1E, the *Disaster Preparedness and Flood Protection Bond Act*. The act sells $4.1 billion of state bonds for rebuilding and repairing "California's most vulnerable flood control structures [levees] to protect homes and prevent loss of life from flood-related disasters, including levee failures, flash floods, and mudslides."[4]

ANOTHER DISASTER LOOMS

Perhaps the greatest disaster to affect the built environment during this century will be global warming. It will be unlike other historical disasters in two ways: It will creep up on us slowly, over decades, and it will be global in scale. It has the potential to permanently eliminate millions of square miles of coastline throughout the world. Because approximately three-quarters of the world's population live in coastal areas, global warming's potential impact on the built environment is unparalleled.

Combating global warming will take unprecedented coordination among local governments and regional, state, and federal agencies. It will require cooperation of the United States with other countries throughout the world to head off the colossal problems associated with the floods, droughts, and famines that global warming can potentially bring. Yet, very few decision makers discuss the problem. Many still ignore it. Those who do discuss it often get wrapped up in the seemingly endless debate over whether natural processes or manmade pollution is causing it. Regardless of its cause, there is a growing body of scientific evidence suggesting that it is occurring. Scientists are becoming more vocal and dire in their predictions.

Because global warming is slow moving, we have the chance to do something to mitigate the damage it could cause. But, for the very same reason, it may not attract enough attention from U.S. and world leaders until it is too late or almost too late to do much about it. The question is, have we learned enough from past disasters to plan and act in advance of a potentially catastrophic disaster? Will enough U.S. and world leaders listen to the growing number of experts suggesting that we do so?

As the many examples in this book illustrate, our two-thousand-year history of disaster planning suggests that we might wait too long. Nevertheless, there is hope. Our approach to disaster planning is not hardwired into us. It is a habit, albeit it is well ingrained. We can change our habits, if we can muster the wisdom, courage, and determination to do so. If we change, we will have turned a historic page. We will have broken our centuries-old habit, and changed how we plan for disaster.

TIME LINE OF DISASTERS

Below is a time line of major disasters in history that have had significant impact on the built environment. Most of them have been discussed in this book, although not all. Note the often-used adjective "great." Not only was the destruction of these disasters great, so too were their effects on the planning and design of the built environment.

Year	Event	Description
27	Fedena Amphitheater Collapse	Amphitheater in outskirts of Rome collapses, killing and injuring an estimated 50,000. Roman Senate enacts law requiring construction inspections and sets minimum financial requirements for developers of large-scale public projects.
64	Great Fire of Rome	Fire destroys 70 percent of Rome. Rome rebuilds with wider streets, noncombustible masonry walls, and water cisterns.
283	Destruction of Roman Forum	Fire destroys much of the Roman Forum.
1066	Couvre-feu Law	"Cover-Fire" Law enacted in Britain by William the Conqueror. Requires all fires to be extinguished at bedtime to reduce house fires. Modern word "curfew" comes from this law.
1212	London's First Great Fire	Fire kills 3,000 Londoners and a large portion of the city is destroyed.

Ca. 1600	London's First Firefighting Equipment	London Fire Brigade invents fire squirts—large syringelike appliances with manual water pumps and water tanks mounted on wagons.
1633	London Fire	Many buildings are destroyed, including those on and around London Bridge. Fire squirts prove ineffectual in fighting the fire. Fire creates a long gap in buildings near London Bridge, which keeps the Great Fire of 1666 from burning over London Bridge and reaching south side of the Thames.
1666	Great Fire of London	Medieval London is destroyed, along with 13,200 houses and 87 churches. Puts an end to the Great Plague of 1665–1666.
1667	London Rebuilding Act	Rebuilding Act reiterates past building laws that were previously ignored and requires buildings to be faced with brick, restricts building height based on street width. Permits only four sorts of houses and limits height to three stories. London rebuilds to new building standards. Act creates conditions for Georgian architectural style.
1835	Great Fire of New York City	Fire destroys an estimated 700 buildings in downtown Manhattan.
1857	Fort Tejon, California, Earthquake	Considered California's "Big One" before the 1906 San Francisco Earthquake. Earth ruptures for over 200 miles along the San Andreas Fault. Ground surface offsets as much as 30 feet. Kern River flows backwards.
1863	New York City Draft Riots	Military draft riot results in fires, vandalism, property destruction, and 100 deaths. Draws city and national attention to deplorable tenement living conditions. Leads to first tenement housing laws
1871	Great Chicago Fire	Destroys one-third of Chicago including most of downtown. Chicago develops first comprehensive building code in the United States. Clears way for construction of first modern skyscrapers.
1886	Charleston, North Carolina, Earthquake	Earthquake with an estimated magnitude of 7.6 on the Ricter scale. Ninety percent of the city and 100 buildings destroyed; 60–110 people die.
1889	First seismograph records earthquake, Germany	Japanese earthquake is measured in Germany. First use of instrument to record ground acceleration due to earthquake.

1900	Galveston Storm	Hurricane storm surge submerges entire city and 75 percent of Galveston is destroyed with 8,000–10,000 lives lost. Largest death toll due to natural disaster in U.S. history.
1903	Chicago's Iroquois Theater Fire	Fire during performance causes smoke inhalation, panic, and stampede that results in 600 patrons killed. Results in numerous building safety regulations including requirements for fire extinguishers, minimum corridor widths, water hoses, fireproof ropes, and scenery drops. Prohibits against locking exit doors from the inside.
1904	Great Baltimore Fire	Destroys downtown Baltimore, destroying 1,500 buildings. Leads to first model building code, the 1905 *National Building Code,* and to standardization of firefighting equipment.
1906	Great San Francisco Earthquake and Fire	Approximately 50 percent of city destroyed by earthquake and subsequent fire, and more than 700 killed. Leads to horizontal load (wind/earthquake) code requirements for tall buildings. Leads to scientific study of earthquakes.
1911	Triangle Shirtwaist Fire, New York City	Garment factory fire kills 146, mostly young women and girls. Fire serves as catalyst for improving workplace safety.
1912	Life Assurance Building Fire, New York City	Fire destroys 7-story-tall building. Replaced with 1.2 million square feet, 42-story-tall building finished in 1915. Leads to first comprehensive city zoning regulations.
1916	New York City Zoning Resolution	First comprehensive zoning requirements in the United States. Divides New York City into use districts, and establishes minimum building setbacks, allowable lot coverages, and building heights. Quickly copied by other cities.
1923	Great Tokyo Earthquake	Earthquake results in 142,000 people killed and approximately 700,000 houses and tall buildings destroyed. Immediate limitation of 100 feet put on height of all future buildings.
1925	Santa Barbara, California, Earthquake	Earthquake with an estimated magnitude of 6.3. Most downtown buildings damaged or destroyed, 13 people killed, and 65 injured. Responsible for city's Spanish-Moorish architectural style. Leads to development of first earthquake code provisions.

1927	*Uniform Building Code* seismic requirements	Based on lessons learned from the 1925 Santa Barbara Earthquake, the UBC contains first-of-a-kind earthquake design provision.
1928	Okeechobee, Florida, Hurricane	Twenty-foot hurricane storm surge over-tops dike at Lake Okeechobee. Hundreds of houses were washed into the Florida Everglades and 2,500 lives lost. The second deadliest storm in U.S. history.
1931	Development of Modified Mercalli (MM) Earthquake Intensity Scale	MM Intensity Scale has 12 Roman-numeral levels of increasing intensity, I–XXII, based on observable effects, not a mathematical basis. Still used in the United States.
1933	Long Beach, California, Earthquake	Earthquake with an estimated magnitude of 6.25 kills 120 people. Many empty K-12 schools collapse, others severely damaged. A wake-up call for earthquake-safe schools. Leads to creation of Field Act and Riley Act.
1933	Field Act Passed	California passes act one month after the Long Beach Earthquake, requiring all school building designs to be reviewed by the State Division of Architecture.
1933	Riley Act	Required all California city governments to establish building departments to review building designs and inspect construction. All new buildings must resist a minimum lateral (earthquake) force 0.02 times the building gravity load.
1935	Nation's first earthquake formula: F = CW	As a result of the 1933 Long Beach Earthquake, the first formula for calculating lateral earthquake forces is included in the *Uniform Building Code*.
1935	Publication of Richter scale	Charles Richter develops a logarithmic scale for determining the intensity of earthquakes by measuring the amplitude of waves recorded by seismographs.
1937	Earthquake research collaboration begins	Caltech, Stanford University, and U.S. Coast and Geodetic Survey begin sharing research data and collaborating in earthquake studies.
1946	Aleutian Islands, Alaska Tsunami	Earthquake with surface-wave magnitude of 7.8 causes tidal wave run-up of 100 feet on Unimak island, Alaska. Almost 5 hours later, tsunami strikes Hilo, Hawaii, with wave run-up of 25 feet, killing 96. Disaster leads to development of tsunami warning system.

1948	Pacific Tsunami Warning System (PTWS)	Early warning system for tsunamis is developed for Pacific Ocean. Called the Seismic Sea Wave Warning System, its name is changed in 1949 to Pacific Tsunami Warning System.
1949	Earthquake Engineering Research Institute (EERI) formed	Purpose of the EERI is to reduce earthquake risks by improving understanding of their impact on physical, social, economic, political, and cultural environment. The EERI advocates comprehensive and realistic solutions to reduce risk.
1952	Arvin-Tehachapi, California, Earthquake	George W. Housner records 1952 Arvin-Tehachapi Earthquake on U.S. Geological Survey instruments in Taft, California, and develops Earthquake Design Spectrum concept.
1958	Lituya Bay, Alaska, Earthquake and Tsunami	The world's biggest tsunami to date. A 7.9 magnitude earthquake causes 40 million cubic yards of dirt and glacier to slide into Lituya Bay, resulting in a tidal wave run-up of over 1,700 feet on opposite bank of bay.
1960	Chilean Earthquake	Largest recorded earthquake with a magnitude of 9.2. Approximately 2,000 killed by earthquake and tsunami. Initiates advancements in seismology, plate tectonics, and tsunami and bay/harbor modeling.
1964	Prince William Sound Earthquake, or Good Friday Earthquake	Friday, March 28, 1964, a 9.2 magnitude earthquake causes a tsunami, killing 106 in Alaska. Causes severe damage to precast concrete structures. Tsunami reaches Crescent City, California, killing 11. Extensive damage as far away as Long Beach Harbor, California.
1964	Niigata, Japan, Earthquake	A 7.5 magnitude earthquake destroys 2,000 houses and kills 28. Damage restricted to structures built on loose fill due to soil liquefaction. Event advances study of liquefaction on buildings and structures.
1967	Establishment of Tsunami Warning System	In aftermath of 1964 Good Friday Earthquake, the United States implements an Alaskan and West Coast early warning system for tsunamis.
1967	Caracas, Venezuela, Earthquake	A 6.5 magnitude earthquake kills more than 200. Leads to a greater understanding of the importance of continuity in concrete reinforcement and interaction between building structural and nonstructural components.

1972	Pruitt-Igoe, St. Louis, Missouri, imploded	High-rise housing complex occupied in 1954 deliberately blown up, bringing to an end one of America's biggest social engineering disasters.
1989	Loma Prieta, California, Earthquake	A 7.1 magnitude earthquake collapses Bay Area double-decker freeway, damages Bay Bridge, and sections of other freeways, houses, and buildings. Death toll of 63.
1992	Hurricane Andrew	Category 5 hurricane strikes Miami-Dade County, Florida, leaving 160,000 homeless and 61 people dead. $27 billion in damage. Leads to development of the Florida State Building Code.
1994	Florida implements nation's first state-wide building code	Florida's *Uniform Building Code* establishes high-wind standards for coastal areas, requiring impact-resistant glazing for new and retrofit windows and doors.
1994	Northridge, California, Earthquake	A 6.7 magnitude earthquake destroys buildings and freeways and causes $40 billion in property damage. The most costly U.S. natural disaster up to that time. Reveals weaknesses in welded connections in steel-framed buildings. Leads to earthquake improvements in building codes.
1995	Kobe, Japan, Earthquake	A 6.9 magnitude earthquake destroys freeways and buildings, killing 5,500 people. Costliest earthquake in history with an estimated $US200 billion in damage.
2001	9/11 World Trade Center attacks	Airplane collisions start fires that cause both World Trade Center Towers to collapse. Engineering and Code groups analyze collapse and recommend numerous improvements for design of tall buildings. New York Port Authority and developer plan construction of "Freedom Tower."
2004	Indian Ocean Tsunami	A 9.1 magnitude earthquake causes tsunami that destroys coastal areas of Sumatra, Anadaman, Nicobar, Thailand, India, and Sri Lanka. Over 140,000 perish. Largest natural disaster in history.
2005	Hurricane Katrina	Category 3 hurricane of enormous size destroys Gulf Coast areas of Alabama, Mississippi, and Louisiana. Levee system protecting New Orleans fails, flooding 80 percent of the city. Third most deadly storm in U.S. history, most expensive natural disaster in U.S. history. Corps of Engineers repairs levees to pre-Katrina conditions. City of New Orleans struggles to rebuild.

I wish to thank my son Andrew for helping me with the research for this book. I also want to thank San Francisco Bay Area and Daly City Historians Bunny and Ken Gillespie. I thank Adam O'Dea, P.E., for his help in preparing some of the figures used in the book and for his technical review of some of the chapters. I thank my wife Persis for her attentive reading, rereading, and helpful suggestions. Writing often becomes a family endeavor, and so I thank the rest of our family, as well, for their support and understanding.

I also want to thank Victoria Smith of Kaplan Publishing for suggesting that I write a book on the subject of disasters from an architect's point of view, and Joshua Martino, development editor, for his helpful suggestions. Finally, I thank Pamela Brodowsky of International Literary Arts for her advice and encouragement.

NOTES

INTRODUCTION

1. The words "firmness, commodity, and delight" actually come from *The Elements of Architecture,* written by the Englishman Sir Henry Wotton (1568–1639), published in 1624. Wotton's work was a free translation of Vitruvius's *de Architecture.* More modern translations use less poetic language than Wotton. For example, Morris Hicky Morgan's 1914 translation calls the three principles "durability, convenience, and beauty." The terms "strength, utility, and aesthetic" are also used. Architects, however, overwhelmingly prefer Wotton's words.
2. Ibid., 84–85.

CHAPTER 1: IT TAKES A DISASTER

1. George Santayana, *The Life of Reason* (New York: Prometheus Books, 1998), 82. Originally published in five volumes as *The Life of Reason or The Phases of Human Progress* (New York: Scribner's Sons, 1905–06).
2. Sylvia Tognetti, "Reviews: Payments for Watershed Services in Coastal Regions: Not Whether But When—and the Cost of Delays," *Flows, Bulletin 14, www.flowsonline.net.*
3. Ibid.

4. Associated Press, "Katrina May Cost as Much as Four Years of War," *www.msnbc.msn.com/id/9281409*.

5. Peirce Edition Project, *The Essential Peirce: Selected Philosophical Writings, Volume 2 1893–1913* (Bloomington and Indianapolis: Indiana University Press, 1998), 95.

6. Ibid., 234.

7. FindLaw for Legal Professionals, "U.S. Supreme Court Yick Wo v. Hopkins, 118 U.S. 356 (1886)," *caselaw.lp.findlaw.com/cgi-bin/getcase.pl?court=us&vol=118&invol=356*.

8. Ibid.

9. Lawrence Veiller, *The Tenement House Reform in New York, 1834–1900* (New York: The Evening Post Job Printing House, 1900), 108.

10. C. C. Knowles and P. H. Pitt, *The History of Building Regulation in London 1189–1972* (London: Architectural Press, 1972), 95.

11. Charles Bastable, *Public Finance* (London: Macmillian and Co., 1917), Book IV, Chapter II. Available at *www.econlib.org/library/bastable/bastbPF22.html*.

12. Robert W. DeForest and Lawrence Veiller, eds., *The Tenement House Problem* (New York: The Macmillan Company, 1903), 81.

13. Ibid., xvii.

14. International Code Council, *International Residential Code for One- and Two-Family Dwellings* (Country Club Hills, IL: International Code Council, 2006), 52, 53. The dimensions for window emergency exits have varied over the years. The dimensions cited here are based on the 2006 *International Residential Code*, which is currently the predominant residential building code used in the United States.

15. Ibid., 48.

16. *The New York Times*, "Lay Cornerstone of New Equitable," 26 April 1914, VIII 3:3.

17. Geoff Tibballs, *Tsunami: The World's Most Terrifying Natural Disaster* (London: Carlton Books Ltd., 2005), 121.

CHAPTER 2: FIRE

1. John Mansley Robinson, *An Introduction to Early Greek Philosophy* (Boston: Houghton Mifflin Company, 1968), 91.

2. Ibid., 91.

3. Thirteen/WNET, *Secrets of the Dead*, New York, 2002. A Public Broadcasting System (PBS) documentary, which included art historian Eric Varner saying, "As many as 100 minor fires broke out in Rome every day. . . ." *www.pbs.org/wnet/secrets/case_rome/clues.html*.

4. Cornelius Tacitus, *Annals of Imperial Rome—Book XV,* 109 AD. Translated by Alfred John Church and William Jackson Brodribb. *classics.mit.edu/Tacitus/annals.11.xv.html,* paragraph 49.

5. Ibid., paragraph 50.

6. Ibid., paragraph 49.

7. Ibid., paragraph 55.

8. Ibid.

9. Gaius Suetonius Tranquillus, *The Lives of the Caesars, Book VI—The Life of Nero.* Believed to be written in 121 AD under the reign of the Emperor Hadrian. Translation by J. C. Rolfe, Loeb Classical Library, 1914. Text is in the public domain. *penelope.uchicago.edu/Thayer/E/Roman/Texts/Suetonius/12Caesars/Nero*.html,* paragraph 16.

10. Ibid., paragraph 31.

11. Tacitus, Op. Cit., paragraph 54.

12. C. C. Knowles and P. H. Pitt, *The History of Building Regulation in London 1189–1972.* (London: Architectural Press, 1972), 9.

13. Ibid., 18.

14. Ibid., 22.

15. Samuel Pepys, *Samuel Pepys Diary 1666—Great Fire. www.pepys.info/fire.html.*

16. Margaret Whinney, *Wren* (London: Thames and Hudson, 1971), 37.

17. C. C. Knowles and P. H. Pitt, Op. Cit., 30.

18. Ibid., 31.

19. Frank A. Randall, *History of the Development of Building Construction in Chicago* (Chicago: University of Illinois Press, 1999), 5.

20. Ibid.

21. Ross Miller, *The Great Chicago Fire* (Chicago: University of Illinois Press, 2000), 58.

22. Horace White, "The Great Chicago Fire," letter to Murat Halstead, October 14, 1871. *www.nationalcenter.org/ChicagoFire.html.*

23. Frank A. Randall, Op. Cit., 12.

24. Barry D. Yatt, *Cracking the Codes: An Architect's Guide to Building Regulations* (New York: John Wiley & Sons, Inc., 1998), 37.

25. Carl W. Condit, *The Chicago School of Architecture: A History of Commercial and Public Building in the Chicago Area 1875–1925* (Chicago: The University of Chicago Press, 1964), 51.

26. Ibid., 83.

27. Louis H. Sullivan, "The Tall Office Building Artistically Considered," *Lippincott's Magazine,* March 1886.

CHAPTER 3: CODES

1. The Code of Hammurabi. *www.wsu.edu/~dee/MESO/CODE.HTM*.

2. Cornelius Tacitus, *Annals of Imperial Rome—Book IV*, 109 AD. Translated by Alfred John Church and William Jackson Brodribb. *classics.mit.edu/Tacitus/annals.11.iv.html*.

3. Henry Thomas Riley, ed., *Liber Albus*, Rolls Series, no. 12, vol. 1, 1889, 328–329, 333–335. Translation of 12th- to 14th-century texts from the Corporation of London Records Office, Liber Albus, ff. 212, 213. Available online at Florilegium Urbanum. *www.trytel.com/~tristan/towns/florilgium/community/cmfabr09.htm*.

4. Ibid.

5. Ibid.

6. Ibid.

7. London Record Society, *London Assize of Nuisance 1301–1431* (London: London Record Society, 1973), entry 191. Available online at British History Online at *www.british-history.ac.uk/report.asp?compid=35972*.

8. New York City Department of Buildings, "Model Code Program." *www.nyc.gov/html/dob/html/model/behistory.shtml*.

9. Holice B. Young, "Our Firemen, The History of the NY Fire Departments, Chapter 14, Part 1," March 2001. *www.usgennet.org/usa/ny/state/fire/11-20/ch14pt1.html*.

10. Egbert Jamieson and Francis Adams, *The Municipal Code of Chicago* (Chicago: Beach, Barnard & Co. Legal Printers, 1881), 255, 256, paragraph 1002.

11. Ibid., 264, paragraph 1044.

12. Casey C. Grant "The Birth of NFPA," *NFPA Journal*, May/June 1995. Also available online as "History of the NFPA Codes and Standards-Making System." *www.nfpa.org/assets/files/PDF/HistoryNFPACodesStandards.pdf*.

13. Chicago Fire Marshall, *Annual Report*, 1903, 10. Available from the Chicago Public Library website at *www.chipublib.org/004chicago/disasters/ful ltext/firerpt.html*.

14. Egbert Jamieson and Francis Adams, Op. Cit., paragraph 1119.

15. Ibid., 276, paragraph 1126.

16. Ibid., 276, paragraph 1127.

17. Ibid., 276, paragraph 1131.

18. Chicago Fire Marshall, Op. Cit.

19. Jamie Stiehm, "Memories of Loss, Inspiration," *Baltimore Sun Times*, 8 February 2004.

20. National Board of Fire Underwriters, *Building Code: Recommended by the National Board of Fire Underwriters* New York: National Board of Fire Underwriters, 1915), forward.
21. Ibid.
22. W. C. Huntington, *Building Construction* (New York: John Wiley & Sons, 1929), 4–5.
23. New York Times, "Stories of Survivors and Witnesses and Rescuers Outside Tell What They Saw," March 26, 1911, 4. Also available online at *www.law.umkc.edu/faculty/projects/ftrials/traingle/trianglenytp4.html.*
24. Arthur F. Cosby, ed. *New Code of Ordinances of the City of New York Including the Sanitary Code, the Building Code and Park Regulations* (New York: The Banks Law Publishing Company, 1915)p.xx

CHAPTER 4: OVERCROWDING

1. Ebenezer Howard, *Garden Cities of To-Morrow* (originally published London, 1902, reprinted London, Faber and Faber, 1946) *www.library.cornell.edu/Reps/DOCS/howard.htm.*
2. Ibid.
3. 240,000 people per square mile equals 375 people per acre, or 116 square feet per person.
4. Robert W. DeForest and Lawrence Veiller, eds., *The Tenement House Problem* (New York: The Macmillan Company, 1903), 78.
5. Ibid., 79.
6. Ibid., 79–80.
7. Ibid., 92.
8. Ibid.
9. Ibid., 101–102.
10. Ibid., 101.
11. Lawrence Veiller, *A Model Housing Law*, Revised Edition. (New York: Russell Sage Foundation, 1920), v.
12. Candice Wheeler, "A Dream City," *Harper's New Monthly Magazine,* 1893, 833.
13. Frank Lloyd Wright, *An Autobiography* (New York: Duell, Sloan, and Pearce, 1943), 126.
14. Jacob A. Riis, *How the Other Half Lives* (New York: Charles Scribner's Sons, 1890). *www.yale.edu/amstud/inforev/riis/introduction.html,* introduction, paragraph 4.
15. Jane Jacobs, *The Death and Life of Great American Cities* (New York: Random House, 1961), quotation is from the 1992 Vintage Books Edition, 25.

CHAPTER 5: EARTHQUAKE

1. John Mansley Robinson, *An Introduction to Early Greek Philosophy* (Boston: Houghton Mifflin Company, 1968), 116.
2. "General Effects of the Shake," *The Daily Alta California*, 8 October 1865. *www.sfmuseum.org/hist1/1865eq.html*.
3. Mark Twain, *Roughing It* (New York: Harper & Row, 1899), 138–139.
4. John A. Veatch, "Earthquakes in San Francisco, and Especially on Their Direction," *S.F. Mining & Scientific Press*, 31 March 1868. *www.sfmuseum.org/alm/quakes1.html*.
5. Staff Writer, *SF Morning Call*, "Destruction of Property in Various Parts of the City," *San Francisco Morning Call*, 22 October 1868. *www.sfmuseum.org/hist1/1868eq.html*.
6. Editors, *SF Morning Call*, "The 'Temblores'—They Prove the Strength and Weakness of San Francisco," *San Francisco Morning Call*, 22 October 1868. *www.sfmuseum.org/hist4/68edit.html*.
7. Staff Writer, *SF Morning Call*, Ob. Cit.
8. Daniel H. Burnham and Edward H. Bennett, *Report on a Plan for San Francisco* (San Francisco: City and County of San Francisco, September 1905), 68.
9. Ibid., 88.
10. Ibid.
11. Walter McElroy, Editor, Northern California Writers Project, *San Francisco* (San Francisco: City and County of San Francisco, 1940), 107.
12. Carl Nolte, "The Dynamite Disaster," *San Francisco Chronicle*, 13 April 2006, A13.
13. John King, "Grand S.F. Plans Never Came to Be" *San Francisco Chronicle*, 12 April 2006, A10.
14. Ibid.
15. Marsden Manson, *Report of Marsden Manson to the Mayor and Committee on Reconstruction on Those Portions of the Burnham Plans which Meet Our Commercial Necessities* (San Francisco: October 1906), preface.
16. City and County of San Francisco, *1906 Building Law of the City and County of San Francisco* (San Francisco: City and County of San Francisco, 1906), paragraph prior to Section 1.
17. Ibid., Section 69.
18. Stephen Tobriner, *Bracing for Disaster: Earthquake-Resistant Architecture and Engineering in San Francisco, 1838–1933* (Berkeley, CA: Heydey Books, 2006), 215.
19. Stephen Tobriner, *The History of Building Codes to the 1920s* (Berkeley, CA: Center for Environmental Design Research, 1984), 55.

20. Jacques DÒArmund, quoted by *The Ojai*, Friday, 3 July 1925. *www.crustal.ucsb.edu/ics/outreach/sb_eqs/SBEQCatlog/SBEQdescrips/SBEQs1921-1925.html.*

21. Robert S. Yeats, *Living with Earthquakes in California: A Survivor's Guide* (Corvallis, OR: Oregon State University Press, 2001), 11.

22. International Conference of Building Officials, *Uniform Building Code 1927 Edition* (Long Beach, CA: ICBO, 1928), 213.

23. Ibid., 214.

24. Orange County and the 1933 Earthquake, *www.anaheimcolony.com/quake.htm.*

25. Ibid.

26. Ibid.

27. International Conference of Building Officials, *Uniform Building Code 1935 Edition* (Long Beach, CA: ICBO, 1935), 244.

28. Ibid., 245.

29. John King, "15 Seconds That Changed San Francisco," *San Francisco Chronicle*, 17 October 2004.

30. Stephen A. Mahin, "Lessons from Steel Buildings Damaged by the Northridge Earthquake," National Information Services for Earthquake Engineering (NIESEE), University of California—Berkeley, December 1997. *nisee.berkeley.edu/northridge/mahin.html.*

CHAPTER 6: WIND AND WATER

1. Keith C. Heidorn, "Dr. Isaac M. Cline Part 2 Converging Paths: A Man and a Storm," 1 September 2000. *www.islandnet.com/~see/weather/history/icline2.htm.*

2. Bill Adair, "10 Years Ago, Her Angry Plea Got Hurricane Aid Moving," *St. Petersburg Times*, 20 August 2002.

3. CNN, "Mayor to feds: 'Get off your asses,'" *CNN.Com*, 2 September 2005. Transcript of radio interview with New Orleans's Nagin. *www.cnn.com/2005/US/09/02/nagin.transcript/.*

4. International Code Council, *2004 Florida Building Code, Building* (Country Club Hill, IL: ICC Publications, 2004), Preface.

5. Ibid., Section 1620.2.

6. Ibid., Section 3105.4.2.

7. Ibid., Section 2410.2.

8. Dennis M. Powers, *The Raging Sea* (New York: Citadel Press, 2005), 31.

9. Geoff Tibballs, *Tsunami: The World's Most Terrifying Natural Disaster* (London: Carlton Books, 2005), 22.

10. International Code Council, *2004 Oregon Structural Specialty Code* (Country Club Hills, IL: International Code Council, 2004), 361R.
11. Ibid.
12. Ibid., 361R–362R.

CHAPTER 7: DISASTERS OF ANOTHER KIND

1. David Cohn, "Appallingly Expensive and Years Late, Yet Bursting with Dreamlike Bravura, the Scottish Parliament May Ultimately be EMBT and RMJM's Bittersweet Masterpiece," *Architectural Record*, February 2005, 99.
2. Parliamentary Business, Official Report, Wednesday, 22 September 2004, Col 10421. *www.scottish.parliament.uk/business/officalReports/meetins/Parliament/or-04/sor0922-02.htm*.
3. James A. Aloisi, Jr., *The Big Dig* (Beverly, MA: Commonwealth Editions, 2004), 10.
4. bid., 9.
5. Ibid., 14–15.
6. Ibid., 26.
7. Tax Payers for Common Sense, "Big Dig Billions Over Budget," 12 April 2000. *www.taxpayer.net/TCS/wastetbasket/transportation/2000-04-12bigdig.htm*.
8. Ibid.
9. Pam Belluck, "Woman Killed as Slab Falls from Big Dig Tunnel," *New York Times*, 11 July 2006.
10. Joe Darst, Mayor of St. Louis quoted, "Slum Surgery in St. Louis," *Architectural Forum*, April 1951, 129.
11. Ibid.
12. James Bailey, "The Case History of a Failure," *Architectural Forum*, December 1965, 22.
13. Mary Delach Leonard, "Pruitt-Igoe Housing Complex," *St. Louis Post-Dispatch*, 13 April 2004.
14. Le Corbusier, translated from the 13th French edition by Frederick Etchells, *Towards a New Architecture* (New York: Dover Publications, Inc., 1986), 54–57. Unabridged and unaltered republication of the work originally published by John Rodker, London, 1931.
15. Ibid., 57–58.
16. Oscar Newman, *Defensible Space* (New York: Collier Books, 1973), 17.

CHAPTER 8: WORLD TRADE CENTER

1. The two towers were not exactly the same height. The South Tower was 1,362 feet tall and North Tower 1,368 feet tall measured to their roofs. The North Tower also supported a 360-foot television and radio transmission tower. Ronald Hamburger et al., *World Trade Center Building Performance Study: Data Collection, Preliminary Observations and Recommendations* (New York: FEMA, May 2002), 2.1.

2. A body falling solely under the influence of earth's gravity is said to be free-falling and accelerates at the rate of 32 feet per second. Aristotle taught that the speed at which an object falls is proportional to its weight, thus, heavier objects fall faster. However, this is not true, and was disproved by Galileo (1564–1642). Legend has it that Galileo dropped a cannon ball and a wooden ball from atop the Leaning Tower of Pisa, observing that they struck the earth at the same time. Because the Leaning Tower is 180 feet tall, it would have taken the balls 4.5 seconds to fall the distance and simultaneously strike the earth (ignoring wind and air friction). However, Galileo never performed the experiment. He used something far less sensational. He rolled different sized balls down incline planes to slow down the process so he could make more exact measurements. The Leaning Tower of Pisa story is just a legend. Others before Galileo had performed the experiment, as did one of Galileo's students, who may have been responsible for starting the legend in the first place. When Galileo's student dropped the ball, he and those watching were astonished. The heavier ball hit the ground slightly before the lighter ball. While this concerned them, it would not have concerned Galileo, who knew that air and friction made a difference and that the lighter ball would be buoyed ever so slightly by the wind and slowed by air friction. By the way, had Galileo dropped the two balls from a height of 1,362 feet—the height of the South Tower—it would have taken the balls 7.25 seconds to strike the ground.

3. Brent Blanchard, "A Critical Analysis of the Collapse of WTC Towers 1, 2 & 7 from an Explosives and Conventional Demolition Industry Viewpoint," 8 August 2006. *www.implosionworld.com.*

4. Ronald Hamburger et al., Op. Cit., Executive Summary, 1.

5. Ibid., 2–15.

6. Ibid., 2–21.

7. Newsweek Editors, "Towers of Mammon," *Newsweek*, 2 July 1973, 56.

8. Eric Dalton, *Divided We Stand: A Biography of New York's World Trade Center* (New York City: Basic Books, 1999), 128.

9. Ibid.

10. *www.archive.salon.com/tech/feature/2001/09/17/wtc-obit/print.html*

11. Paul Heyer, *Architects on Architecture: New Directions in America* (New York: Walker and Company, 1966), 186.

12. Ronald Hamburger, et al., Op. Cit., 2–22.

13. Ibid., 2–15.

14. Ibid., 2–22.

15. A.E. Cote, Editor, *Fire Protection Handbook 17th Edition* (Quincy, MA: National Fire Protection Association, 1992), 6–62 to 6–70.

16. Thomas W. Eagar and Christopher Musso, "Why Did the World Trade Center Collapse? Science, Engineering, and Speculation," *JOM*, December 2001, 8–11.

17. John L. Gross and Therese P. McAllister, *Structural Fire Response and Probable Collapse Sequence of the World Trade Center Towers* (Washington, D.C.: National Institute of Standards and Technology, September 2005), xxx.

18. Phil Hirschkorn, "Freedom Tower to Rise 1,776 Feet from Ashes," CNN, Saturday, 20 December 2003. *www.cnn.com/2003/US/Northeast/12/19/wtc.plan/*.

19. Ibid.

20. Charles V. Bagli, "A Plan to Rebuild by 2012, and Doubts on the Big Rush," *New York Times,* Thursday, 27 April 2006.

21. William M. Connolly, Chairman, International Code Council Ad Hoc Committee on Terrorism Resistant Buildings, *Code Change Proposal: 403.15 Additional Exit Stair,* International Code Council, 15 November 2005. *www.iccsafe.org.*

22. Barbara A. Nadel, Editor, *Building Security: Handbook for Architectural Planning and Design* (New York: McGraw-Hill, 2004), 5.4.

23. William M. Connolly, Chairman, International Code Council Ad Hoc Committee on Terrorism Resistant Buildings, *Code Change Proposal: 403.15 Structural Integrity of Exit stair Enclosures,* International Code Council, November 15, 2005. *www.iccsafe.org.*

24. International Code Council News, "Media Background Information NIST WTC Related Code Changes to the *International Building Code* (IBC) and *International Fire Code* (IFC)." *www.iccsafe.org/news/NIST-WTC.html.*

CHAPTER 9: HURRICANE KATRINA

1. Ivor van Heerden and Mike Bryan, *The Storm: What Went Wrong and Why During Hurricane Katrina—The Inside Story from One Louisiana Scientist* (New York: Viking, 2006), 90.

2. Joby Warrick and Michael Grunwald, "Investigators Link Levee Failures to Design Flaws," *Washington Post,* 24 October 2005.

3. Ibid.

4. Rosemary James, Editor, *My New Orleans: Ballads to the Big Easy by Her Sons, Daughters, and Lovers* (New York: Simon & Schuster, 2006), 22–23. Poem "Nasty Water," by James Nolan, originally published by L-pantheon Press, 1997.

5. FEMA, *Summary Report on Building Performance: Hurricane Katrina 2005,* FEMA Report No. 548 (Washington, D.C.: FEMA, April 2006), 1–7.6 Douglas Brinkley, *The Great Deluge: Hurricane Katrina, New Orleans, and the Mississippi Gulf Coast* (New York: Harper Collins, 2006), 79–80.

7. *USA Today* Editors, "Census Outlines Face of Today's New Orleans, *USA Today,* 7 June 2006.

8. Josh Drobnyk, "Mississippi Approves Onshore Gambling as Biloxi Looks to Rebuild," *Online Newshour & LPB Louisiana Public Broadcasting,* October 2005. *www.pbs.org.newshour/local/gulfcoast/background/rebuilding_biloxi.html.*

9. Ibid.

10. Ibid.

11. Ibid.

12. State of Mississippi Bill HB 1406, signed 14 April 2006.

13. Lieutenant General Carl Strock, White House Press Briefing, 2:00 PM, 6 March 2006. *www.whitehouse.gov/news/releases/2006/03/print/20060306-4.html.*

14. Ibid.

15. R.G. Bea and Independent Levee Investigation Team, *Investigation of the Performance of the New Orleans Flood Protection Systems in Hurricane Katrina on August 29, 2005* (Berkeley, CA: University of California, May 22, 2006), xix.

16. Ibid., xxi.

17. Ibid.

18. USACE, Task Force Hope, "June 1, 2006: An Important Day for New Orleans," *Status Report Newsletter,* 4 June 2006.

19. ASCE External Review Team, *Hurricane Katrina One Year Later: What Must We Do Next?* (Reston, VA: American Society of Civil Engineers, 2006), 12.

20. Evan Thomas, Jonathan Darman, and Sarah Childress, "New Orleans Blues," *Newsweek,* 4 September 2006, 33.

21. C. Ray Nagin, Mayor, City of New Orleans Mayor's Press Office, 5 July 2006. *www.cityofno.com.*

22. *USA Today* Staff, "N.O. Recovery Slow Process," *USA Today,* 23 August 2006.

23. Gwen Filosa, "Experts Excoriate Recovery Leaders," *Times Picayune*, 29 July 2006.

24. Sack, Kevin and Ann Simmons, "Memories fill the void on a block in New Orleans," *Los Angles Times*, 25 December 2006.

CHAPTER 10: LEARNING FROM DISASTERS

1. ASCE External Review Team, Op. Cit., 5.

2. George Santayana, Op. Cit., 82.

3. Ibid., 68.

4. Warren Slocum, Chief Elections Officer, *Sample Ballot and Official Voter Information Pamphlet*, County of San Mateo, California, 2006.

BIBLIOGRAPHY

The bibliography is an alphabetical listing, by author, of the various works consulted, quoted, or cited in this book. It includes books, articles, and Internet sources. The author does not claim that the bibliography is a comprehensive listing of books on the subject nor is it necessarily a listing of all the works that influenced the text of this book.

Adair, Bill. "10 Years Ago, Her Angry Plea Got Hurricane Aid Moving," *St. Petersburg Times*, 20 August 2002.

ASCE External Review Team. *Hurricane Katrina One Year Later: What Must We Do Next?* Reston, Virginia, American Society of Civil Engineers, 2006.

Bailey, James. "The Case History of a Failure," *Architectural Forum*, December 1965, 22–25.

Bea, R. G., and Independent Levee Investigation Team. *Investigation of the Performance of the New Orleans Flood Protection Systems in Hurricane Katrina on August 29, 2005*. Berkeley, CA: University of California, May 22, 2006.

Blanchard, Brent. "A Critical Analysis of the Collapse of WTC Towers 1, 2 & 7 from an Explosives and Conventional Demolition Industry Viewpoint." August 8, 2006. *www.implosionworld.com*.

Burden, Amanda, Director of Department of City Planning. *Zoning Handbook*. New York: The City of New York, 2006.

Burnham, Daniel H., and Edward H. Bennett. *Report on a Plan for San Francisco*. San Francisco, City and County of San Francisco, September 1905.

Condit, Carl W. *The Chicago School of Architecture: A History of Commercial and Public Building in the Chicago Area, 1875–1925*. Chicago: The University of Chicago Press, 1964.

Cosby, Arthur F., editor. *New Code of Ordinances of the City of New York Including the Sanitary Code, the Building Code and Park Regulations*. New York: The Banks Law Publishing Company, 1915.

———. *Code of Ordinances of the City of New York*. New York: The Banks Law Publishing Company, 1922.

Cote, A. E., editor. *Fire Protection Handbook 17th Edition*. Quincy, MA: National Fire Protection Association, 1992.

Darst, Joseph M. "St. Louis Rebuilds with Balanced Civic Improvement Program," *The American City* (August 1950), 100–101.

Darton, Eric. *Divided We Stand: A Biography of New York's World Trade Center*. New York: Basic Books, 1999.

Davis, Mike. *Ecology of Fear: Los Angeles and the Imagination of Disaster*. New York: Vintage Books, 1998.

DeForest, Robert W., and Lawrence Veiller. *The Tenement House Problem*, Volume 1. New York: The Macmillan Company, 1903.

Drobnyk, Josh. "Mississippi Approves Onshore Gambling as Biloxi Looks to Rebuild," *Online Newshour and LPB Louisiana Public Broadcasting*, October 2005. *www.pbs.org.newshour/local/gulfcoast/background/rebuilding_biloxi.html*.

Dyson, Michael Eric. *Come Hell or High Water: Hurricane Katrina and the Color of Disaster*. New York: Basic Civitas Books, 2006.

Eagar, Thomas, and Christopher Musso. "Why Did the World Trade Center Collapse? Science, Engineering, and Speculation," *JOM* (December 2001) 8–11.

FEMA. *Above the Flood: Elevating Your Floodprone House*. FEMA Report No. 347. Washington, D.C.: FEMA, May 2000.

———. *Summary Report on Building Performance: Hurricane Katrina 2005*. FEMA Report No. 548. Washington, D.C.: FEMA, April 2006.

Filosa, Gwen. "Experts Excoriate Recovery Leaders," *Times Picayune,* 29 July 2006.

Gillespie, Angus Kress. *Twin Towers: The Life of New York City's World Trade Center.* New Brunswick, NJ: Rutgers University Press, 1999.

Goldberger, Paul. *Up from Zero: Politics, Architecture, and the Rebuilding of New York.* New York: Random House, 2004.

Gross, John L., and Therese P. McAllister. *Structural Fire Response and Probable Collapse Sequence of the World Trade Center Towers.* Washington, D.C.: National Institute of Standards and Technology, September 2005.

Hamburger, John, et al. *World Trade Center Building Performance Study: Data Collection, Preliminary Observations, and Recommendations.* New York: FEMA, May 2002.

Heyer, Paul. *Architects on Architecture: New Direction in America.* New York: Walker and Company, 1966.

Huntington, W. C. *Building Construction.* New York: John Wiley & Sons, 1929.

Husock, Howard. "Public Housing as a 'Poorhouse,'" *National Affairs,* 1997. *webmail.pas.earthlink.net/wam/rintable.jsp?msgid=1904&x=626923280.*

International Code Council. *2004 Oregon Structural Specialty Code.* Country Club Hills, IL: International Code Council, 2004.

———. *2006 International Building Code.* Country Club Hills, IL: International Code Council, 2006.

———. *International Residential Code for One and Two-Family Dwellings.* Country Club Hills, IL: International Code Council, 2006.

International Conference of Building Officials. *Uniform Building Code 1927 Edition.* Long Beach, CA: ICBO, 1928.

———. *Uniform Building Code 1935 Edition,* Long Beach, CA: ICBO, 1935.

Jacobs, Jane. *The Death and Life of Great American Cities.* New York: Random House, 1961. Vintage Books Edition, 1992.

Jamieson, Egbert, and Francis Adams. *The Municipal Code of Chicago: Comprising the Laws of Illinois Relating to the City of Chicago, and the Ordinances of the City Council; Codified and Revised.* Chicago: Beach, Barnard & Co., Legal Printers, 1881.

Jardine, Lisa. *On a Grander Scale: The Outstanding Life of Sir Christopher Wren.* New York: Harper Collins Publishers, 2002.

Kay, Jane Holtz. "Architecture." *The Nation*, 24 September 1973, 284.

King, John. "15 Seconds That Changed San Francisco." *San Francisco Chronicle*, 17 October 2004.

————. "Grand S.F. Plans Never Came to Be." *San Francisco Chronicle*, 12 April 2006, A1 and A10.

Knowles, C. C., and P. H. Pitt. *The History of Building Regulation in London 1189–1972*. London: Architectural Press, 1972.

Kostof, Spiro. *A History of Architecture: Settings and Rituals*. New York: Oxford University Press, 1995.

Le Corbusier, translated from the 13th French edition by Frederick Etchells. *Towards a New Architecture*. New York: Dover Publications, Inc., 1986. Unabridged and unaltered republication of the work originally published by John Rodker, London, 1931.

Leonard, Mary Delach. "Pruitt-Igoe Housing Complex." *St. Louis Post-Dispatch*, 13 April 2004.

Lüsted, Marcia Amidon. *The Empire State Building*. Farmington Hills, MI: Thomson Gale, 2005.

Manson, Marsden. *Report of Marsden Manson to the Mayor and Committee on Reconstruction on Those Portions of the Burnham Plans which Meet Our Commercial Necessities*. San Francisco, October 1906.

Massie, Allan. *The Caesars*. New York: Franklin Watts, 1984.

McCue, George. "$57,000,000 Later." *Architectural Forum*, May 1973, 42–45.

McElroy, Walter, editor, Northern California Writers Project. *San Francisco*. San Francisco: City and County of San Francisco, 1940.

Mitchell, Margaret. *Gone with the Wind*. New York: Macmillan Publishing Company, 1975 edition.

Mogilevich, Mariana. "Architecture: Big Bad Buildings: The Vanishing Legacy of Minoru Yamasaki." *The Next American City*. *www.americancity.org/article.php?id_article=62*.

Moyer, Susan M., editor. *Katrina: Stories of Rescue, Recovery and Rebuilding in the Eye of the Storm*. Champaign, IL: Spotlight Press L.L.C., 2005.

Nadel, Barbara A., editor. *Building Security: Handbook for Architectural Planning and Design.* New York: McGraw-Hill, 2004.

National Review Editors. "Pruitt-Igoe, RIP." *National Review,* 15 December 1970, 1335–1336.

Newman, Oscar. *Defensible Space.* New York, Collier Books, 1973.

Newsweek Editors. "Towers of Mammon." *Newsweek,* 2 July 1973, 56.

Nolte, Carl. "The Dynamite Disaster." *San Francisco Chronicle,* 13 April 2006, A13.

Peterson, Jon A. *The Birth of City Planning in the United States, 1840–1917.* Baltimore: The Johns Hopkins University Press, 2003.

Poinsett, Alex. "Countdown in Housing: Shortage of Low-Income Dwellings Generates Explosive Pressures in Nation's Cities," *Ebony,* September 1972, 60–68.

Powers, Dennis M. *The Raging Sea.* New York: Citadel Press, 2005.

Rabun, J. Stanley. *Structural Analysis of Historic Buildings: Restoration, Preservation, and Adaptive Reuse Applications for Architects and Engineers.* New York: John Wiley & Sons, Inc., 2000.

Ramroth, William G., Jr. *Pragmatism and Modern Architecture.* Jefferson, North Carolina: McFarland & Company, Inc., Publishers, 2006.

Randall, Frank A. *History of the Development of Building Construction in Chicago.* Chicago: University of Illinois Press, 1999.

Rasmussen, Steen Eiler. *London: The Unique City—Part 1.* Cambridge, Mass.: The MIT Press, 1974. First published in 1934.

Reddaway, T. F. *The Rebuilding of London After the Great Fire.* London: Jonathan Cape LTD, 1940.

Reps, John W. *Cities of the American West: A History of Frontier Urban Planning.* Princeton, NJ: Princeton University Press, 1965.

Riis, Jacob A. *How the Other Half Lives.* New York: Charles Scribner's Sons, 1890. Available at *www.yale.edu/amstud/inforev/riis/title.html.*

Robinson, John Mansley. *An Introduction to Early Greek Philosophy.* Boston: Houghton Mifflin Company, 1968.

Russell, James S. "Can New Orleans and the Gulf Coast Face the Hard Questions?" *Architectural Record,* June 2006, 130–138.

Santayana, George. *The Life of Reason.* New York: Prometheus Books, 1998. Originally published in five volumes as *The Life of Reason* or *The Phases of Human Progress.* New York: Scribner's Sons, 1905–1906.

Scarre, Chris. *Chronicle of the Roman Emperors: The Reign-by-Reign Record of the Rulers of Imperial Rome.* London: Thames and Hudson, Ltd., 1995.

Schurr, Sam H., editor. *Energy, Economic Growth, and the Environment.* Baltimore: The Johns Hopkins University Press, 1972.

Stewart, Gail B. *Catastrophe in Southern Asia: The Tsunami of 2004.* Detroit: Lucent Books, 2005.

Thirteen/WNET. *Secrets of the Dead.* New York: 2002 Educational Broadcasting Corporation. *www.pbs.org/wnet/secrets/case_rome/clues.html.*

Thomas, Evan, Jonathan Darman, and Sarah Childress. "New Orleans Blues." *Newsweek,* 4 September 2006, 28–36.

Tibballs, Geoff. *Tsunami: The World's Most Terrifying Natural Disaster.* London: Carlton Books, Ltd., 2005.

Time Magazine Editors. Hurricane Katrina: The Storm That Changed America. New York: Time Inc., 2005.

Time Magazine Editors. "The Tragedy of Pruitt-Igoe." *Time,* 27 December 1971, 38.

Tobriner, Stephen. *Bracing for Disaster: Earthquake-Resistant Architecture and Engineering in San Francisco, 1838–1933.* Berkeley, CA: Heydey Books, 2006.

———. *The History of Building Codes to the 1920s.* Berkeley, CA: Center for Environmental Design Research, 1984.

Twain, Mark. *Roughing It.* New York: Harper & Row, 1899.

USA Today Editors. "Census Outlines Face of Today's New Orleans." *USA Today,* 7 June 2006.

Vale, Lawrence J., and Thomas J. Campanella. *The Resilient City: How Modern Cities Recover from Disaster.* Oxford: Oxford University Press, 2005.

van Heerden, Ivor, and Mike Bryan. *The Storm: What Went Wrong and Why During Hurricane Katrina—The Inside Story from One Louisiana Scientist.* New York: Viking, 2006.

Veatch, John A. "Earthquakes in San Francisco, and Especially on Their Direction." *S.F. Mining & Scientific Press,* 31 March 1868.

Veiller, Lawrence. *A Model Housing Law,* Revised Edition. New York: Russell Sage Foundation, 1920.

Von Hoffman, Alexander. "Why They Built the Pruitt-Igoe Project." Joint Center for Housing Studies, Harvard University. www.soc.iastate.edu/sapp/PruittIgoe.html.

Warrick, Joby, and Michael Grunwald. "Investigators Link Levee Failures to Design Flaws." *Washington Post,* 24 October 2005.

Wheeler, Candace. "A Dream City." *Harper's New Monthly Magazine,* 1893, 833.

Whinney, Margaret. *Wren.* London: Thames and Hudson, 1971.

Yeats, Robert S. *Living with Earthquakes in California: A Survivor's Guide.* Corvallis, OR: Oregon State University Press, 2001.

A

Abduction, 234–35

Achmitz, Eugene E., 106

Adler, Dankmar, 45

Aesop, 1–2

Age of Reason, 32

Alaska Earthquake, Tsunami (1958), 247

Albert, Prince, 75

AIA. *See* American Institute of Architects

Aleutian Islands, Alaska tsunami (1946), 246

Alfred P. Murrah Federal Building (Oklahoma City), 186, 187

American Institute of Architects (AIA), 91

American Society of Civil Engineers (ASCE), 182, 207, 222–24, 237
   Hurricane Katrina External Review, 224–25, 233

Anadaman Island, 143

Anaximenes, 123

Annals of Imperial Rome, 20–24

Annan, Kofi, 18

Antium, 22

Architectural Forum, 164, 165

Architecture, importance of, 6–7

Aristotle, 259

Boston
  Big Dig, 157–63
  building code in, 52
  height limits in, 85–86
Boston Fire, 65, 238
Boston Harbor, 160
Boston Harbor Islands State Park, 163
Bourbon Street, 203
Brick standards, 28
Bring New Orleans Back Commission (BNOB), 226, 228, 230
Britannicus, 22
Brown Jr., Arthur, 110
Budget controls, 155
Buffalo, tenement housing, 86
Building code, 146, 237
  earliest in London, 49–52
  fire's effect on, 15–17
  first, 41–42, 44–46
  first American, 52–54
  handrails in, 12
  Hurricane Katrina and, 218
  importance of, 8–12
  NFPA, 54–56
  origins of, 47–49
  room sizes in, 11
  shower stalls in, 11
  stairs in, 11–12
  statewide, 248
  window placement in, 11
Building Code: Recommended by the National Board of Fire Underwriters, 64
Building department, 44
Building elevation, 145–46
Building Law of the City and County of San Francisco 1906, The, 107–10
Building materials, 146
Building Officials & Code Administration International, Inc., 65
Building orientation, 146
Building Performance Study (BPS), 182, 184, 185–86
Building utility core strength, 197
Burnham, Daniel H., 38, 45, 87–88, 90–91, 103, 106, 110
Bush, George H., 134

G

H

W